The Sixties in America
Almanac

**Tom Pendergast
and Sara Pendergast**

Allison McNeill,
Project Editor

U·X·L

*An imprint of Thomson Gale,
a part of The Thomson Corporation*

THOMSON
GALE

Detroit • New York • San Francisco • San Diego • New Haven, Conn. • Waterville, Maine • London • Munich

The Sixties in America: Almanac

Tom Pendergast and Sara Pendergast

Project Editor
Allison McNeill

Editorial
Kathleen J. Edgar

Rights Acquisition and Management
Mari Masalin-Cooper

Imaging and Multimedia
Denay Wilding, Lezlie Light, Mike Logusz

Product Design
Kate Scheible and Pamela Galbreath

Composition
Evi Seoud

Manufacturing
Rita Wimberley

LIBRARY OF CONGRESS CATALOGING-IN-PUBLICATION DATA

Pendergast, Tom.
   Sixties in America. Almanac / Tom Pendergast and Sara Pendergast.
     p. cm.
   Includes bibliographical references and index.
    ISBN 0-7876-9246-8 (hardcover : alk. paper)
   1. United States—History—1961–1969—Juvenile literature. 2. Almanacs, American—Juvenile literature. I. Pendergast, Sara. II. Title.

E841.P38 2004
973.923—dc22
                                  2004016601

Printed in the United States of America
10 9 8 7 6 5 4 3 2 1

Contents

Reader's Guide

Many Americans realized by the middle of the 1960s that their nation was going through a period of intense change and disruption. The decade had begun in relative peace, with the election of a vibrant, young president, John F. Kennedy, a Democrat. Yet Kennedy faced several key issues that would come to define the decade. First, he clashed with the Soviet Union over the spread of communist influence in Europe and in Cuba. Then, he faced domestic tensions as the civil rights movement in the South grew increasingly intense and even violent. When Kennedy was assassinated in November of 1963, the nation was shocked and saddened, for many Americans had invested great hopes in Kennedy.

Kennedy's successor, Lyndon B. Johnson, struggled with the existing tensions and new pressures as well. He had an ambitious agenda for domestic policies that he called the Great Society, which included passing civil rights legislation, using federal funds to wage a "war on poverty," and creating programs to support public education, housing, and jobs. He succeeded in passing many of his programs. But Johnson's political career was undone by American involvement in the expanding war in Vietnam, which American combat troops entered in 1965. A powerful grassroots movement rose up against the war, and its dramatic demonstrations helped turn public sentiment against the war. Johnson did not seek reelection in 1968. Republican Richard M. Nixon won a hard-fought election by promising to return law and order to what he depicted as an unruly nation.

Domestic and international politics were not the only source of high drama in the 1960s. The colorful hippie subculture emerged as a growing youth movement, bringing changes in music, education, fashion, art, and other areas of culture. Thanks to television, American sports became more commercial and more dramatic, and American sports figures like Muhammad Ali, Vince Lombardi, and Joe Namath became important cultural figures. Riots in major cities and the assassinations of the Rev. Dr. Martin Luther King Jr., Malcolm X, and Robert Kennedy caused many Americans to worry about rising violence in their society. An increase in sexual content in books and movies, as well as a new openness about homosexuality at the end of the decade, raised worries about declining morality. There was, of course, much, much more, as changes in one area of American society encouraged or clashed with other movements and trends.

The dramatic, stirring, and sometimes violent events of the 1960s make it an important decade for students to study in their quest to understand American society as it exists today. Many aspects of American culture in the 2000s can be traced back to that era. In some ways, the 1960s are still close at hand. Classic rock radio stations continue to play music from the decade. In fact, the Beatles remain one of the top-selling bands, just as they were in the 1960s. Fashion trends introduced in the 1960s—bell-bottoms and paisley fabric, for example—make periodic comebacks. Politicians continue to refer to the legacy of President John F. Kennedy and civil rights leader Martin Luther King Jr. to inspire audiences. Political leaders and activists also point to the lessons of the Vietnam War to help Americans understand foreign policy. Many Americans who experienced the 1960s firsthand are in positions of power in American society in the 2000s, and their experiences of that decade inform their actions.

In some ways, however, the 1960s can seem quite distant. For example, during that era, television was still a relatively new phenomenon. Nightly coverage of war on television was something new to Americans. In addition, the Cold War (1945–91) between the United States and the Soviet Union—and the threat of nuclear war—informed every decision about foreign policy. And, sexuality, especially homosexuality, was never discussed in polite company, much less on television. One of the features that make this decade so fascinating is the fact that the 1960s are so close, yet so far away.

The Sixties in America: Almanac presents, in fifteen chapters, a comprehensive overview of the events that occurred within the United States during the 1960s. The volume concentrates on the political, social, and cultural impact of the decade. The introduction asks readers to consider the themes that make the decade worthy of study. This includes: the unfolding dramas of the civil rights movement; the Vietnam War, and antiwar movement; the expansion of the federal government under Democratic presidents; the birth of a counterculture and its impact on American entertainment; and a variety of other cultural developments. These issues and others are considered closely in the thematic chapters that follow. Finally, the conclusion asks readers to consider the extent to which the experiences and events of the 1960s shaped American society in the years that followed.

Features

The Sixties in America: Almanac contains numerous sidebar boxes that highlight people and events of special interest, and each chapter offers a list of additional sources that students can go to for more information. More than seventy black-and-white photographs illustrate the material. The volume begins with a timeline of important events in the history of the 1960s, a "Words to Know" section that introduces students to difficult or unfamiliar terms, and a "Research and Activity Ideas" section. The volume concludes with a general bibliography and a subject index so students can easily find the people, places, and events discussed throughout *The Sixties in America: Almanac*.

The Sixties in America Reference Library

The Sixties in America: Almanac is only one component of the three-part U•X•L Sixties in America Reference Library. The other two titles in this set are:

- *The Sixties in America: Biographies* (one volume) presents the life stories of twenty-six men and women who played crucial roles in the social, cultural, and political developments of the 1960s. Readers will find coverage of the most notable figures of the decade, including John F. Kennedy, Lyndon B. Johnson, Martin Luther King Jr., and Malcolm X. Essays are also provided on a number of lesser-known though no less interesting figures, including labor activist Dolores Huerta, atheist activist Madalyn Murray O'Hair, scientist Frances Oldham Kelsey, feminist author and activist Betty Friedan, and Native American activist Richard Oakes.

- *The Sixties in America: Primary Sources* (one volume) tells the story of the 1960s in the words of the people who lived and shaped the decade. The volume gives readers firsthand contact with some of the key documents of the era, including material pertaining to the civil rights movement, the formation of U.S. policy in Vietnam, the growth of the antiwar movement, the rise of feminism and the women's movement, and the emergence of television as a cultural force in the United States. Also included are expressions of political radicalism from such diverse groups and individuals as the Students for a Democratic Society, Young Americans for Freedom, Barry Goldwater, and the Yippies. Some of these primary sources use specialized or complex language, so efforts have been made to place these documents in context as well as define terms that may be otherwise inaccessible to young readers.

- A cumulative index of all three titles in the U•X•L Sixties in America Reference Library is also available.

Special Thanks

The authors wish to thank U•X•L's Allison McNeill for being the ideal editor for this set, pointing out pitfalls to avoid while ably steering us toward creating books that would best serve an audience of young readers.

The authors note that work on this book was both enriched and complicated by the growing and diverse body of historical knowledge that exists on the 1960s. The 1960s may be considered a part of the distant past to many of the readers of this book, but many of those who have written about the period lived through it or, in the case of the authors of this book, had parents who lived through it. It was such a dramatic, eventful decade that those with direct experience have not always seen it clearly. As such, the authors have tried to develop an approach to the decade that is without undue bias, though it may take another generation before the decade is seen clearly.

Comments and Suggestions

We welcome your comments on *The Sixties in America: Almanac* and suggestions for other topics to consider. Please write: Editors, *The Sixties in America: Almanac,* U•X•L, 27500 Drake Rd., Farmington Hills, Michigan 48331-3535; call toll-free: 1-800-877-4253; fax to (248) 699-8097; or send e-mail via http://www.gale.com.

Timeline of Events

1960 Dolores Huerta and César Chávez form the United Farm Workers of America (UFW), an agricultural workers labor union.

January 4, 1960 The United Steel Workers agree on a settlement to end the longest steel strike in U.S. history. The strike had started in July 1959.

February 1, 1960 Four black students request service at a whites-only lunch counter at a Woolworth's store in Greensboro, North Carolina. They politely begin a "sit-in" to protest not being served. Their nonviolent protest sparks a new form of civil rights protest that quickly spreads throughout the American South.

May 1960 The oral contraceptive pill, known as "the pill," is approved for distribution throughout the United States.

May 6, 1960 The Civil Rights Act of 1960 is approved to protect black voting rights. However, the law's loopholes make it very difficult for blacks to register or to vote.

May 10, 1960 Nashville, Tennessee, becomes the first large city to desegregate public places.

May 13, 1960 College students protesting the House Un-American Activities Committee hearing outside the San Francisco, California, city hall are dispersed by police who blast the protestors with fire hoses.

July 25, 1960 The first African American eats a meal at the Woolworth's lunch counter in Greensboro, North Carolina.

September 1960 The Young Americans for Freedom, a group of conservative activists, release a set of principles known as the "Sharon Statement." This is considered the founding document on the modern conservative movement.

Fall 1960 Democrat John F. Kennedy and Republican Richard M. Nixon engage in a series of televised presidential debates, the first such debates to air on national television.

January 3, 1961 The United States severs diplomatic ties with Cuba.

January 20, 1961 In his inaugural speech as president, John F. Kennedy urges Americans to "Ask not what your country can do for you—ask what you can do for your country." Kennedy takes office with Lyndon B. Johnson as vice president.

January 31, 1961 The United States launches a chimpanzee into space in a test flight of Project Mercury, a space mission of the National Aeronautics and Space Administration (NASA).

February 17-23, 1961 A six-day airline strike grounds flights by American, Eastern, Flying Tiger, National, and TWA airlines.

March 20, 1961 Louisiana's legislation enforcing segregation is deemed unconstitutional.

April 12-May 5, 1961 Two Soviet cosmonauts become the first men in space.

April 17, 1961 U.S.-supported Cuban exiles invade Cuba in the Bay of Pigs invasion. To the embarrassment of President Kennedy, they are defeated within three days.

May 4, 1961 Black and white civil rights activists begin their "freedom rides" to various southern cities in an attempt to end segregation in interstate transportation.

May 9, 1961 In a speech to the National Association of Broadcasters, Federal Communications Commission chairperson Newton Minow makes the famous statement that television is a "vast wasteland."

May 14, 1961 Ku Klux Klan members attack freedom riders and burn the riders' bus in Anniston, Alabama.

May 25, 1961 President Kennedy announces that the United States intends to land a man on the moon and return him safely, beginning the "space race" between the Soviets and Americans.

July 21, 1961 Astronaut Gus Grissom blasts off in the second American manned rocket flight, though he does not enter orbit.

August 13, 1961 East Germany begins construction of the Berlin Wall.

October 26-28, 1961 U.S. and Soviet tanks confront each other along the border of East and West Berlin.

November 3, 1961 U.S. government officials return from South Vietnam and suggest that decisive military action will lead to a quick victory.

December 1961 President Kennedy forms the Commission on the Status of Women to investigate barriers to women's full enjoyment of basic rights.

1962 Nationally distributed *Harper's Bazaar* magazine includes a full-page color advertisement featuring a nude model, making nudity in advertising a subject of national discussion.

1962 Scientist Rachel Carson publishes *Silent Spring,* which is credited with giving birth to the modern environmental movement.

January 12, 1962 The U.S. State Department denies Americans who are members of the Communist Party the ability to travel abroad.

February 20, 1962 U.S. astronaut John Glenn is the first American to orbit Earth; all three television networks cover the event.

February 26, 1962 The Supreme Court rules that segregation in interstate and intrastate transportation is unconstitutional.

June 1962 The Students for a Democratic Society (SDS) issues the "Port Huron Statement," a manifesto for the emerging New Left student movement.

June 25, 1962 The Supreme Court ruling in *Engel v. Vitale* holds that prayer in schools is unconstitutional.

July 8, 1962 The U.S. government initiates a study on the impact of television on young children.

July 9-August 1, 1962 Artist Andy Warhol exhibits a series of paintings of Campbell's soup cans at the Ferus Gallery in Los Angeles, California.

July 26, 1962 The public schools in Prince Edward County, Virginia, are opened by federal order after being closed for three years in an attempt to avoid desegregation. The schools remain closed on appeal, however, and the case is sent to the U.S. Supreme Court.

October 1962 President Kennedy faces off with Soviet Premier Nikita Khrushchev over the Soviets' placement of long-range missiles on the island nation of Cuba, eventually forcing the removal of the missiles.

October 1, 1962 James Meredith becomes the first black student to enroll at the University of Mississippi. The event sparks fifteen hours of rioting, leaving two dead. He had been blocked from enrollment by Mississippi governor Ross Barnett on September 24, by Lt. Governor Paul Johnson on September 26, and by riots on campus on September 30.

1963 Betty Friedan publishes *The Feminine Mystique*, a major book on the role of women in U.S. society.

January 14, 1963 In his inaugural speech as governor of Alabama, George Wallace declares his support for "segregation now, segregation tomorrow, segregation forever!"

January 26, 1963 A New York City newspaper strike ends after 114 days with lost revenues of $100 million. It becomes the costliest newspaper strike in history.

January 28, 1963 The first black student enrolls at Clemson College in South Carolina—without incident.

April 2, 1963 The Rev. Dr. Martin Luther King Jr. and the Southern Christian Leadership Conference begin efforts to desegregate the city of Birmingham, Alabama.

June 11, 1963 Alabama Governor George Wallace blocks the steps of the University of Alabama to prevent the enrollment of two black students. However, a court order secures the enrollment of the students.

June 17, 1963 In the case of *Murray v. Curlett,* the U.S. Supreme Court issues a definitive ruling against prayer in public schools. The case launched the career of Madalyn Murray O'Hair, who became America's most vocal atheist activist.

June 26, 1963 President John F. Kennedy pledges that the United States will help West Germany resist communism, proclaiming "Ich bin ein Berliner" (I am a Berliner).

July 16, 1963 Barry Goldwater accepts the Republican presidential nomination, announcing that "extremism in the defense of liberty is no vice."

August 18, 1963 James Meredith becomes the first black to graduate from the University of Mississippi with a bachelor's degree.

August 28, 1963 At the March on Washington for Jobs and Freedom, attended by more than 100,000 supporters of the civil rights movement, the Rev. Dr. Martin Luther King Jr. delivers his "I Have a Dream" speech.

September 15, 1963 Four young black girls are murdered when a bomb explodes under the steps of the Sixteenth Street Baptist Church in Birmingham, Alabama.

November 1, 1963 South Vietnamese president Ngo Dinh Diem is killed in a U.S.-backed coup.

November 22, 1963 President John F. Kennedy is assassinated in Dallas, Texas. Lyndon B. Johnson is sworn in as president.

December 16, 1963 President Lyndon B. Johnson signs an aid-to-higher-education bill into law as a "monument to President Kennedy."

January 8, 1964 President Johnson declares a "War on Poverty."

February 1964 The Beatles begin their first U.S. concert tour.

February 1964 Boxer Cassius Clay defeats Sonny Liston to become world heavyweight champion. The next day he publicly changes his name, first to Muhammad X and then to Muhammad Ali. He also embraces the Nation of Islam as his religion.

March 1964 Black activist Malcolm X breaks with the Nation of Islam, a black separatist group, and begins his own group, the Organization of Afro-American Unity. The new association promotes peaceful coexistence between whites and blacks as well as equal rights for blacks.

May 25, 1964 The U.S. Supreme Court holds that the Prince Edward County, Virginia, schools must open.

June 1964 Three civil rights workers are killed during the voter-registration drive called "freedom summer" in Mississippi.

July 2, 1964 President Johnson signs the Civil Rights Act of 1964 into law.

July 18, 1964 Riots break out in the black neighborhoods of New York City.

August 3, 1964 North Vietnamese patrol boats attack U.S. ships in the Gulf of Tonkin.

August 7, 1964 The U.S. Congress passes the Tonkin Gulf Resolution, granting President Lyndon B. Johnson congressional approval to wage war in Vietnam.

August 30, 1964 President Johnson signs the Equal Opportunity Act, which provides $950 million for anti-poverty programs, small-business loans, and youth programs, and also forms the Job Corps.

September 1964 The Warren Commission issues a report declaring that Lee Harvey Oswald acted alone in the assassination of John F. Kennedy.

October 12, 1964 The first space flight with more than one man is launched by the Soviet Union.

December 3, 1964 Nearly eight hundred students sitting in at the administration building of the University of California, Berkeley, are arrested.

December 10, 1964 The Rev. Dr. Martin Luther King Jr. is awarded the Nobel Peace Prize for his work promoting equal rights for all Americans.

January 25, 1965 The federal budget contains the largest increase in welfare and education spending since President Franklin Delano Roosevelt's New Deal of the 1930s.

February 8, 1965 The Soviet Union commits military support to the North Vietnamese.

February 21, 1965 Black leader Malcolm X is shot and killed after delivering a speech in Harlem, New York.

March 2, 1965 U.S. bombing campaigns begin over North Vietnam.

March 7, 1965 Civil rights activists, marching from Selma to Montgomery, Alabama, to protest the lack of voting rights for blacks, are attacked by Alabama state police.

March 8, 1965 The first U.S. combat troops leave for Vietnam; earlier on-ground personnel were advisers or other support personnel.

March 18, 1965 Soviet cosmonaut Aleksei Leonev walks in space for ten minutes.

March 25, 1965 Twenty-five thousand civil rights activists gather in Montgomery, Alabama.

April 17, 1965 The first mass protest against the Vietnam War is organized by Students for a Democratic Society and attracts more than 15,000 protestors to Washington, D.C.

April 25, 1965 The United States confirms that North Vietnamese troops are fighting within South Vietnam.

June 5, 1965 U.S. officials announce the active engagement of U.S. troops in combat in Vietnam.

June 18, 1965 Nguyen Cao Cy becomes South Vietnamese premier.

June 28, 1965 President Johnson increases the military draft from 17,000 to 35,000 men per month.

July 17, 1965 The first close-up photos of Mars taken in space are sent to Earth by U.S. spacecraft *Mariner 4.*

July 28, 1965 125,000 U.S. troops are committed to the fight in Vietnam.

August 6, 1965 President Johnson signs the Voting Rights Act of 1965 into law.

August 11-16, 1965 The Watts section of Los Angeles, California, erupts in riots that kill thirty-five people and damage $200 million in property.

September 16, 1965 Labor leader Dolores Huerta helps organize a strike of 5,000 United Farm Workers of America (UFW) farmworkers in Delano, California. The strike ends in 1970—following a two-year national boycott of grapes—with the recognition of the labor union.

October 15, 1965 Protests against the war in Vietnam spread to forty U.S. cities.

November 27, 1965 Twenty-five thousand antiwar demonstrators converge on Washington, D.C.

December 20, 1965 U.S. field commanders pursue enemy troops into Cambodia, which borders on South Vietnam.

December 21, 1965 The Soviet Union announces increased support for North Vietnam.

1966 The National Organization for Women (NOW), a political action group formed to win equal rights for women, is founded with author Betty Friedan as its first president.

1966 The Student Nonviolent Coordinating Committee (SNCC) changes its official policy from integration to separatism, changes its name to the Student National Coordinating Committee, and expels all whites from its organization.

January 1966 In the Haight-Ashbury neighborhood of San Francisco, California, a group of young people organize the Trips Festival, which is widely seen as the start of the hippie movement. Within months, Haight-Ashbury becomes the center of this loosely based youth movement.

February 3, 1966 The unmanned Soviet spacecraft, *Luna 9,* makes the first landing on the moon.

February 4, 1966 Televised congressional hearings on U.S. policy regarding the Vietnam War begin.

March 16, 1966 With *Gemini 8,* U.S. astronauts Neil Armstrong and David Scott perform the first space docking of an orbiting spacecraft.

April 3, 1966 The unmanned Soviet spacecraft, *Luna 10,* becomes the first man-made object to orbit the moon.

April 6, 1966 The National Farm Workers Union, headed by César Chávez, is recognized as the bargaining agent for farmworkers at Schenley Industries after nearly a year-long strike.

May 12, 1966 To protest the University of Chicago's cooperation with the military draft, students stage a sit-in at the administration building.

May 15, 1966 Ten thousand antiwar demonstrators picket the White House.

July 1, 1966 The first U.S. health-insurance plan for the elderly, Medicare, starts.

July 11, 1966 The Soviet Union refuses to send athletes to participate in the annual U.S.–Soviet track meet because of U.S. policy in Vietnam.

July 12, 1966 Riots erupt in Chicago, Illinois, and occur in twenty other cities during the summer.

August 30, 1966 Communist China agrees to send aid to North Vietnam.

September 1966 In a famous *Playboy* magazine interview, LSD advocate Timothy Leary urges Americans to "turn on, tune in [and] drop out."

September 1, 1966 French President Charles de Gaulle asks the United States to withdraw from Vietnam.

September 9, 1966 The Traffic Safety Act is signed by President Johnson. It enforces safety standards for automobiles.

October 1966 Huey P. Newton and Bobby Seale establish the Black Panthers, a militant black nationalist group.

1967 College student protests of the Vietnam War and the draft increase throughout the country.

1967 The "summer of love" begins when more than 75,000 young people migrate to San Francisco's Haight-Ashbury district with the hope of building a new society based on peace, "free love," and drugs. During the summer, bad drug experiences, crime, rape, and violence escalate in the district. The summer ends with a march proclaiming the death of the hippie movement.

1967 The use of LSD is made illegal nationwide.

January 15, 1967 Led by fiery coach Vince Lombardi, the Green Bay Packers win the National Football League's inaugural (first) Super Bowl.

January 27, 1967 Gus Grissom, Edward White, and Roger Chaffee are killed aboard the rocket *Apollo 1* after a fire on the launch pad.

April 1967 Large antiwar protests occur in San Francisco and New York City.

May 13, 1967 New York City hosts a pro-Vietnam War parade that attracts 70,000 people.

June 23-25, 1967 In Glassboro, New Jersey, Soviet Premier Aleksei Kosygin and U.S. President Johnson discuss nuclear arms control, Vietnam, and the Middle East.

July 12, 1967 Riots break out in Newark, New Jersey.

July 23, 1967 Riots in Detroit, Michigan, kill forty-three people and damage $200 million in property; the National Guard is called in to restore order.

August 3, 1967 President Johnson announces plans to send 45,000 to 50,000 additional troops to Vietnam in order to raise troop strength to 525,000 by the end of 1968.

October 21-22, 1967 More than 250,000 people organized by the National Mobilization to End the War in Vietnam (MOBE) gather to protest the Vietnam War in Washington, D.C. The protest ends in a lighthearted attempt, led by activist Abbie Hoffmann, to levitate the Pentagon.

January 25, 1968 Secretary of Health, Education, and Welfare John Gardner's doubts about the "Great Society" lead him to resign.

January 31, 1968 The North Vietnamese army launches the Tet Offensive, a major military campaign against South Vietnamese and American forces in South Vietnam.

February 6, 1968 Sweden grants asylum (political protection) to six American soldiers opposed to the war in Vietnam.

February 27, 1968 News anchor Walter Cronkite announces on national television that he believes the war in Vietnam has become a stalemate (a situation in which progress is at a standstill).

March 8, 1968 The first statewide teacher's strike in U.S. history ends after almost half of Florida's public-school teachers spend more than two weeks on picket lines.

March 16, 1968 The My Lai massacre leaves hundreds of South Vietnamese men, women, and children dead at the hands of U.S. soldiers. (Reports of the deaths are suppressed for more than a year.)

March 31, 1968 President Johnson announces that he will not seek reelection as president of the United States.

April 4, 1968 Civil rights leader Rev. Dr. Martin Luther King Jr. is assassinated in Memphis, Tennessee.

May 6-30, 1968 Student demonstrations in Paris, France, spark a general strike throughout the country that eventually involves 10 million workers.

May 12, 1968 Peace talks to end the Vietnam War begin in Paris.

June 5, 1968 Democratic presidential candidate Robert Kennedy is assassinated in Los Angeles shortly after winning the California primary.

August 26-29, 1968 At the Democratic presidential nominating convention in Chicago, Illinois, Vice President Hubert Humphrey secures the party's nomination. Protests rage, both inside and outside the convention center, and police and National Guard forces attack and beat demonstrators on national television. A radical group known as the Yippies nominates a pig for president.

September 7, 1968 More than one hundred women's liberation protestors gather outside the Miss America Pageant proceedings to throw out bras, girdles, and high-heeled shoes to protest women's subordination to men in American society.

October 14-28, 1968 American 200-meter-dash gold medalist Tommie Smith and bronze medalist John Carlos bow their heads and raise their fists in a Black Power salute during the playing of the "Star-Spangled Banner" at the Olympic Games in Mexico. As a result, they are stripped of their medals and suspended from their team.

November 5, 1968 Republican Richard M. Nixon is elected president, defeating Democrat Hubert Humphrey and independent candidate George Wallace.

December 4, 1968 The U.S. government enforces the 1964 Civil Rights Act in the North by ordering the public schools in Union, New Jersey, to comply with desegregation.

December 21, 1968 With *Apollo 8*, the United States becomes the first to orbit a manned spacecraft around the Moon.

1969 The "Great Society" programs give educational aid to 9 million children from low-income families, offer Head Start primary care to 716,000, and support the vocational education of 4 million high school and 845,000 technical students.

1969 President Nixon continues negotiations to end the Vietnam War.

1969 The Supreme Court orders the immediate desegregation of all public schools.

June 8, 1969 President Nixon orders the removal of 25,000 American troops from Vietnam, thus beginning the American withdrawal from the war.

June 18-22, 1969 The Students for a Democratic Society holds its national convention, which concludes with the organization breaking up into the Progressive Labor Party and the Revolutionary Youth Movement (RYM).

June 27, 1969 Homosexuals and police clash at the Stonewall Inn in New York following a police raid on the bar; the Stonewall riot is the symbolic start of the gay liberation movement.

July 20, 1969 The United States lands the first manned spacecraft, *Apollo 11,* on the Moon. Neil Armstrong and Edwin "Buzz" Aldrin walk on the Moon's surface.

August 1969 Members of the Manson Family, a cult led by Charles Manson, murder seven people outside Los Angeles, California.

August 15-17, 1969 The Woodstock Music Festival is held in upstate New York, drawing more than 500,000 music lovers.

September 3, 1969 North Vietnamese president Ho Chi Minh dies at age seventy-nine.

October 15, 1969 Various antiwar groups label this day "Moratorium Day" and organize hundreds of thousands of marchers in protests across the United States.

November 15, 1969 250,000 antiwar demonstrators march on Washington, D.C.

November 21, 1969 A group of Native American activists, led by Richard Oakes, takes possession of Alcatraz Island in the bay near San Francisco, California. The event marks one of the most dramatic moments in the growing Native American rights movement.

1973 Following the landmark decision by the U.S. Supreme Court in *Roe v. Wade,* abortion is legalized in the United States. For many involved in the struggle for women's rights, particularly women's reproductive rights, this is a major victory for their cause.

April 23, 1975 President Gerald Ford, who succeeded Richard Nixon, announces that the war in Vietnam is "finished."

April 30, 1975 The South Vietnamese surrender to officially end the war in Vietnam.

January 21, 1977 President Jimmy Carter fulfills his campaign promise to pardon those who had peacefully avoided the draft during the Vietnam War. This allowed draft dodgers, who had fled the country to avoid mandatory military service, to return home to the United States without fear of being prosecuted for their actions.

1980 The conservative movement, begun under Senator Barry Goldwater, shows its strength as Republican Ronald Reagan soundly defeats incumbent president Jimmy Carter in the presidential election.

1982 The Equal Rights Amendment, which states that equal legal rights cannot be denied based on gender, fails to be ratified. Although the amendment passed in both the House and Senate in 1972, it needed to be ratified by three-fourths (thirty-eight) of the states before it could become part of the U.S. Constitution. The ERA fell three states short of ratification by its deadline in 1982. President Ronald Reagan was among those opposed to the amendment; earlier, he became the first major presidential candidate to voice his opposition to the ERA.

November 13, 1982 The Vietnam Veterans Memorial, also known as "The Wall," is dedicated in Washington, D.C. Designed by twenty-one-year-old artist/architect Maya Lin, the memorial records the names of the more than 58,000 American men and women who did not return from the war.

1991 The communist government of the Soviet Union collapses, thus ending the Cold War between the United States and the Soviet Union.

November 2000 The first crew takes up residence on the International Space Station, a joint effort by the Canadian, European, Japanese, Brazilian, Russian, and U.S.

space agencies. The crew consists of two Russians and one American.

August 2003 On August 20, Alabama Chief Justice Roy Moore refuses to abide by a U.S. District Court order to remove a Ten Commandments monument from the state's judicial building. The U.S. District Court had ruled that the monument violated the separation of church and state. On August 27, workers remove the monument from public view. Later, Moore loses his job for refusing to comply with the court order. The monument itself begins a tour of U.S. cities in mid-2004.

2004 Twin robots, part of NASA's Mars Exploration Rover program, transmit photos to scientists back on Earth as the agency studies the geology of the red planet.

2004 Senator John Kerry, a Vietnam veteran who later spoke against the war, runs for president against incumbent George W. Bush.

Words to Know

A

activist: A person who campaigns vigorously for or against a political, social, or economic issue.

authentic: True to one's spirit or character. In the 1960s, the idea of being authentic was important to many young people because they considered the behavior of their parents to be inauthentic or something that compromised their own values.

B

black nationalism: An ideology held among militant groups of American blacks that called for the formation of self-governing black communities that were separate from those of whites.

Black Power: A movement among American blacks to gain economic and political rights and improve their social condition.

C

civil rights: The legal, political, and human rights guaranteed by the U.S. constitution and various legislative acts, including the right to vote, the right to equal protection under the law, to right to equal use of public facilities, and the right to freedom of speech.

Cold War: A prolonged conflict for world dominance from 1945 to 1991 between the two superpowers, the democratic, capitalist United States and the communist Soviet Union. The weapons of conflict were commonly words of propaganda and threats, not military conflicts.

communal living: A shared living space formed by a group of like-minded individuals. Those living in communes work together for the common good of the group and share material possessions.

communism: A political system in which most aspects of social and economic life are dictated by the government. Under communism, all property is owned by the government and, theoretically, wealth is distributed evenly throughout society.

conservatism: A political ideology based on the concept of a limited federal government, one that protects individual's freedoms by maintaining domestic order, providing for national defense, and administering justice. This ideology is generally opposed to the use of federal powers for the protection or preservation of civil rights.

counterculture: Literally, a cultural group whose values run counter to the majority. In the late 1950s and through the 1960s, several distinct groups criticized developments in American society and worked for social change. Some historians use the term to refer only to hippies, but the counterculture also included groups such as the New Left and racial and ethnic political action groups.

D

democracy: A political system that places the power of the government in the hands of citizens. During the Cold

War, democracy was generally considered to include a capitalist economic system, in which individual property owners made the decisions that determined economic activities.

desegregation: To end the practice of separating races, as in schools, buses, restaurants, or other public facilities.

discrimination: The singling out of minority groups for unfavorable treatment.

draft (selective service): A system by which persons are chosen for mandatory service in a nation's military.

draft dodgers: Persons who hide in or flee from a country in order to avoid mandatory military service.

drop out: To reject the social and economic norms of society by living an alternative lifestyle.

E

establishment: A term used by members of the counterculture to refer to the established power structures and authority figures of the time, including parents, employers, and the government.

F

feminism: A theory and organized social movement based on the idea that male and female genders are socially, politically, and economically equal.

G

grassroots: An effort formed by ordinary people at a local community level.

Great Society: The social vision of President Lyndon B. Johnson that would use the federal government to improve the American quality of life. This would be achieved by enacting legislation to regulate air and water quality, to offer medical care, to provide civil

Space Race: A competition between the United States and the Soviet Union to build space programs that launched rockets and men outside the Earth's orbit. One of the chief objectives of the Space Race was to land a man on the moon.

U

Uncle Tom: A derogatory term used to refer to a black person who acts in submissive ways toward whites.

V

Vietcong: Guerilla forces in South Vietnam who allied themselves with the North Vietnamese Army in an effort to unify the country under communist rule. The Vietcong fought the U.S. forces that came to aid South Vietnam in its quest to remain independent. Guerilla forces are those involved in unconventional warfare practices, including sabotage and terrorist activities.

W

War on Poverty: The central program of President Lyndon B. Johnson's "Great Society," this effort tried to end poverty by providing poor Americans with education, job training, food, housing, and money.

welfare: Government aid to the needy in the form of money or other necessities, such as foodstuffs or housing.

Research and Activity Ideas

The following ideas and projects are intended to offer suggestions for complementing your classroom work on understanding various aspects of the 1960s in America:

The 1960s Outside America: You know that the 1960s were a turbulent, exciting decade in the United States, but did you know that similar disruptions shook some of the other major countries around the world? In the summer of 1968, student walkouts and union strikes paralyzed much of France, especially the capital city of Paris. That same year, an uprising against communist rule in Czechoslovakia led to an invasion of that country by troops sponsored by the Soviet Union. Research the events that happened in France, Czechoslovakia, or some other country and compare and contrast them with events in the United States.

A Decade of Movements: The 1960s is often seen as a decade of movements. The civil rights movement, the antiwar movement, the student movement, the Native American rights movement, the gay liberation movement, and the women's movement all achieved important gains during the decade. Using what you know or what you can learn about these movements, construct a project that analyzes the relationships between two or more movements. You might consider whether the movements share common underlying themes or ideas, analyze whether their methods proved to be effective for reaching their goals, or even compare some of the political statements or "manifestos" produced by these groups. Your project might be a research paper, a multimedia presentation, or a comparative timeline.

Then and Now: Historians of rock 'n' roll music often look to the 1960s as the starting point of trends that carried forward into the twenty-first century. For example, the Beatles are often said to be the biggest influence on U.S. pop music. Using the medium of music, create a project that shows the continuity across decades. You could present several clips of music from across the decades that show the influence of bands from the 1960s on bands from the 1970s, 1980s, 1990s, or 2000s, or you could write an essay examining how certain themes or trends in music have emerged since, or as a result of, the 1960s. You might research your favorite band. Do they cite any acts from the 1960s as influences on their music today? Use your imagination to create a project that is both useful and entertaining.

Kennedy: The Myth and the Reality: A survey conducted in 2003 showed that Americans consider John F. Kennedy to be one of the greatest presidents in American history, second only to Abraham Lincoln. Yet most Americans cannot point to specific programs or accomplishments of the Kennedy administration. Consider the reasons for Kennedy's enduring popularity. Does he deserve such high esteem or not? How do his actual accomplishments as president compare with popular memories of his presidency?

Oral History: If you ask around, it is likely that you will find people in your community—perhaps even in your school—who were involved in some of the important events of the 1960s, such as a civil rights march or an antiwar demonstration. You may even know someone who fought in the Vietnam War. Interview this person to learn about his or her memories of the events of the 1960s and how they impacted his or her life. Then write an oral history that relates the memories of your subject, or compares those memories to other accounts of the event remembered.

A Movement for Today: People who got involved in the different movements of the 1960s—such as the civil rights movement or the antiwar movement—believed strongly in the need for people to work together to bring about social change. Is there something in today's culture that you would like to change? Working with others, create a new organization to promote the change you would like to see. Then, write a "manifesto," or a written statement of purpose, and a plan for recruiting volunteers. You might even work together to stage a public event to draw support for your cause.

A Museum of the 1960s: You have just been hired by a wealthy philanthropist (a person who is dedicated to helping the welfare of others, through charitable means) to create a museum of the 1960s. She has asked that you have four sections to relate the major experiences of the decade. Working alone or with classmates, create a plan for your museum. How will you organize the four sections of the museum? What kinds of exhibits will you use to help people understand the decade? You might either write a plan to present to the philanthropist, or lay out a floor plan for the museum that shows the different elements you hope to incorporate.

The 1960s on the Web: Plenty of information about the 1960s is available on the Internet—but not all of it is worthwhile. Students like you would benefit from a guide to the 1960s on the Web that pointed out what is worthwhile and what is not. Choose an area of the 1960s that interests you—such as hippies, or John F. Kennedy, or the Vietnam War—and research your subject on the Web. Then provide an annotated list of the five top Web sites (an annotated list provides the

Web address and a brief description that discusses the site), as well as a list of those sources that you do not think are worthwhile. Or, create a Web site of your own with links to the best sites.

Debating the Vietnam War: America's involvement in the Vietnam War was one of the most controversial issues in American history, both at the time and ever since. Do you understand why the United States got involved in the war, and why the war did not turn out like the strategists planned? Do you understand why some people spoke out so strongly against the war? With at least one partner, take some time to research both sides of the issue. Then present a debate in class. As an alternative, pretend that you and your partner are opposing presidential candidates in 1968, when the war in Vietnam was a very important issue. Both candidates should present opening statements about their positions, then defend their position as they accept questions from the audience.

Personal Top Ten: It is late December 1969 and you are the feature writer for a major national newspaper. Your editor just asked that you put together a list of the top ten stories of the 1960s. What do you think are the top ten events of this decade? Write up your list, with a paragraph describing why each event is important.

The Sixties in America

Almanac

Grand Dreams for a Better Society: Conflicting Visions of the 1960s

The 1960s were years of great and shocking events: assassins gunned down three national figures, including a president; President John F. Kennedy (1917–1963; served 1961–63) narrowly averted a nuclear war with a high-stakes bluff; civil rights activist Martin Luther King Jr. (1929–1968) inspired the nation with his grand dream for a better nation; President Lyndon Johnson sent soldiers to fight a war in distant Vietnam; President Richard Nixon launched a spaceship that placed a man on the moon; the Beatles, an English rock band, "invaded" America; hippies "turned on, tuned in, and dropped out"; African Americans rioted in the streets of American cities; and the Green Bay Packers formed a football dynasty. With the exception of the assassinations, these were not isolated events. In fact, they were expressions of larger social movements or trends, dramatic distillations of widespread social tumult and tension. The dramatic events of the 1960s continued to have an impact on American social, political, and cultural practices into the early 2000s. One way people can understand who they are is to take a look at an earlier era in which their ancestors worked out their visions of the American dream.

Those who grew into adulthood in the 1960s also looked back to an earlier era to make sense of their lives. They looked back especially to the Great Depression (1929–41) and to World War II (1939–45), the most momentous events of the recent years. Members of this earlier generation endured severe economic troubles and then wartime civilian hardships and military service when the United States joined the Allied powers of Great Britain, France, and others against the Axis powers of Germany, Italy, and Japan. Following the end of World War II, the United States was perceived as the most powerful nation on earth, both economically and militarily. By the late 1950s, the great question facing the nation was how it could live up to this great legacy—how to ensure that the nation lived up to the ideals fought for by those of an earlier generation. In the years to come, numbers of Americans—politicians, social reformers, students, and other kinds of people—dreamed about how they could affect their world. Their dreams—announced in speeches, chanted while marching, written in law, sung over the radio, beamed back to Americans from the moon via television, countered by those with different visions, and sometimes paid for in blood—gave shape to the decade.

Some of the grandest dreams of the decade were announced in the political programs of major party politicians. Democrat John F. Kennedy, elected president in 1960, called his package of policies the New Frontier, for he wanted to push Americans into a new age of accomplishment. "Ask not what your country can do for you," he implored his countrymen in his inaugural address, "ask what you can do for your country." Kennedy was an inspiration to many Americans, yet he was resisted by a Congress unwilling to move at the speed Kennedy desired. Before the end of his first term, Kennedy was assassinated. His successor, Democrat Lyndon Johnson also had dreams, which he called the Great Society. He wanted to see an end to poverty in the United States and the extension of equal rights to all Americans, regardless of race, color, or creed. The dreams of these Democratic politicians rested upon the excellent economic performance enjoyed by the United States during most of the decade, and Kennedy and Johnson worked to greatly expand the federal government. Republican Richard Nixon, who was elected in 1968, did not share the liberal dreams of big government

As presidents, John F. Kennedy (left) and Lyndon Baines Johnson (right) each had a dream for America, but neither was able to see his vision fulfilled. Kennedy was cut down by an assassin's bullet while Johnson got derailed by the war in Vietnam. *Courtesy of the John F. Kennedy Library.*

pursued by the two Democratic presidents before him. In fact, Nixon represented the growing conservative political movement of the period, a movement that believed in limiting the size and power of the federal government and returning power to state and local governments and whenever possible to the people themselves. This conservative vision proved a strong force in American politics into the 2000s.

One opinion held by many Republican and Democratic politicians during the 1960s was that Communism, the form of government in the Soviet Union and the People's Republic of China, was the biggest threat to the United States. U.S. politicians committed themselves to stopping the spread of Communism throughout the world in a long conflict known as the Cold War (1945–91). America's Cold War policy was shaped by the belief that a democratic political system and a free-market economy (one which let individual property owners make the majority of economic decisions) provided the best opportunities for the people of the world and that

Communism was a tool of oppression. These beliefs led to dramatic encounters with the Soviet Union over its missiles placed in Cuba and over the Berlin Wall, a wall that divided the German capitol, Berlin, into east and west sections.

The political commitment to stop the spread of Communism was part of the explanation for the U.S. involvement in a civil war in Vietnam. American foreign policy was based, in part, on two beliefs: Communism must be contained, and other nations should use democratic means to achieve self-rule. These two beliefs came into deep conflict during the Vietnam War. In order to stop the spread of Communism, the United States supported the corrupt and brutal pro-Western South Vietnamese government that thwarted the majority preference for communist rule. The conflict between these two guiding principles of American foreign policy complicated the already difficult matter of conducting a war in Vietnam and helped inspire the largest antiwar movement in American history. Starting on college campuses in 1965, the antiwar movement became a powerful force in American politics by the late 1960s, drawing hundreds of thousands of participants and using its dream of global peace to change American foreign policy.

When Martin Luther King Jr. stood on the steps of the Lincoln Memorial in Washington, D.C., on August 28, 1963, he looked out over an audience of 250,000 supporters of civil rights for African Americans. He told this audience and the nation: "I have a dream that one day...sons of former slaves and the sons of former slave owners will be able to sit down together at the table of brotherhood." King's dream, shared by millions of Americans, black and white, was one public expression of a powerful civil rights movement that drew increasing attention during the 1960s. In fact, the struggle for civil rights was expressed publicly in many ways during the 1960s, from marches to sit-ins to violent riots. By the mid-1960s, landmark legislation granted American blacks full civil and voting rights, nearly 100 years after the slaves were freed. By the middle of the 1960s, other groups began to grasp the significance of the dream: women, Native Americans, Chicanos, and homosexuals all lay claim to this dream as they too agitated for equal rights in a diverse American society.

The dream of a society in which people would not be judged on the basis of race, class, gender, or sexual orienta-

Martin Luther King, Jr. delivered his famous "I Have a Dream" speech during the March on Washington in 1963. In his address he said that people should not be judged based on their skin color but on the content of their character. *UPI/Corbis-Bettman.*

tion posed very real challenges to long-held American traditions, beliefs, and institutions. Across the American South, whites resisted, sometimes violently, the destruction of their long-standing racist behavior. Many people argued against granting legal protections to minorities, women, and homosexuals. Yet by the end of the decade, protest groups had made important gains in eroding persistent American biases and prejudices. Their gains did not completely erase these prejudices, but the movement for equal rights for all Americans that gained ground in the 1960s was one of the most significant shifts in social consciousness and behavior of the twentieth century.

Americans pursued a variety of other dreams during the 1960s. The National Aeronautics and Space Administration (NASA) raced to place a man on the moon before the Soviet space program, and NASA succeeded in 1969. Hippies pursued their dream of peace, while engaging in drug use and unconventional sexual behavior. Other changes swept through American society: television use became nearly universal, though people worried about the quality of programming; the arts and literature reflected the turbulence of social and political change; and sports became more highly commercialized. For those immersed in pushing for social and political change, it was an intensely stimulating decade. For those who wanted to keep things the way they had been, the 1960s were disturbing and threatening years. By the end of the decade, many people felt exhausted by the pace of change, and they shifted their attention from world affairs and politics to their own private lives, a shift that earned the 1970s the nickname "The Me Decade." Were the 1960s more turbulent, more highly charged, than other decades? Were the great dreams pursued by Americans realized? These are some of the questions explored in the following chapters.

For More Information

Books

Archer, Jules. *The Incredible Sixties: The Stormy Years that Changed America*. San Diego, CA: Harcourt Brace Jovanovich, 1986.

Dudley, William, ed. *The 1960s*. San Diego, CA: Greenhaven, 2000.

Isserman, Maurice, and Michael Kazin. *America Divided: The Civil War of the 1960s*. New York: Oxford University Press, 2000.

The Innocent 1960s: Politics in the Kennedy Years

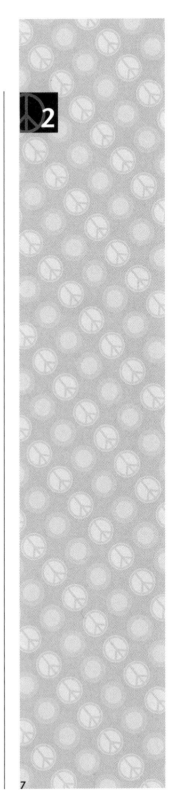

2

In the early 2000s, President John F. Kennedy (1917–1963; served 1961–63) was widely esteemed as one of the most important leaders in U.S. history. In fact, a 2003 poll conducted by Ohio University and the Scripps Howard News Service revealed that 14 percent of Americans listed Kennedy as their favorite president, placing him second only to Abraham Lincoln (1809–1865; served 1861–65), who led the United States during the Civil War. Yet it is difficult to point to tangible reasons for Kennedy's popularity: on domestic issues, he promised far more than he accomplished and passed no important legislation; in foreign policy, he fumbled an invasion of Cuba, narrowly averted a nuclear war with the Soviet Union, and enmeshed the United States in what became the protracted war in Vietnam. Clearly, it was not his lackluster record of political accomplishments that won Kennedy the love and respect of Americans, both at the time and in the following decades. What Kennedy offered instead was an inspiring challenge for Americans to live up to their higher ideals and, for Americans looking back, a nostalgic reminder of a less complicated time in American life. In the early twenty-first century, Kennedy remained a symbol of the simpler side of the 1960s.

The election of 1960: religion, Cold War politics, and television

As the presidential election of 1960 drew nearer, Americans were faced with a choice between two very different candidates. Richard M. Nixon (1913–1994), the Republican Party's nominee, was well known to voters. He had served as vice president for eight years under Republican president Dwight D. Eisenhower (1890–1969; served 1953–61), who was the popular hero of World War II (1939–45). Nixon ran on Eisenhower's record, which called for minimal government involvement in the economy and a mild commitment to civil rights reforms, then an emerging political issue. Nixon also presented himself as a staunch opponent of Communism, the political system favored by the Soviet Union and the People's Republic of China. Loved by few, Nixon was yet the choice of the Republican establishment, and he faced no serious challenges to his nomination bid.

Kennedy, on the other hand, offered a real change from the go-slow politics of the Eisenhower era. Just forty-three years old when he ran for president, the youthful son of a powerful political family told Americans that it was time for their country to accomplish great things. That message was positive, but Kennedy had one great liability: he was Catholic. No Catholic had ever been elected president, for many Americans feared that a Catholic president would take orders from the pope, the leader of the Roman Catholic Church. In the primary race and again in the general election, Kennedy was forced to confront the issue. For example, in a September 12, 1960, speech he said, according to Theodore White's *The Making of the President 1960*: "I believe in an America where the separation of Church and State is absolute, where no Catholic prelate would tell the President (should he be a Catholic) how to act, and no Protestant minister would tell his parishioners how to vote." Once he put this issue to rest, Kennedy was able to focus on his campaign goals to improve the country's economic performance—which had been stalled for several

years—and make the United States a more powerful world leader in part by encouraging its people to commit themselves to public service.

Early polls showed that the race between the candidates was too close to call, and as the November election neared every campaign statement was scrutinized for how it would affect the outcome of the election. In September, the two candidates agreed to a series of nationally televised debates—the first presidential debates ever seen on national television. The more experienced Nixon believed he could beat the man he considered a political lightweight, but under the hot glare of the TV lights a different impression was conveyed. Kennedy's youthful, handsome appearance and cool, easy demeanor came off well on TV; Nixon, by contrast, had had his makeup applied poorly and he looked tired and tense. Though people listening to the debates on the radio felt that Nixon had mastered the issues, the 115 to 120 million TV viewers judged Kennedy the clear winner.

Richard Nixon (left) squares off against John F. Kennedy (right) in the first presidential debates broadcast on national television, September 1960. © Bettmann/Corbis.

After these debates, Kennedy began to win more supporters. Just before the election, Kennedy won the endorsement of Martin Luther King Sr., father of the emerging civil rights leader. The endorsement helped swing the African American vote to Kennedy in the South, which contributed to his ultimate victory in North Carolina and Texas. On election night, however, the vote was nearly too close to call. With 64 percent of Americans voting, Kennedy received 49.7 percent of the vote (34,227,096 votes), while Nixon won 49.5 percent (34,107,646 votes). In the end, Kennedy won by just over 119,450 more votes than Nixon. (The margin was greater in the electoral college, where Kennedy took 303 votes to Nixon's 219.)

Kennedy's dream

Kennedy entered the office of the presidency with no clear mandate from the American voting public and with a reduced Democratic majority in both the House and Senate. Yet the narrowness of his victory did not prevent him from announcing an ambitious agenda for his presidency and for the American public. In his inaugural address—delivered on a day so cold that the event was nearly cancelled—Kennedy delivered a stirring call to action to the American people, as quoted on the Library of Congress *Presidential Inaugurations* Web site. The speech was focused primarily on foreign policy, and he committed America to protecting the world from the spread of communism when he stated: "Let every nation know, whether it wishes us well or ill, that we shall pay any price, bear any burden, meet any hardship, support any friend, oppose any foe, in order to assure the survival and the success of liberty." When it came to domestic policy, Kennedy asked Americans, simply and elegantly, to "ask not what your country can do for you—ask what you can do for your country."

With his impassioned address, the dashing president helped launch the Kennedy myth. In fact, much of Kennedy's legacy rests on what he said and not necessarily what he did. Kennedy frequently appealed to the highest ideals of American politics: love of freedom and equality, and commitment to public service. He asked Americans to "struggle against the common enemies of man: tyranny, poverty, disease, and war itself." He told them that they were part of a "new generation" of Americans who would shape the world of tomorrow, and though he believed that the United States faced great obstacles, he encouraged people to face those problems with hope and energy. (Many of Kennedy's speeches are collected on the John F. Kennedy Library and Museum Web site.) Kennedy's inspiring words, his youthful energy, his dynamic and charming wife, Jacqueline Bouvier Kennedy (1929–1994), and the group of young, talented assistants he brought into office—all of these fed the image of Kennedy as a dynamic and forceful leader.

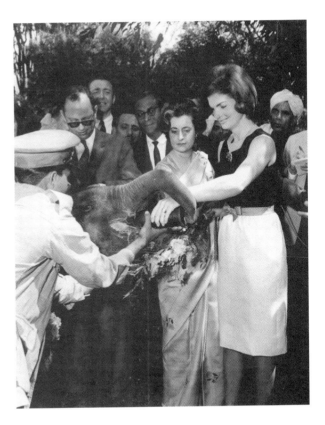

Kennedy's public words were bold, stirring, and somewhat vague, yet he had definite and pragmatic goals for his presidency. In foreign policy, he wanted to improve relations with the communist world, even while demonstrating that he would stand up to any aggression on the part of the Soviet Union or China. Kennedy wanted to establish America as the clear world leader by increasing American economic and military assistance to countries in Africa, Latin America, and Asia. And he wanted to strengthen the American military. At home, Kennedy wanted to jump-start the economy by creating jobs, reducing widespread poverty, and improving government aid for urban housing, education, and health care. He also pledged that he would take actions to end racial discrimination. He labeled his plans the New Frontier, for he wanted to take the United States forward into a new era of accomplishment. In truth, Kennedy accomplished few of his goals, for his presidency focused on frequent foreign policy crises and continual domestic policy frustrations.

Many American admired Jacqueline Kennedy's style and grace. As First Lady, she was involved in various diplomatic trips, such as a visit to India in 1962 where she met Indira Gandhi, who later became prime minister of India. *AP/Wide World Photos. Reproduced by permission.*

Cold War foreign policy: Missteps and triumphs

When he took office, John F. Kennedy inherited from his predecessor a series of difficult foreign policy situations, all of them informed by the ongoing conflict known as the Cold War (1945–91). The United States and the Soviet Union, the two most powerful countries in the world, had very different political and economic systems. The United States was committed to democratic political systems, free-market economies, and freedom of religion and expression. The Soviet Union, on the other hand, had a totalitarian political system (one in which powerful leaders made the important decisions without consulting citizens) and a communist economy. Communist Party leaders controlled all elements of Soviet life. Following the end of World War II (1939–45), both the United States and the Soviet Union had committed themselves to world leadership. The two countries did not want to fight a war with each other; both sides possessed nuclear weapons, with the capacity to destroy each other and possibly the entire world. In fact, both sides were interested in signing treaties to eliminate the possibility of nuclear warfare. Rather than fighting directly, the two countries sought to attain influence over other countries, especially smaller countries that were struggling to define or change their own political systems. This competition to establish their irreconcilable political systems was called the Cold War, and during the Kennedy administration it was fought in diplomatic clashes over Cuba, the German city of Berlin, and the civil war in Vietnam.

During his presidential campaign, Eisenhower had been involved in a dramatic confrontation with the Soviets over Soviet charges that Americans had been spying on them. On May 1, 1960, a high-altitude U.S. spy plane called a U-2 was shot down over the Soviet Union. Eisenhower denied that the plane was spying; he said it was a weather research plane that had strayed off course. Delighted to catch the American president in a lie, the Soviets produced the captured American pilot, Francis Gary Powers. Soviet premier Nikita Khrushchev (1894–1971) spoke out publicly against the spying and demanded an apology. He proclaimed: "Our country is a strong and mighty state.…If the U.S.A. has not yet suffered a real war on its territory and wants to start a war, we will fire rockets and hit their territory a few minutes later," as quoted in Gini Holland's *The 1960s*. This angry rhetoric frightened the world and proved deeply embarrassing to Eisenhower, but he steadfastly refused to apologize. In

The Peace Corps: The Softer Side of the Cold War

In most dramatic expressions of the Cold War between the United States and the Soviet Union, such as in Cuba and Berlin, military forces stood on guard and leaders brought the world to the brink of nuclear destruction. While shows of military strength were an important means of waging the war for world dominance, they were not the only means. In fact, one of the most effective means of communicating American values was the Peace Corps, created by President John F. Kennedy in 1961.

In the late 1950s, Democratic congressmen Henry S. Reuss of Wisconsin and Hubert H. Humphrey of Minnesota had argued for sending U.S. volunteers into developing nations to help relieve the suffering from poverty, disease, and illiteracy (the inability to read). Kennedy took up this idea in his 1960 campaign for the presidency, and on March 1, 1961, he signed a bill establishing the Peace Corps and appointed his brother-in-law, Sargent Shriver, to head the organization. The Peace Corps recruited, trained, and supplied mostly youthful volunteers to travel to countries around the world. Kennedy promoted the Peace Corps as one of the many ways that Americans could commit themselves to higher ideals. He believed that this volunteer service was a good way to show the world the true meaning of American values.

Though some critics have accused the Peace Corps of serving American political interests, in fact the agency worked to distance itself from political issues. Peace Corps volunteers were not out to promote American political causes but rather to help people in poor countries to develop successful farming practices, healthcare facilities, and businesses. Between its formation in 1961 and the early 2000s, the Peace Corps sent some 170,000 volunteers to 137 countries, and it continued to receive bipartisan (Republican and Democrat) support in Congress into the twenty-first century.

the end, the incident derailed a summit conference between the two superpowers, Great Britain, and France and increased tensions between the countries.

Other tensions from the Eisenhower years carried over into the first days of the Kennedy administration as well. In the Caribbean island nation of Cuba in 1959, revolutionary forces led by Fidel Castro (c. 1927–) overthrew the Cuban government of Fulgencio Batista (1901–1973), a longtime U.S. ally. Within the following year, relations between the United States and Cuba deteriorated, and Castro's government began to side with the Soviet Union, which was eager to provide assistance to a newly communist nation just ninety miles off the coast of the United States. Cuba's acceptance of Soviet-style Communism was deeply troubling to U.S. policy makers. They worried that other countries in the Caribbean might follow Cuba's example and also that the Soviet Union would put missiles in Cuba.

At the request of President Eisenhower, in 1960 the U.S. Central Intelligence Agency (CIA) laid plans for an invasion of Cuba to bring down the Castro government. Kennedy inherited these plans, but he changed them. He ordered U.S. troops to not to become directly involved in the invasion, which was carried out by pro-U.S. Cubans who had fled or were kicked out of the country following Castro's takeover. The Bay of Pigs invasion, named for the bay in Cuba where it took place, was launched on April 17, 1961, and soon turned into a disaster. U.S. intelligence predictions that there would be little armed opposition and widespread civilian support proved wrong, and the Cuban invasion forces were quickly routed: their boats were sunk and those men who landed on the beach were gunned down or captured, all while U.S. ships and planes stood by and watched. According to historian George Moss, writing in *America in the Twentieth Century*, "America stood exposed as both imperialistic and inept, a pathetic combination of wickedness and weakness." It had funded and helped organize the invasion, but did not possess the strength of will to put its own troops into action.

The United States fared better in its clash with the Soviets over of the German city of Berlin. Ever since the end of World War II, Germany had been divided in two, with communist East Germany allied with the Soviets and democratic West Germany allied with the United States. The split between the two Germanies was mirrored by the split in the city of Berlin, which lay entirely within the borders of East Germany and was divided into East and West Berlin. On August 13, 1961, the East Germans closed the border between the two halves of the city in order to prevent East German citizens from "defecting," or leaving their country, to the West. Backed by the Soviets, the East Germans began to build a wall along the border to block free passage across the border. Soviet and East German soldiers shot and killed anyone attempting to escape East Germany for the freedom of West Berlin. In 1963, President Kennedy traveled to West Berlin and announced, to an adoring audience of West Berliners: "There are many people in the world who really don't understand, or say they don't, what is the great issue between the free world and the Communist world. Let them come to Berlin.... Freedom has many difficulties and democracy is not perfect. But we have never had to put a wall up to keep our people in—to prevent them from leaving us.... All free men, wherever they may live, are citizens of Berlin. And, therefore, as a free man, I take pride in the words 'Ich bin ein Berliner,' [I am a Berliner]" as quoted at the *American Rhetoric* Web site. Thanks in part to Kennedy's speech, the wall came to stand as a symbol for the way the governments in Soviet Bloc countries repressed their citizens. The wall's destruction in November 1989 signaled the beginning of the end of the Cold War.

Cuban missile crisis

In 1962, the United States and the Soviet Union clashed once again, in what became the single most dangerous clash in the long history of the Cold War. Following the Bay of Pigs invasion of Cuba, the Soviet Union agreed to provide military advice and assistance to the tiny nation. The United States monitored as carefully as it could the interactions between the two communist nations, and on October 14, 1962, the worst fears of American strategists were realized. On that date, a U.S. U-2 spy plane flying over Cuba took photos that revealed that the Soviets were assisting in the construction of launch sites for both medium-range and intermediate-range ballistic missiles, which were capable of delivering nuclear warheads to major American cities—including Washington, D.C. Intensified spy missions revealed that the missile sites—twelve in all—could be operational as early as the end of October.

Kennedy quickly convened his top military and political advisors to help him decide how to confront this serious threat to U.S. security. These advisors (including the president's brother, Attorney General Robert F. Kennedy [1925–1968] and Secretary of Defense Robert McNamara [1916–]) presented Kennedy with several options, including going public with the information and demanding negotiations, conducting negotiations in private, placing a

MISSILE EQUIPMENT
MARIEL PORT FACILITY
4 NOVEMBER 1962

LAUNCH STANDS

17 MISSILE ERECTORS

Aerial intelligence photos revealed that the Soviets were placing missiles in Cuba for a possible attack on the United States. This view of the Mariel Port facility in Cuba reveals some of those locations. *© Corbis.*

naval blockade around the island, launching a tactical air strike on the missile sites, or conducting an all-out U.S. invasion of Cuba. For an agonizing week, Kennedy's team, named Excomm, for Executive Committee of the National Security Council, deliberated over what was the correct path for the nation to follow. Each of the members believed that the future of the country, and perhaps of the world, was at risk.

On October 22, the president briefed Congress and then gave a dramatic, televised address to a shocked nation. He described the Soviet presence in Cuba and his decision to impose a naval blockade on Cuba that would bar any military materiel (military equipment and supplies) from reaching the island. He also warned that a missile attack on the United States would trigger a U.S. nuclear attack on the Soviet Union, with consequences that no one could foretell. Across the globe, the armed forces of both countries were placed on alert, and U.S. military vessels soon stopped and searched Soviet ships en route to Cuba. On October 25, several Soviet ships stopped in mid-route rather than risk search.

Publicly, leaders from both sides presented a stern demeanor and demanded that the other side back down. Behind the scenes, however, intense, back-channel negotiations began. TV reporters delivered messages to Soviet spies, while diplomats exchanged terse letters. Soviet premier Nikita Khrushchev sent one letter offering to withdraw the missiles in exchange for a U.S. promise not to invade Cuba; less than a day later, he sent a rambling letter demanding that the United States also withdraw missiles from the country of Turkey. While Kennedy pondered his response on October 27, events worsened: Soviet radio broadcast Khrushchev's demands, and Cuban forces shot down a U.S. U-2 plane flying over their country. That night, Kennedy made what many historians consider to be a brilliant tactical move: he responded to Khrushchev's first request (not to invade Cuba) and ignored the second (removing the missiles from Turkey). On October 28, Soviet radio announced the acceptance of Kennedy's terms. People across the globe breathed a sigh of relief. Through careful diplomacy, Kennedy had negotiated the best possible outcome. Within a month, Soviet forces had dismantled the missile sites. In a goodwill gesture, the United States eventually removed their missiles from Turkey as well.

The intense standoff known as the Cuban Missile Crisis was a pivotal moment in the Cold War. Both sides seemed to come to the realization that they could not play bluffing games in which the risk was so great for the entire world. Following the crisis, both sides worked harder to communicate with the other. They installed "hot lines," or direct telephone links, to provide instant communication between American president and Soviet premier, and committed themselves to treaties limiting nuclear testing. Though the Cold War continued until 1991, during those years the world did not again so closely approach nuclear annihilation.

Vietnam: Trouble to come

Of the many foreign policy problems Kennedy inherited when he took office in 1960, the brewing conflict in the distant nation of Vietnam hardly seemed to be the most pressing. The United States had had a tortured relationship with the small East Asian country for nearly twenty years. American forces had supported Vietnamese forces when they fought against Japanese occupation during World War II. After the war, however, the French had reestablished control in a region that they had controlled since the late nineteenth century. Faced with either supporting Vietnamese patriots led by a man named Ho Chi Minh (c. 1890–1969) or supporting their historical European ally, the United States made the difficult decision to back French rule. This decision was made easier by Ho Chi Minh's embrace of Communism.

From 1945 to 1954, the United States provided financial and military support to the French as they fought an increasingly intense war against Ho Chi Minh and his forces, called the Vietminh. By 1954, the war had killed 95,000 French soldiers, 300,000 Vietnamese soldiers, and as many as a million Vietnamese civilians. In that year France withdrew from the area by negotiating a peace treaty that divided Vietnam in half and granted Cambodia and Laos independence. North Vietnam was controlled by communists led by Ho Chi Minh, and South Vietnam was ruled by a corrupt government led by Ngo Dinh Diem (1901–1963) and backed by the United States. American policy after 1954 consisted of supporting the South Vietnamese regime with economic assistance, arms, and military training. Over the years, however, their support for the Diem regime in South Vietnam became increasingly embarrassing. Diem enjoyed little support in his own country, and he ruled by oppressing, even torturing and killing, those who opposed him. Increasingly, people within South Vietnam began to join guerilla forces fighting against their own government. These people were known as the Vietcong; "cong" means "commies," a slang term for communists, because they supported communist North Vietnam.

The rumblings of American involvement in the Vietnam War preceded the Kennedy Administration. However, the situation began to intensify in the 1960s and eventually led to U.S. troops being sent to Vietnam to fight. *National Archives.*

Kennedy did not like the policy of support for South Vietnam that he had inherited, but he felt that it was important for the United States to help the South Vietnamese defeat the communist uprising among its own citizens. He subscribed to what is known as the "domino theory," the idea, first described in 1947 by President Harry S. Truman (1884–1972; served 1945–53), that if one Asian nation fell to Communism, others would follow (as in a row of dominoes, once the first domino falls it knocks down all the rest of the dominoes in sequence). Kennedy committed to sending more money and U.S. weapons to South Vietnam, and though he did not send combat troops, he did increase the number of military advisors to 12,000 in 1963. He hoped that with this additional support, the South Vietnamese could defeat the communists and give the United States an excuse to withdraw by declaring victory. This policy of gradually increasing support existed when Kennedy was assassinated in November of 1963. It would be up to Kennedy's successor to guide American policy in Vietnam. (For complete coverage of the Vietnam War, see Chapter Five.)

Kennedy's domestic policies

For much of his brief term in office, Kennedy was occupied with foreign policy issues. With regard to foreign policy, the U.S. Constitution gave him wide latitude to act as chief executive. In terms of domestic policy, however, Kennedy was constrained by the need to seek support and approval from a Congress that was not willing to move quickly on the major issues Kennedy supported.

Though Kennedy is often remembered as a champion of justice and civil rights, in fact he accomplished little in these areas. During his campaign in 1960 and while in office, Kennedy publicly proclaimed that he supported major civil rights legislation. Yet he failed to introduce such legislation, knowing that he could not win votes for his programs from the Congress. Despite the fact that his party controlled Congress with a majority of 263 to the Republican's 174, Kennedy knew that a voting bloc of conservative southern Democrats would side with the Republicans to stop his more ambitious programs. Kennedy issued an executive order establishing the Committee on Equal Employment Opportunity in 1961, but this action was not enough to settle the criticism he faced from civil rights leaders who complained that he supported the movement in word only.

Over the three years of his presidency, however, Kennedy was pushed to deepen his commitment to civil rights. Several dramatic civil rights actions—including the "Freedom Rides" and the attacks of civil rights demonstrators ordered by Montgomery, Alabama, police chief Eugene "Bull" Connor (1897–1973) in 1961; the integration of the University of Mississippi in 1962; and the famous "March on Washington" of 1963—demanded presidential reaction, and Kennedy increasingly committed himself to the cause. He issued several executive orders and sent federal authorities to ensure the safety of demonstrators in the South; increasingly, he grew willing to use federal power to force states to live up to promises of equality. By mid-1963, Kennedy had prepared a full civil rights legislative package, but he was unable to see its passage because of his unexpected death in November of that year. (For complete coverage of the civil rights movement, see Chapter 8.)

Perhaps the greatest domestic accomplishment of the Kennedy administration was the stimulus Kennedy gave to the U.S. economy. Unlike Eisenhower, Kennedy was willing to use the power of the federal government to improve the economy. He proposed and passed a number of measures to expand the economy, including a large cut in the income tax and tax breaks for businesses. But he also continued a Democratic tradition of providing support and protections for working Americans. He increased the minimum wage from $1.00 to $1.25 per hour, expanded Social Security benefits to a larger group of people, and presented legislation to help farmers and improve federal housing (housing provided for the poorest Americans). The stimulus package began to work quickly, prompting the economy to expand continuously almost to the end of the decade. Thanks in large part to Kennedy's programs, the 1960s were prosperous years in the United States.

Starting the space program

Kennedy also created a space program capable of placing a man on the moon. When Kennedy took office in 1961, the United States lagged far behind the Soviet Union in what was widely known as the "space race," the effort to launch satellites and eventually men into space. The Soviets had placed the first satellite, called Sputnik, in space in 1957, and in 1960 they had launched two dogs into space and returned them safely to earth. Then, on April 12, 1961, the Soviet astronaut Yuri Gagarin became the first man to orbit Earth. Though the United States' space program followed with a manned spaceflight on May 5, 1961, few were satisfied with coming in second—especially President Kennedy.

Kennedy viewed the space race as an important part of the American competition with the Soviet Union. Along with many Americans, he wanted the United States to win that competition. He told Congress in May of 1961 that the United States should have the goal of sending a man to the moon by the end of the decade. This challenge led to unprecedented spending on space exploration: by 1965, the nation's space agency, the National Aeronautics and Space Administration (NASA), received $5.25 billion in funding, its highest level in the decade. Within two years of Kennedy's challenge, Project Mercury astronaut Leroy Gordon Cooper had orbited Earth for thirty-six hours. Though Kennedy did not live to see it, American astronauts eventually became the first to orbit and even-

Leroy Gordon "Gordo" Cooper (foreground) and Charles Conrad Jr. were two of the first astronauts in the NASA space program. *NASA Johnson Space Center.*

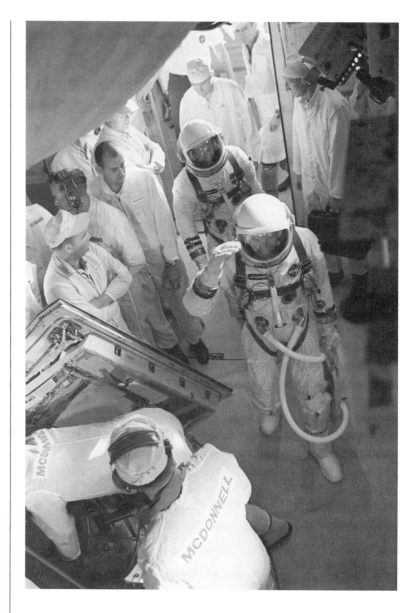

tually land on the Moon, with Neil Armstrong taking the first steps on the Moon on July 16, 1969.

Assassination shocks nation

By mid-1963, Kennedy was hitting his stride as president: his economic incentive program had spurred the Ameri-

Who Really Killed JFK?:
The Warren Report and Conspiracy Theories

On November 29, 1963, just a week after the assassination of John F. Kennedy, President Lyndon B. Johnson appointed an independent commission to investigate the circumstances leading to the shooting and to the subsequent murder of suspect Lee Harvey Oswald. To head the commission, Johnson appointed Supreme Court Chief Justice Earl Warren (1891–1974), one of the most respected men in the United States. In the course of its investigation, the Warren Commission questioned 552 witnesses and sifted through mountains of data, including a grainy film shot by a Texan named Abraham Zapruder, known later as the Zapruder Film. The commission's report, known as the Warren Report, was released to the public on September 24, 1964. Designed to put questions about the assassination to rest, the report instead stirred up controversies and conspiracy theories that continued into the early 2000s.

The key conclusion of the Warren Report was that Lee Harvey Oswald acted alone in killing the president. The report also sought to dispel a total of twenty-two myths and rumors concerning the involvement of the Central Intelligence Agency (CIA), the Federal Bureau of Investigation (FBI), the Soviet Union, mysterious Cubans, and others who might have planned together with Oswald to kill the president. Over the years, however, many contested the conclusions drawn in the Warren Report. A New Orleans, Louisiana, district attorney named Jim Garrison attempted unsuccessfully to convict a local businessman for his involvement in the killing in 1967. In 1991, filmmaker Oliver Stone brought the issue back to the public's attention with the movie *JFK: The Untold Story,* which was seen by fifty million people. The movie explored several different theories, including the idea that high U.S. government officials might have been involved in a conspiracy to kill the president. In the early 2000s, conspiracy theories regarding Kennedy's death continued to surface on the Internet.

can economy to substantial gains; he had stood up to the Soviet challenge in Cuba, earning the respect of the world; he stood prepared to introduce significant civil rights legislation; and he looked forward to seeking reelection in 1964. Though Kennedy had his detractors, he was among the most popular presidents in American history, with an approval rating that never fell below 59 percent during his time in office. People admired his personal style and his charming wife and were encouraged by his stirring speeches challenging Americans to work to fulfill their nation's great destiny. And so it was a

Schlesinger, Arthur, Jr. *A Thousand Days: John F. Kennedy and the White House.* New York: Houghton Mifflin, 1965.

Semple, Robert, ed. *Four Days in November: The Original Coverage of the John F. Kennedy Assassination.* New York: St. Martin's Press, 2003.

Uschan, Michael V. *John F. Kennedy.* San Diego, CA: Lucent Books, 1999.

White, Theodore. *The Making of the President 1960.* New York: Atheneum, 1961.

Wyden, Peter. *Bay of Pigs: The Untold Story.* New York: Simon and Schuster, 1979.

Web sites

"Bay of Pigs: 40 Years After." *The National Security Archive.* www.gwu.edu/~nsarchiv/bayofpigs (accessed on June 14, 2004).

"The Cuban Missile Crisis, 1962: The 40th Anniversary." *The National Security Archive.* www.gwu.edu/~nsarchiv/nsa/cuba_mis_cri/ (accessed on June 14, 2004).

"Favorite Presidents." *Scripps Howard News Service.* www.shns.com/shns/g_index2.cfm?action=detail&pk=PREZ-CHART-02-06-03 (accessed on June 11, 2004).

"John F. Kennedy." *Presidential Inaugurations.* http://memory.loc.gov/ammem/pihtml/pi051.html (accessed on June 11, 2004).

"John F. Kennedy: 'Ich bin ein Berliner.'" *American Rhetoric.* http://www.americanrhetoric.com/speeches/jfkichbineinberliner.html (accessed on June 11, 2004).

John F. Kennedy Library and Museum. www.jfklibrary.org (accessed on June 14, 2004).

Johnson, Thomas R., and David A. Hatch. "NSA and the Cuban Missile Crisis." *National Security Agency Central Security Service.* www.nsa.gov/cuba/index.cfm (accessed on June 14, 2004).

Peace Corps. www.peacecorps.gov (accessed on June 14, 2004).

The Triumph and Collapse of the Johnson Administration

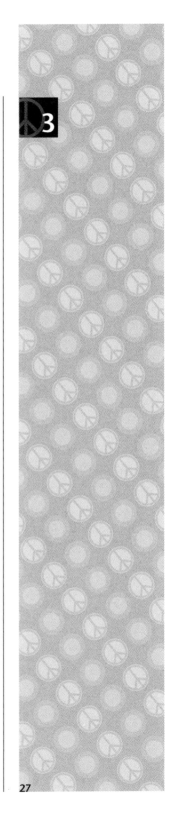

3

Few presidents have entered office under more difficult circumstances than Lyndon B. Johnson (1908–1973; served 1963–69). Johnson had been elected as vice president along with President John F. Kennedy in 1960, and he had served for three years with the customary lack of public attention endured by American vice presidents. Then, on a fateful visit to Dallas, Texas, on November 22, 1963, American political life changed. An assassin's bullets killed President Kennedy, and in the unsetting hours after the shooting, Johnson was sworn in as the president. When he appeared on national television that evening, he greeted a nation in deep grief over the death of one of the most beloved presidents in American history.

In some ways, Kennedy's shoes would be hard to fill. Few politicians in the twentieth century matched Kennedy's personal appeal and charm, and few were so able to inspire the American people to set aside their political differences and embrace lofty ideals about the ability of government to contribute to social justice and world peace. When it came to matters of substance, however, Kennedy had accomplished

Shortly after the assassination of President Kennedy, Lyndon Johnson took the oath of office aboard the president's plane, Air Force One. He was flanked by Jacqueline Kennedy (on his left) and his wife, Lady Bird Johnson (on his right). *AP/Wide World Photos. Reproduced by permission.*

relatively little. Lacking strong backing in Congress, and without the political skills needed to push through his ambitious agenda, Kennedy died without notable accomplishments. But Johnson, a skilled political operator with years of experience in Congress, seized upon the sentimental public embrace of Kennedy's vision to push through one of the most ambitious and sweeping expansions of government power and programs in U.S. history.

Johnson's accomplishments as president were many: his vision of a "Great Society" required passage of major civil rights legislation, the use of federal funds to wage what Johnson called a "war on poverty," and important programs to support public education, housing, and jobs. Were he judged solely on the accomplishments of his first three years in office—1964, 1965, and 1966—he might well be recalled as one of the greatest American presidents. Johnson was undone, however, by the tragic unraveling of the Vietnam War (1954–75), by the rising tide of violence produced by unrest in ghettoes (areas of a city where the poorest residents live) and a growing antiwar movement, and by a conservative political backlash (reaction against the existing trend). By 1968, Johnson was so staggered by the difficulties of managing these multiple problems that he did not run for reelection. The story of Johnson's presidential career thus highlights all the promise and all the pitfalls of politics in the tumultuous 1960s.

Walking in Kennedy's footsteps: The Civil Rights Act of 1964

In 1962 and 1963, pressure built on politicians to secure the passage of a civil rights bill that would make illegal the racial discrimination (the singling out of minority groups for unfavorable treatment) that existed throughout all areas of American life. The civil rights movement was growing increasingly vocal in its calls for the federal government to secure the rights that had been guaranteed by the U.S. Constitution but ignored in reality, especially in southern states. The "Freedom Rides" of 1961 and the attacks on civil rights demonstrators ordered by Montgomery, Alabama, police chief Eugene "Bull" Connor (1897–1973) and other public officials, the forced integration of the University of Mississippi in 1962, and the famous "March on Washington" of 1963—which concluded in Martin Luther King Jr.'s famous "I Have a Dream" speech—helped build public support for federal protections for African Americans and other minorities. In 1963, President Kennedy began preparing such legislation, and he sent his multi-part civil rights bill to Congress just two days before his assassination. (For full coverage of the civil rights movement, see Chapter 8.)

When Johnson took office, he asked Congress to honor the memory of President Kennedy by passing his landmark legislation. The bill, now known as the Civil Rights Act of 1964, passed out of the House quickly, was presented to the Senate in February of 1964, and hit a roadblock. Southern senators, several of whom held powerful committee chairs, objected to federal civil rights legislation. They believed that states ought to be able to set their own course with regard to the desegregation of schools and other public facilities. (Desegregation was the elimination of separate facilities based on race.) For forty-seven days, senators conducted a filibuster, a legislative technique designed to delay a vote, usually through extended discussion or debate. Finally, on June 10, 1964, senators reached a compromise and passed the bill.

On July 2, 1964, President Johnson signed the Civil Rights Act into law. It is difficult to overestimate the importance of the act: it was to date the most important civil rights law in the United States since Abraham Lincoln's 1863 Emancipation Proclamation freed the slaves during the American Civil War (1861–65). Perhaps the most important provisions in the Civil Rights Act were those forbidding all public facilities from discriminating or refusing service based on race, color, religion, or national origin. From this point forward, hotels, restaurants, service stations, bus stations, and all government-run facilities were legally required to operate with equal treatment for all. The Civil Rights Act also placed restrictions on segregation (or separation by race) in housing and education, though some school systems still found ways to provide separate facilities. Finally, it banned discriminatory practices in employment, declaring that no employer of more than twenty-five people could discriminate on the basis of race, color, religion, national origin, or gender. The last provision had slipped into the legislation nearly unnoticed, but it provided an important guarantor of equal employment rights for women, an issue that was just beginning to come to widespread public attention. One significant item was excluded from the act: voting rights. This key issue was not be addressed for another year.

War on poverty

In his first State of the Union address, delivered in January of 1964, Johnson announced that it was time to conduct a war on poverty. In a time of increasing prosperity for the majority of Americans, Johnson argued that it was inexcusable for nearly 20 percent of Americans to live in poverty. By the summer of that year, he signed into law the Economic Opportunity Act of 1964, which created a new agency, the Office of Economic Opportunity, to administer programs to help the poor. These programs included Head Start, a preschool education program; job training programs for youths and adults; loans to companies willing to hire the unemployed; and a program called VISTA (Volunteers in Service to America), a domestic version of the Peace Corps that sends youthful volunteers into U.S. communities to assist poor people. Johnson also signed into law programs to provide food stamps, extend legal counsel to the poor, and fund urban mass transit programs.

The 1964 election

The presidential election year of 1964 began with the incumbent, President Johnson, possessing nearly every advantage. Johnson had managed a near-seamless transition to power following the assassination of John F. Kennedy, and he wisely leveraged Kennedy's popularity to gain passage of significant civil rights and antipoverty legislation. More importantly, Johnson began to broaden his ideas on what he would do were he reelected. He proposed a vision that drew on Kennedy's knack for encouraging Americans to look to the federal government as a tool to address long-standing social inequities. This vision, which Johnson termed the "Great Society," was first laid out in a speech at the University of Michigan on May 22, 1964, as quoted in Bruce J. Schulman's *Lyndon B. Johnson and American Liberalism*:

Lady Bird Johnson worked to support her husband's war on poverty by serving as the national chair of the Head Start program. Taking bullhorn in hand, she addresses people at the Head Start center in New Jersey in August 1965.
© *Bettmann/Corbis*.

> The Great Society rests in abundance and liberty for all. It demands an end to poverty and racial injustice, to which we are totally committed in our time. For better or worse, your generation has been appointed by history to deal with those problems and to lead America to a new age.... You can help build a society where the demands of morality, and the needs of the spirit, can be realized in the life of the Nation. So will you join in the battle to give every citizen the full equality which God enjoins and the law requires, whatever his belief or race, or the color of his skin? Will you join in the battle to give every citizen an escape from the crushing weight of poverty?

Warren Court

When President Dwight D. Eisenhower appointed California politician Earl Warren (1891–1974) to the United States Supreme Court in 1953, Eisenhower could not have known that Warren would lead one of the most influential courts in history. In fact this former district attorney and Republican politician became chief justice of the Court in 1954 and led a series of precedent-setting rulings pertaining to individual rights, religious freedom, censorship, and the rights of the accused.

Warren became the chief justice of a Supreme Court divided over its role: some justices believed that the role of the court was to actively protect the rights of individuals from intrusions by the state or federal government; other justices believed that the Court should restrain itself from ruling on any issue unless there was a clear contradiction with the U.S. Constitution. From the very beginning, Warren used his finely honed political skills to craft some of the most famous legal decisions of the twentieth century. One of the most important decisions came in 1954, in *Brown v. Board of Education of Topeka, Kansas*, in which the Court struck down state laws allowing "separate but equal" educational institutions; after *Brown*, all public education facilities were required to be racially desegregated.

The Warren Court made a series of important rulings in the 1960s. Among the most important were:

• *Baker v. Carr* (1962): In this case, the Supreme Court established the principle of "one man, one vote," which required that political jurisdictions at the national, state, and local levels be drawn in such a way as to assure equal representation in comparable districts. By the end of the decade, thanks to

Though Johnson's vision was cloaked in classic American idealism, what it proposed was a very substantial increase in the size of government bureaucracy and in government spending. According to Frederick F. Siegel, author of *Troubled Journey: From Pearl Harbor to Ronald Reagan,* what Johnson proposed to do was no less than the passage of a "twenty-five-year backlog of liberal Democratic legislation on health, education, racial discrimination, and conservation that had been sitting on the rear burner" since the end of major New Deal legislation in the late 1930s, the program of President Franklin D. Roosevelt (1882–1945; served 1933–45) that had been put in place to promote economic recovery and social reform.

several additional clarifying rulings, virtually every election district in the United States had been redrawn.

- *School Dist. of Abbington v. Schempp* (1963): In this case, tried alongside a case publicized by noted atheist Madalyn Murray O'Hair (1919–1995), the Court ruled that prayer in public schools violates the Constitutional separation of church and state.

- *New York Times v. Sullivan* (1964): In this case, the Court made it very difficult for public officials to pursue libel cases (cases that claim a person's reputation is ruined by unfavorable coverage) against newspapers or other sources of public information. This ruling was widely credited with protecting the freedom of the press.

- *Miranda v. Arizona* (1966): In this case, the Court ruled that individuals in police custody must be informed of their rights. This *Miranda* ruling not only protected the rights of individuals but made widely known the phrase beginning "You have the right to remain silent..." to millions of TV viewers who heard the *Miranda* warning read to suspects on crime programs.

These and many other rulings by the Warren Court were supported and appreciated by the Democratic governments of Presidents Kennedy and Johnson. However, they angered many conservatives, who complained that the Supreme Court under Warren had overstepped its bounds. Richard Nixon had the opportunity to appoint a new chief justice when Warren retired in 1969. Nixon chose the conservative Warren Burger (1907–1995).

Remarkably, Johnson was able to campaign on an extremely ambitious program of legislative change. Johnson's program was well to the left of the political center of American politics, if the "left" indicates a belief that the federal government should play a larger role in regulating the economy and should be willing to assert its authority with social issues so as to assure equality and protect civil liberties. Johnson was able to move so far left precisely because his opponent in the 1964 presidential election moved so far to the right. The Republican nominee, Barry Goldwater (1909–1998), argued emphatically that the federal government should intervene as little as possible in the free play of economic markets and that it should leave most social issues to local governments. These

Texas supporters of conservative politician Barry Goldwater wave campaign signs at a state convention in 1964. *National Archives.*

views alone, however, were not what doomed Goldwater's candidacy and pushed moderate voters into the Johnson camp. Rather, it was a combination of Johnson's polished political skills and Goldwater's poor campaigning and unfortunate public statements that made it possible for Johnson to dominate the election so convincingly.

Goldwater had succeeded at capturing the Republican nomination by convincing many Republicans that it was time to limit the size and scope of the federal government and to return control to state and local government. He built a coalition of white southerners who resented the federal government interfering in racial matters, western businessmen who wanted lower taxes and fewer regulations on business activity, and conservative young people who resisted the social and cultural changes sweeping American universities. He thrilled the conservative faithful in his nomination acceptance speech in July of 1964 when he proclaimed: "I would remind you that extremism in the defense of liberty is no vice. And let me remind you that moderation in the pursuit of justice is no virtue," as quoted in Robert Alan Goldberg's *Barry Goldwater*.

In fact, Goldwater's brand of extremism proved to be a vice that would prevent his election. Without a strong campaign staff helping him, Goldwater often made verbal mistakes when he spoke publicly. He suggested that poor people suffered from laziness and stupidity, that the eastern seaboard ought to be cut off and let float out to sea, and, infamously, that the United States should consider using atomic weapons in Vietnam. Johnson seized on these missteps and argued convincingly that Goldwater was too extreme to trust with the presidency. In one of the most dramatic political TV commercials of all time, a young girl was shown plucking the petals of a daisy, one by one, as a male voice began an urgent countdown. As the countdown reached zero, a mushroom cloud from an atomic bomb filled the screen. Then President Johnson's voice declared: "These are the stakes—to make a world in which all of God's children can live, or to go into the dark. We must either love each other, or we must die." (The commercial can be viewed online at the American Museum of the Moving Image's *Living Room Candidate* Web site.)

In November, Americans elected Johnson by one of the biggest landslides in modern political history. Johnson received just over 61 percent of the popular vote, coming close to doubling Goldwater's total. Perhaps even more importantly, the Democrats gained thirty-seven seats in the House and two seats in the Senate, further padding their already substantial majorities. Johnson had a clear mandate for pushing his political program.

Creating a great society

Johnson had served in the United States Congress for twenty-four years, long enough to know that he did not have long to build on the positive feelings generated by his 1964 victory, and so he set quickly to work. The very first bill he introduced in Congress created programs that assured health care for the elderly and the poor. These programs—called Medicare and Medicaid, respectively—guaranteed access to adequate health care for those over age sixty-five and for those too poor to afford health insurance. The programs also pumped millions and millions of dollars into hospitals and healthcare providers, such as nursing homes and clinics, across the nation. Johnson followed the Medicare/Medicaid bills with a lot of other healthcare legislation, including programs funding immunizations, research on the handicapped and disabled, funding for a variety of healthcare facilities, and loans for students in medical professions. Before this legislation was even signed, Johnson urged the passage of the Elementary and Secondary Education Act of 1965, which dramatically increased the amount of federal funding made available to public schools (which had, to this point, been funded almost entirely through local taxes).

Another essential piece of Johnson's ambitious social agenda was the elimination of obstacles placed in the way of black voters, especially in the South. Despite the protections of the Fifteenth Amendment, which declared in 1870 that voting rights could not be abridged or limited on the basis of "race, color, or previous condition of servitude," many southern states had erected barriers that kept black citizens from voting, including special taxes, tests of literacy (the ability to read), and other requirements very difficult for blacks to meet. The only way to attack those barriers was through costly legal actions. The Voting Rights Act of 1965, signed into law on August 6, 1965, specifically outlawed discriminatory practices in states where voter turnout in the 1964 presidential elections had been less than 50 percent of potentially eligible voters—that is, the majority of southern states. The law allowed the federal government to intervene if local officials failed to eliminate barriers to black voter registration. The results were immediate: within six months, 300,000 new African American voters were registered, and by 1970 the number of blacks registered to vote in the South had nearly doubled. Members of the civil rights movement, who had pushed first Kennedy and then Johnson to support such legislation, cheered the Voting Rights Act of 1965 as one of their most significant victories of the decade.

Johnson's Great Society also included a variety of smaller programs. These were additional programs to provide financial support for inner-city housing; public works projects in depressed rural areas, especially Appalachia; laws requiring

truth in packaging and safety provisions in cars, toys, and other items commonly used by Americans; rules requiring that government decisions be made transparent to citizens through the Freedom of Information Act; and the creation of the National Endowment for the Arts and Humanities, organizations that channeled public funding to arts and humanities projects across the nation. There was, quite literally, something for everyone in the Great Society, and in the early twenty-first century many of these programs continued to be established parts of federal government.

Though Johnson's political skills were essential to passing such legislation, the the Great Society was also made possible by America's great prosperity. Between 1960 and 1965 the growth rate of the American economy had nearly doubled, from 2.1 percent to 4.5 percent. According to Siegel, "This 'social surplus,' the excess of revenues over expenditures, provided nearly four billion dollars a year for new public spending.... Johnson's economic advisors assured him

Following the passage of the Voting Rights Act of 1965, African Americans who had previously been denied access to the polls were finally allowed to vote. Here, residents of Wilcox County, Alabama, line up at the polling station at the local general store. *© Bettmann/Corbis.*

that the unprecedented surpluses would continue indefinitely." This surplus of revenues (in excess of what budget planners had predicted) was so great that Johnson was able to increase federal spending while offering Americans a substantial tax cut. To many, it appeared that the Great Society could be built without the pain of higher taxes. As long as economic growth continued to surge, Johnson and his advisors saw no reason for pessimism. What they could not have predicted in 1964 or 1965, however, was that a distant war in Vietnam would soon claim large portions of the Johnson administration's financial and political capital. By 1967, expansion of the Great Society had been stopped and Johnson's future political prospects lay in ruins.

The politics of Vietnam

Like President Kennedy before him, Lyndon Johnson inherited from his predecessor the fact of American involvement in Vietnam, a tiny and divided country in Southeast Asia. Ever since the French withdrew from the region in 1954, the United States had been supplying money, arms, and military advisors to the South Vietnamese government. The goal of the United States was to maintain a pro-Western government in South Vietnam in the face of attempts by the communist government of North Vietnam—and by the Vietcong, a sympathetic guerilla army within South Vietnam—to unite the two Vietnams under communist rule. As Johnson began his run for the presidency in 1964, his desire was to contain the spread of Communism in Vietnam without letting this distant conflict distract him from his domestic policy goals. But he did not get his wish: the conflict quickly grew into what is generally considered America's greatest military disaster. (For full coverage of the Vietnam War, see Chapter 5.)

In the summer of 1964, twin pressures pushed Johnson into increasing U.S. involvement in Vietnam. First, North Vietnamese attacks on the South grew more persistent and effective, and U.S. military planners urged Johnson to step up aerial bombing and send additional American military advisors (the U.S. had not yet committed soldiers to combat). Second, Republican Barry Goldwater charged that Johnson was about to "lose" Vietnam to Communism. Johnson needed a way to send a message both to North Vietnam and to American voters. He found it in the Gulf of Tonkin incident. American ships patrolling in the Gulf of Tonkin, off the coast of North Vietnam, claimed that they had been fired upon by North Vietnamese torpedoes (whether missiles were actually fired has never been determined). Declaring that the United States was now the victim of North Vietnamese aggression, President Johnson asked Congress for authorization to "take all necessary measures to repel any armed attack against the forces of the United States and to prevent further aggression." In a very nearly unanimous show of support, on August 7, 1964, Congress passed the Gulf of Tonkin Resolution and the United States found itself in a war against North Vietnam.

After the Gulf of Tonkin Resolution passed, U.S. involvement in Vietnam grew steadily. There were 23,300 American troops in Vietnam in 1964, most of them classified as advisors. Following Johnson's election in November, the number of combat troops grew steadily, to 184,300 by the end of 1965; 385,300 in 1966; 485,600 in 1967; to a high of 536,100 troops in 1968. From the very beginning of combat operations in 1965, the war did not go as hoped. Most of the fighting took place on South Vietnamese territory, against an enemy who sneaked in and out under cover of darkness and jungle. There were few traditional battles in which the United States could use its decisive advantage in firepower. Instead, the U.S. military measured its success in "body counts," tallies of enemy dead that were often inflated to create American "victories." The problem was, no one knew how many Vietcong and North Vietnamese would have to be killed to win the war.

As the war went on, problems mounted: U.S. soldiers killed civilians, and more and more of the South Vietnamese population came to support the communists. Military strategists from field commanders to generals to the president were challenged in trying to fight a determined, crafty foe. Marine platoon commander Philip Caputo, quoted in *The Columbia Guide to America in the 1960s,* lamented: "Without a front, flanks, or rear, we fought a formless war against a formless enemy who evaporated like the jungle mists, only to materialize in some unexpected places." And all the while, the costs of waging war rose, both the costs in American lives and American dollars. By the end of the war in 1975, 45,941 sol-

☮ Acting Presidential: LBJ's Image Problem

Few politicians in the late 1990s and early 2000s were able to compare with John F. Kennedy in terms of personal style, appeal, and culture. Kennedy was a young, vigorous man when he was elected president, and he had a charming, beautiful wife, Jacqueline, who used her education and sophistication to make the White House a center for culture. By contrast, Kennedy's vice president and successor in office, Lyndon B. Johnson, appeared to be a crude and rough-edged politician. It was an image problem that Johnson struggled with throughout his presidency.

Johnson's background could not have been more different than the Kennedys', who had grown up surrounded by great wealth. Johnson was from a middle-class family; he attended public schools and graduated from Southwest Texas State College. As a United States congressman and later as a senator, Johnson, or LBJ, as he was often called, made a name for himself for his hard work and also for his willingness to use his folksy charm and humor to bring people over to his position. Johnson was a gregarious, friendly man who loved to tell folksy stories and off-color sexual jokes. Such traits perhaps were fine for a congressman—but they were a liability for a president.

As president, Johnson tried to appear more sober and "presidential," but when he did so critics complained that he looked stiff and awkward. His attempts to appear warm and friendly frequently backfired. Asked to pose with his dogs, he picked up the two beagles by the ears. Dog lovers wrote critical letters to newspapers and magazines. When Johnson

diers had died in combat, another 10,420 had died in noncombat situations, and the United States had spent some $140 billion.

Coming apart

Not long after Johnson sent the first combat troops to Vietnam, the first wave of a rising tide of organized protest emerged to speak out against U.S. involvement in the war. This antiwar movement grew out of a loosely organized student political movement called the New Left. The New Left first emerged in 1962 as the Students for a Democratic Society (SDS), which announced its political position in a docu-

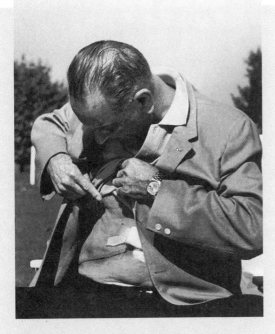

President Lyndon Johnson shows reporters his surgery scar. *AP/Wide World Photos. Reproduced by permission.*

porters his lengthy scar and his paunchy belly. The widely published photograph brought renewed protests about his unsophisticated personal style. Johnson sometimes played up his crude reputation, as when he conducted interviews with highly educated reporters (he called them "The Harvards") while sitting on the White House toilet, or when he intentionally overdid his Texas accent.

Johnson's sometimes crude behavior was an amusing pet peeve of reporters and the public when Johnson was at the height of his popularity, as he was in 1965 and 1966. But when his troubles with Vietnam and the antiwar movement began to make him the subject of much more pointed public criticism, his personal mannerisms were emphasized by those who wanted to drive him from office.

was recovering from gallbladder surgery in 1965 he lifted his shirt to show re-

ment called the Port Huron Statement. The SDS caused political activism on college campuses across the United States. Beginning in 1965, the SDS and a variety of other, less formally organized student groups began to direct their efforts to protesting the war.

The first major event in the American antiwar movement occurred on April 17, 1965, when more than 15,000 demonstrators met in Washington, D.C., to hear a speech by SDS president Paul Potter. Potter argued that the American government was ignoring the will of the American people and offering deceitful reasons for going to war. Over the next two years, these charges were leveled again and again as antiwar protests grew ever more frequent. In October of 1965

For the first time ever, Americans witnessed a war as it happened. Via television, the bloody images of the Vietnam conflict were brought into homes on a nightly basis. *National Archives.*

there were demonstrations in forty American cities; in 1966 and 1967 the demonstrations grew larger and more intense. In April of 1967, some 100,000 protestors marched in New York City, and in October of that year 35,000 marched on the Pentagon, the headquarters of the U.S. military. Increasingly, antiwar demonstrations drew from a broad spectrum of Americans, including members of the civil rights movement. (For a complete discussion of the antiwar movement, see Chapter 6.)

These protests, combined with the rising number of combat deaths and the dramatic television coverage of the war, began to have a real impact on American support for the war. Surveys showed that support for the war dropped from 61 percent in 1965, to 50 percent in late 1966, to 40 percent in the spring of 1968, and to 35 percent on the dawn of the presidential election in 1968. What began for Johnson as a way to demonstrate his resolve in opposing Communism became, by the mid-1960s, a serious political problem.

There were other pressures facing Johnson during his first term as elected president. Among the most dramatic troubles were violent urban race riots, which spread from New York City in 1964 to a number of other American cities. The riots were a reflection of rising discontentment among blacks in northern cities, who complained about the brutality of white police forces, the lack of jobs, and the poor quality of urban housing, among other concerns. In the Watts section of Los Angeles, riots raged for five days in the summer of 1965; there were forty race riots in 1966 and another 160 in the summer of 1967. In Detroit, Michigan, and Newark, New Jersey, National Guard troops had to be called out to restore order, and there was massive destruction of property. These riots, combined with the antiwar demonstrations and the increasing visibility of the hippie movement, which celebrated drug use and rock'n' roll, convinced many Americans that the United States was coming apart at the seams.

The combination of these events—the difficulties of waging war in Vietnam, antiwar protests, race riots, and a general fear of lawlessness—effectively doomed Johnson's presidency after 1966. The Republican Party gained forty-seven seats in the House of Representatives in the mid-term elections of 1966. More energetic because of its success, the party stepped up its attacks on Johnson and effectively put a halt to any further Great Society legislation. As Johnson put it in his colorful language, as quoted by Schulman, "That bitch of a war [was destroying] the woman I really loved—the Great Society."

Johnson was challenged by both the left and the right, and he had trouble governing. As the presidential elections of 1968 drew near, it became clear that several people from within Johnson's own Democratic Party were willing to challenge him for the party's nomination. By the spring of 1968, there were several contenders for the nomination (though they had not all yet entered the race): Senator Robert F. Kennedy (1925–1968), the former president's younger brother; Vice President Hubert Humphrey (1911–1978); Eugene McCarthy (1916–) of Minnesota; and George McGovern (1922–) of South Dakota. With polls indicating that he would likely be defeated in the primaries (elections to choose the Democratic nominee), President Johnson made the following announcement on March 31, 1968: "I shall not seek and I will not accept the nomination of my party for another term as your President," as quoted in Robert Dallek's *Lyndon B. Johnson: Portrait of a President.* The election year politics of 1968 went on without Johnson, who departed the office a bitter and broken man.

1968: A defining year

Johnson's decision not to run for reelection was only one of many startling events that made 1968 both dramatic and historic. The year began with the Tet Offensive, a massive, two-month-long attack by combined North Vietnamese and Vietcong forces on American and South Vietnamese positions throughout the South. Though the assault was not successful in toppling the South Vietnamese government, it did shatter the U.S. government's assertion that the war was under its control and helped convince Johnson that he should not run for reelection. On February 27, 1968, in the midst of the Tet Offensive, a highly respected newsman and the host of the *CBS Evening News,* Walter Cronkite, expressed the opinion that "...it seems now more certain than ever that the bloody experience of Vietnam is to end in a stalemate." This statement echoed the conclusion being drawn by an increasing number of Americans.

The events of the spring pushed the antiwar movement to new heights. Protestors targeted the Democratic nominating convention, held in Chicago, as the site in which to protest the ongoing war. Unlike many other demonstrations, this one did not end peacefully. Some of the most radical protestors of the antiwar movement, including the Yippies (a group of hippies committed to making dramatic political statements), gathered in Chicago, despite being warned by Chicago mayor Richard Daley (1902–1976) that his police would not tolerate trouble. For nearly the entire week of the convention, protestors and police clashed violently on the streets. On the night of the presidential nomination, police clubbed and teargassed protestors and bystanders as the crowd chanted, "The whole world is watching!" In fact, the world was, for the events were carried on live television, which also was covering the nomination of candidate Hubert Humphrey for the presidency inside the convention hall.

Following his brother's legacy, Robert F. Kennedy was gunned down by an assassin in 1968. Bobby Kennedy was campaigning to run for president on the Democratic ticket. *AP/Wide World Photos. Reproduced by permission.*

The dramatic scenes at the Chicago convention compounded the worries of everyday Americans that violence had become commonplace in the United States. Already that year, two prominent Americans had been assassinated: on April 4, 1968, civil rights leader Martin Luther King Jr. was shot and killed in Memphis, Tennessee, and on June 5, 1968, Robert Kennedy was gunned down in Los Angeles while campaigning for the presidency. Both men had come out strongly against the war in Vietnam. Riots followed King's death, similar to those that flared in several American cities during the summer of 1967.

In the context of all this violence and protest, Republican presidential nominee Richard M. Nixon (1913–1994; served 1969–74) presented himself as the candidate of "law and order," and the representative of the "silent majority" of Americans who wanted to see a return to more traditional American values and lifestyle. He ran on the promise that he would extract the United States from the war in Vietnam, though he did not provide specifics. (Nixon eventually did lead the removal of troops, though he also ordered a massive intensification of bombing.) In addition, he promised to put a halt to the massive public spending that characterized the Johnson administration. Despite the unpopularity of the war, Nixon only narrowly defeated Democratic candidate Hubert Humphrey, thanks in large part to an effective third-party campaign led by Alabama governor George Wallace (1919–1998). With Nixon's victory, a conservative Republican took control of the executive office. Nixon would lead a nation troubled by its lack of confidence in the government, and his own behavior in office would only deepen that distrust. (For full coverage of the conservative rise to power, see Chapter 4.)

For More Information

Books

Breuer, William B. *Race to the Moon: America's Duel with the Soviets.* Westport, CT: Greenwood Publishing, 1993.

Burner, David. *Making Peace with the 1960s.* Princeton, NJ: Princeton University Press, 1996.

Colbert, Nancy A. *Great Society: The Story of Lyndon Baines Johnson.* Greensboro, NC: Morgan Reynolds. 2002.

Dallek, Robert. *Lyndon B. Johnson: Portrait of a President.* New York: Oxford University Press, 2004.

Dudley, William, ed. *The 1960s.* San Diego, CA: Greenhaven, 2000.

Farber, David. *The Age of Great Dreams: America in the 1960s.* New York: Hill and Wang, 1994.

Farber, David, and Beth Bailey, with others. *The Columbia Guide to America in the 1960s.* New York: Columbia University Press, 2001.

Goldberg, Robert Alan. *Barry Goldwater.* New Haven, CT: Yale University Press, 1995.

Helsing, Jeffrey W. *Johnson's War/Johnson's Great Society: The Guns and Butter Trap.* Westport, CT: Praeger, 2000.

Holland, Gini. *The 1960s.* San Diego, CA: Lucent, 1999.

Just, Ward. *Reporting Vietnam: Part One: American Journalism 1959–1969.* New York: Library of America, 1998.

Levy, Debbie. *Lyndon B. Johnson.* Minneapolis, MN: Lerner, 2003.

Moss, George. *America in the Twentieth Century.* Upper Saddle River, NJ: Prentice-Hall, 1988.

Schulman, Bruce J. *Lyndon B. Johnson and American Liberalism: A Brief Biography with Documents.* Boston, MA: Bedford, 1995.

Schuman, Michael. *Lyndon B. Johnson.* Springfield, NJ: Enslow, 1998.

Siegel, Frederick F. *Troubled Journey: From Pearl Harbor to Ronald Reagan.* New York: Hill and Wang, 1984.

Witcover, Jules. *1968: The Year the Dream Died: Revisiting 1968 in America.* New York: Warner Books, 1997.

Periodicals

"Message to Congress, August 5, 1964." *Department of State Bulletin,* Washington, D.C. (August 24, 1964).

"House Joint Resolution 1145, August 7, 1964." *Department of State Bulletin,* Washington, D.C. (August 24, 1964).

Web sites

"The Living Room Candidate: 1964, Johnson vs. Goldwater." *American Museum of the Moving Image.* www.ammi.org/livingroomcandidate/index_2000.html (accessed on June 15, 2004).

Lyndon Baines Johnson Library and Museum. www.lbjlib.utexas.edu (accessed on June 17, 2004).

"Lyndon B. Johnson." *American Presidents Life Portraits.* www.americanpresidents.org/presidents/president.asp?PresidentNumber=35 (accessed on June 17, 2004).

"Lyndon B. Johnson." *The White House.* www.whitehouse.gov/history/presidents/lj36.htm (accessed on June 17, 2004).

Another Dream for America: The Conservative Vision

4

The 1960s is known as a decade of political movements. The civil rights movement, the New Left student movement, the feminist movement, and the antiwar movement all attracted a great deal of attention. Each of these movements had its own goals, yet each shared one characteristic: they were dominated by those who believed that through direct public action the government could be convinced to respond to the needs and demands of the people. Colorful and dramatic, these movements attracted the largest share of media coverage in the decade that they helped to define. There was another movement, however, one that was equally important in terms of its long-term impact on American politics. Driven by people who wanted to decrease the size and influence of the federal government, and to combat the spread of Communism, the modern conservative movement appealed to those on the opposite end of the political spectrum from civil rights and antiwar protestors. In response to the defeat of Republican Richard Nixon (1913– 1994; served 1969–74) by Democrat John F. Kennedy (1917– 1963; served 1961–63) in the presidential election of 1960, American conservatives began to craft a set of political positions that came to characterize Republican Party politics into the 2000s.

The center in American politics

Politics in America is often described as existing along a spectrum of opinion that ranges from left to right. This entire spectrum is typically known by the term "liberalism," a complicated set of beliefs with a long history in the United States and other modern democratic nations, like the United Kingdom, France, and other European countries. Some of liberalism's basic tenets are the belief in progress, the protection of civil liberties, and the support of free competition in the economy. But within this broad political philosophy there is much room for disagreement. Those on the left have typically argued that the federal government should play a larger role in regulating the economy and should be willing to assert its authority with social issues so as to assure equality and protect civil liberties. Those on the right have typically argued that the federal government should intervene as little as possible in the free play of economic markets and that it should leave most social issues to local governments, which best reflect the interests of the people. For the better part of American history, politicians have fought over which version of political liberalism should inform the actions of the federal government at any one time.

In the 1950s, however, many Americans believed that the age-old contest between the left and the right for control of government had been resolved. It appeared that most Americans shared the view that government should provide a safety net of social programs for the truly disadvantaged, take steps to ensure a healthy economy, and otherwise allow local and state government to handle the interests of citizens living within the local area. The Democratic Party, taking a moderate-left viewpoint, was nearly indistinguishable from the Republican Party, which held a moderate-right viewpoint. And both parties were united in their opposition to Communism, the system of government in the rival Soviet Union.

This apparent consensus, or general agreement, broke down dramatically in the 1960s. Several factors encouraged those on the left to push for more rapid social changes than the United States had experienced in years. The election of John F. Kennedy was a crucial factor. Kennedy was a youthful, dynamic leader; in his impassioned campaign speeches and in his inaugural address of 1961, in which he had urged Americans to "ask not what your country can do for you, ask what you can do for your country," he encouraged people to commit themselves to making the United States a greater country by working hard for the causes that mattered most to them. Many young people took Kennedy's words to heart as they sought to reshape the policies of the colleges that they attended. Members of the civil rights movement, which had been working for the expansion of civil rights to African Americans for years, also believed that the time might have come for them to make real gains. Similarly, American women sought ways to enlarge their role in economic and political life. Youth groups, civil rights groups, and women all believed that through committed activism they could enlist the federal government in their quest to improve conditions for all Americans.

Conservatives looked critically on the rise of leftist activism. They did not want to see the federal government expand, and they feared that a minority of liberal activists would trample on the rights of a majority. In the early 1960s, however, they had no organized basis for asserting their political viewpoints. Many who had supported the Republican Party were disappointed by that party's lack of vision. And so, on college campuses across the country, and in governor mansions in Alabama and Arizona, conservative thinkers and activists began to put together a movement of their own, one that they hoped could take back power from the federal government.

Student roots of American conservatism

Like much of the activism on the left, activism on the right began in the nation's universities—and for some of the same reasons. U.S. campuses were in the middle of a huge surge in enrollments, from two million students in 1950 up to seven million in 1968. College enrollments in the 1960s showed the influence of the "baby boom," a name given to the huge generation of children born in the years immediately following World War II (1939–45). This large

generation, some 76 million strong, had come of age during the politically quiet 1950s, but they would not remain quiet for long. Told again and again how important they were to the nation's future, baby boomer college students became more interested in their future roles. Some of the earliest student activism began in 1957, the year that professors in universities who received grants from the federal government were forced to sign an oath of loyalty renouncing Communism. This oath became a source of controversy on college campuses. Students who protested the oath discovered that they shared political leanings, and many of them later joined the leftist Students for Democratic Society (SDS). But there was also a group of students who supported the oath, and they too found that they had much in common. Before too long, they had joined together to form the first important conservative organization, Young Americans for Freedom (YAF).

The Young Americans for Freedom participate in the Loyalty Day Parade in Philadelphia, Pennsylvania, June 1966. The parade is to show loyalty to the U.S. in spite of the growing number of anti-Vietnam War protests.
© Leif Skoogfors/Corbis.

The Godfather of Conservatism: William F. Buckley Jr.

Well before Barry Goldwater and George Wallace helped to define American conservatism in the 1960s, William F. Buckley Jr. (1925–) was working behind the scenes to create an intellectually respectable conservative movement in the United States. Buckley first came to public attention in 1951, when he published *God and Man at Yale*. This book charged that the faculty at Yale University, Buckley's alma mater, taught secular values (values that were not based on a belief in God) and moral relativism (the belief that all values are relative), not the respect for God and sense of moral rightness that he believed were at the heart of American values. In 1955 he founded the *National Review*, a magazine of opinion that published the best thinking of American conservatives.

In 1960, the wealthy Buckley gathered together a group of young conservatives, called Young Americans for Freedom, at his Connecticut estate, and he helped them form the "Sharon Statement," a manifesto for conservative politics. Buckley's efforts to guide the movement did not stop there, however. In 1962 he began publishing a weekly newspaper column, "On the Right," which appeared in more

William F. Buckley Jr, August 1965. *AP/Wide World Photos. Reproduced by permission.*

than 300 papers. In 1966 he became host of *Firing Line*, an Emmy-award-winning television debate show that remained on the air until 1999.

Whether organizing, editing, hosting a television show, or writing one of his many fictional and non-fictional works, Buckley was one of the most consistently intelligent and witty conservative political voices in the twentieth-century United States, praised by those on both the left and the right. He is truly the godfather of American conservatism.

The Young Americans for Freedom formed in September of 1960, when some ninety students from forty-four colleges in twenty-four states gathered at the Sharon, Connecticut, estate of conservative spokesman William F. Buckley Jr.

(1925–; see sidebar). They appointed a national director and set out plans to recruit members between the ages of eighteen and thirty-five. Most importantly, they drafted a set of principles designed to guide their growing political movement. That set of principles became known as the "Sharon Statement."

Short and direct, the "Sharon Statement" made clear several crucial positions for the conservative movement. It declared that the role of government should be limited to preserving internal order, providing for national defense, and administering justice; that the Constitution reserves primary power to the states and the people; that the economy works best with minimal government intervention; and that America must commit itself to victory over, and not coexistence with, international Communism. In declaring such clear-cut principles, YAF intended to break with an earlier generation of conservatives, who its members said had been primarily interested in generating profits for businesses. In the words of William F. Buckley Jr., writing to the subscribers of the *National Review* in 1960, as quoted in *Conservatism in America since 1930,* YAF was committed to a political program that went beyond economic issues and included "the moral aspect of freedom; ... transcendent values; ... the nature of man. All this together with a tough-as-nails statement of political and economic convictions...."

At first, YAF drew its greatest support from its fervent anti-Communism position. YAF initiated a "Stop Red Trade" campaign that urged American companies to withdraw from any trade with Soviet bloc countries. The group staged letter-writing campaigns, boycotts, and demonstrations, and claimed to have blocked Firestone from building a rubber plant in Romania. YAF's strong anti-communist agenda helped draw nearly 20,000 people to a 1962 rally in New York's Madison Square Garden. YAF also attracted attention when its members spoke out against leftist groups like the SDS and staged counter-demonstrations at antiwar rallies. But YAF truly had its biggest impact when it supported the political career of Arizona governor Barry Goldwater (1909–1998).

Conservative icon Barry Goldwater

As they prepared for the presidential election season of 1964, members of the Republican Party had good reason

Supporters of Barry
Goldwater don signs and
black-eye makeup
proclaiming "Goldwater
people would rather fight
than switch [candidates],"
in support of the
Republican presidential
nominee, in Montgomery,
Alabama, September 1964.
© Bettmann/Corbis.

to be discouraged. Richard M. Nixon's loss to Kennedy in the
1960 election had divided the party. The party's most conservative members distrusted Nixon, and they wanted a true
conservative to run against the liberal incumbent (which,
after Kennedy was assassinated late in 1963, was Lyndon B.
Johnson [1908–1973; served 1963–69]). But the party's Eastern Establishment, so known because of their location in the
East and their long-standing ties to banking and business interests, wanted a more moderate candidate. The stage was set
for a battle for the heart of the Republican Party.

The champion of the conservative cause was Arizona
senator Barry Goldwater. A handsome, fiery former Air Force
pilot, Goldwater had jumped straight from Phoenix, Arizona,
city politics to the U.S. Senate, where he made his mark as a
die-hard conservative. In 1960, he published *The Conscience of
a Conservative,* which outlined his approach to politics. In this
book, he asserted: "I have little interest in streamlining government or in making it more efficient, for I mean to reduce its

size. I do not undertake to promote welfare, for I propose to extend freedom. My aim is not to pass laws, but to repeal them." Such statements—along with Goldwater's willingness to take a clear stand on Communism—endeared him to many conservatives who worked for his nomination, including YAF members.

Committed conservatives threw themselves behind Goldwater in the Republican presidential primaries, but he received strong opposition from the moderates, who backed Eastern Establishment candidate Nelson Rockefeller (1908–1979). When Goldwater won the nomination at the Republican nominating convention held July 13-16, 1964, Americans recognized that the conservative wing had taken over the Republican Party. Goldwater capped his acceptance speech with words that thrilled conservative listeners: "Our people have followed false prophets. We must, and we shall, return to proven ways—not because they are old, but because they are true.... I would remind you that extremism in the defense of liberty is no vice. And let me remind you that moderation in the pursuit of justice is no virtue," as quoted in Robert Alan Goldberg's book, *Barry Goldwater.*

Goldwater's fiery conservatism, so appealing to those on the far right, turned out to be too strong for the general electorate. In the era before political candidates were so carefully coached on how to speak to the media, Goldwater made statements that came back to haunt him. He suggested that poor people suffered from laziness and stupidity, that the eastern seaboard ought to be cut off and let float out to sea, and—infamously—that the United States should consider using atomic weapons in Vietnam. To a nation that was terrified of the effects of a worldwide nuclear war, this was too much. In the end, Johnson crushed Goldwater, winning 61.2 percent of the popular vote. Yet Goldwater had won the Deep South—Alabama, Georgia, Louisiana, Mississippi, and South Carolina—something no Republican had ever achieved. It gave Republicans hope that eventually they could break the hold that the Democratic Party had traditionally held on southern states.

George Wallace's working-class conservatism

Barry Goldwater's was a clean-cut brand of American conservatism: it was focused on issues like Communism and

shrinking the size of the federal government. Supported by the youthful conservative members of YAF and the hard-charging businessmen of the American West, Goldwater was clearly in the American mainstream. The other prominent conservative leader of the mid-1960s could claim no such air of respectability. George Wallace (1919–1998), the colorful governor of Alabama, tapped into very different sources of dissatisfaction and anger as he united southerners and many other working-class Americans behind his conservative movement. Wallace joined the anti-communist, small-government conservatism of Goldwater with appeals to common-sense, old-fashioned values, resistance to federal intervention in local issues, and, especially in the South, with coded calls for a continuation of white political and social dominance. By 1968 Wallace's strength was so great that he mounted a highly successful third-party candidacy (a candidacy that was not backed by one of the two major parties, the Democrats and the Republicans) for the presidency.

From the moment he returned from his service in the Air Force in World War II (1939–45), Wallace began to leave his mark on Alabama politics. As a state attorney general and then a state representative, Wallace was known as a political liberal. But when he first ran for governor in 1958 he was soundly defeated by an opponent who openly promoted segregation—the policy of restricting access to schools, restaurants, and other facilities on the basis of race. Recognizing that he would never claim the governorship in Alabama by supporting civil rights for blacks, Wallace switched his position and won the Alabama governorship in 1962, thanks to the support of the racist group the Ku Klux Klan (an organization whose members kept their identity secret as they terrorized black citizens). In his inaugural speech in January 1963, Wallace defined his position when he stated: "In the name of the greatest people that ever trod this earth, I draw the line in the dust and toss the gauntlet before the feet of tyranny, and I say: segregation now, segregation tomorrow, segregation forever!" as quoted in *Our Nation's Archive.*

Wallace's speech captured the attention of southerners who believed the federal government had overstepped its authority by passing federal desegregation laws, but he did not stop there. Later in 1963 Wallace stood on the steps of the University of Alabama, physically blocking black students from access to the school. President Kennedy was forced to order National Guard troops to help integrate the state's schools, thus ending the separation of the races. The graphic image of Wallace staring down federal authorities was televised across the nation. Wallace was a hero to southern racists—but how would his belligerence play to northern audiences?

Wallace had always been known as a political chameleon; he was capable of shifting his presentation to suit voters' views, and he did it again as he rose to national prominence. The key to his rise to fame was his recognition that northerners were facing some of the same issues as southerners. While northerners had supported civil rights for blacks in theory, they felt very differently when African Americans moved into white neighborhoods and competed for white jobs. Moreover, many northern whites were becoming more concerned with the rising violence that occurred alongside or because of the civil rights movement and the growing antiwar movement. According to Wallace biographer Dan T.

The Radical Right

Though some Americans found conservative politicians Barry Goldwater and George Wallace frightening and extreme, there were several right-wing political groups whose strident beliefs and angry rhetoric made Goldwater and Wallace seem quite moderate. The John Birch Society and the American Nazi Party were two of the most extreme. The John Birch Society was the largest such group, claiming 80,000 members in 1967. Founded by wealthy businessman Robert Welch (1899–1985) in 1958 and named after an American missionary who was killed by Chinese communists in the late 1940s, the John Birch Society took anti-Communism to new heights. Welch and his followers believed that communists had infiltrated all levels of the U.S. government, and at one time they had even charged former president Dwight D. Eisenhower and Supreme Court justice Earl Warren with being corrupted by communists. The John Birch Society was highly organized and well funded, and it often supported the more conservative Republicans (who usually did not admit to having the Society's support).

Even the most conservative politicians wanted nothing to do with the American Nazi Party, formed in 1958 by George Lincoln Rockwell (1918–1967). A self-proclaimed disciple of German Nazi leader

George Lincoln Rockwell, front, leader of the American Nazi Party, May 1961. *AP/Wide World Photos. Reproduced by permission.*

Adolf Hitler, Rockwell preached anti-Jewish, anti-black hatred to his small group of followers. The small Nazi Party won national media coverage with its attention-grabbing stunts, such as harassing civil rights workers with a "hate bus" that traveled through the South and picking fights with protestors at anti-war demonstrations. Rockwell ran for the governor of Virginia in 1965 and received over 5,000 votes (just over 1 percent). He was shot and killed in 1967 by a disgruntled former party member, though his party survived into the early 2000s.

Carter, author of *The Politics of Rage,* "Without using the cruder vocabulary of traditional racism, George Wallace began his national career by skillfully exploiting [the] fears and hatreds [of working-class, northern whites]. For the age-old southern cry of 'Nigger, nigger,' he substituted the political equivalents of apple pie and motherhood: the rights to private property, community control, neighborhood schools, union seniority." Through the mid-1960s, Wallace refined his message, adding to it criticisms of the women's rights movement and the sexual promiscuity and drug use of the younger generation. Increasingly he appealed to what political analysts have called "white backlash," "the silent majority," or "alienated voters," all terms used to refer to Americans who did not like the violence and upheaval of protests led by students, civil rights demonstrators, and women, and wanted a return to stability in American political life.

Since he did not receive the Republican presidential nomination in 1968, George Wallace ran for president as the candidate of the American Independence Party. He got on the ballot in all fifty states, and polls showed that his support was at 21 percent of the electorate as late as September 1968. Wallace hoped that he could win the southern states, where his support was strongest, take a few border states (such as Maryland and Missouri), and throw the election into confusion. But as the election became more intense, Wallace's weaknesses proved too great. A powerful speaker in person, Wallace came off as overheated and extreme on television; many people were turned off by his apparent racism, which he steadfastly denied; and his running mate, General Curtis LeMay (1906–1990), publicly stated his willingness to use nuclear weapons in Vietnam. In the end, Wallace's support faltered as election day neared, and he ended up with just over 13 percent of the vote—a solid number for an independent candidate, but not enough to stop the election of Republican candidate Richard M. Nixon.

Wallace's career continued after 1968, though he was never again so prominent. He won reelection as governor of Alabama in 1970 with an actively racist campaign, then decided to run for president as a Democrat in 1972. On May 15, 1972, a deranged gunman shot four bullets into Wallace at a campaign stop, causing injuries that resulted in his using a wheelchair for the rest of his life. Wallace continued his campaign, but George McGovern eventually won the Democratic nomination. In 1982, while campaigning once again for governor of Alabama, Wallace renounced his past racism and won the support of African Americans. He died in 1998.

Return to mainstream conservatism: The Nixon presidency

Richard Nixon was no one's favorite candidate when he ran for the presidency in 1968. Nixon was hard driving, intensely competitive, and fearful; not even his closest aides claimed to personally like him. Yet Nixon was capable of bridging the divide that separated moderate and right-wing Republicans, and he beat out several rivals for the nomination. Nixon was accepted by mainstream, big business Republicans who had long provided major funding for the party, for he supported their pro-business interests. More importantly, Nixon appealed to the growing majority of Republicans who wanted an end to violence in American cities (riots flared in urban centers in 1967 and 1968), to antiwar demonstrations, and to the lifestyle excesses of the counterculture. Promoting himself as the "law-and-order" candidate and the representative of the "silent majority," Nixon was elected to the presidency. He led a Republican Party that had been much influenced by the conservative movements led by Goldwater and Wallace.

As president, Nixon worked to please both sides of the party. In terms of domestic policy, Nixon was limited by the miserable state of the economy, which was suffering from the combined effects of funding a war in Vietnam and expanded social aid programs created by Democratic president Lyndon Johnson. Nixon might have liked to scale back the social programs, but he hesitated to do so out of fear of damaging the already fragile economy. Instead, Nixon used the power of the federal government to freeze wages and prices in selected areas of the economy. In fact, Nixon's greatest impact on domestic policy was symbolic: he spoke out publicly against the lawlessness of antiwar protestors and the immorality of drug use and sexual freedom. His messages created a climate of intolerance for these behaviors, but Nixon left it up to local authorities to enforce these values. When local officials cracked down on demonstrations, Nixon remained conspicuously silent. It was under this policy that, in May of 1970, members of the Ohio National Guard fired on protesting students at Kent State University, killing four and wounding several others.

Nixon's greatest achievements as president were in foreign policy, an area in which Nixon and his secretary of

"The Eagle Has Landed": Placing a Man on the Moon

In 1961, President John F. Kennedy (1917–1963; served 1961–63) challenged the nation to place a man on the Moon. Like many of Kennedy's bold political statements, this challenge was intended to push Americans to strive for greatness. But it was also motivated by the fear that the Soviet Union, which had been first to place both a satellite and a man in orbit around Earth, would beat the United States once again. Kennedy wanted the United States to win what became known as the space race, and space missions were continued under Presidents Johnson and Nixon.

Progress in the space race came slowly but surely. NASA—the National Aeronautics and Space Administration—put two men in space on March 23, 1965, in the first manned mission in Project Gemini. The goal of this project was to perfect the techniques needed to separate, maneuver, and dock spacecraft while in orbit, and also to allow men to "walk" in space, tethered to their spacecraft. Over a span of eighteen months, Project Gemini achieved ten successful manned missions in space, and paved the way for a trip to the Moon.

Project Apollo, the next stage in NASA's mission to send men to the Moon, began in disaster. On *Apollo 1*, a problem during testing led to a fire in the spacecraft that incinerated three astronauts. (The Soviet's first voyage in their Moon-landing project, Project Soyuz, was equally ill-fated: *Soyuz 1* made it into space, but mechanical malfunctions left the craft spinning out of control. The craft plummeted to Earth, killing the lone cosmonaut on board.) Later manned Apollo missions were more successful. On December 25, 1968, *Apollo 8* became the first spaceship to orbit the Moon.

On July 16, 1969, NASA launched *Apollo 11*, carrying astronauts Neil Armstrong (1930–), Michael Collins (1930–), and "Buzz" Aldrin (1930–). Four days later the craft reached the Moon, and Neil Armstrong announced the successful arrival on the moon with the famous words: "The *Eagle* has landed" (referring to the lunar landing module). Across the nation, jubilant Americans watched on television the grainy image of Neil Armstrong bouncing across the surface of the Moon, and they thrilled to his statement: "That's one small step for man, one giant leap for mankind." The astronauts then successfully returned to their ship, and to Earth.

With its successful landing, the United States won the space race, and the Soviet Union eventually abandoned its plans for a Moon landing after a series of problems. Eventually, the two countries would coordinate their efforts to put men and women in an orbiting space station.

state, Henry Kissinger (1923–), shared a deep interest. Nixon wanted to open foreign markets to U.S. trade, and it was very difficult to do so when tensions between the United States,

Richard Nixon addresses the media in California.
AP/Wide World Photos. Reproduced by permission.

the Soviet Union, and the communist People's Republic of China were so high. Nixon sought out high-level contacts within the Chinese government and visited the nation in February of 1972. He also opened talks with the Soviet Union about improving U.S.–Soviet relations. In the early 2000s these actions were considered Nixon's most important achievements as president.

Nixon also understood one point very clearly: that the United States could not afford to remain involved in a distant and expensive war in Vietnam. Once he took office, however, he discovered how difficult it would be to get the United States out of the war. Although it took several years, Nixon's policies in Vietnam—which relied on a combination of negotiations, increased bombing, and the slow withdrawal of U.S. troops—did result in the end of U.S. involvement in the conflict. A cease-fire between U.S. and North Vietnamese forces was finally signed on January 27, 1973. (For more details on the Vietnam War, see Chapter 10.) Moreover, Nixon announced that in the future the United States would avoid direct military involvement overseas and would instead provide economic and military aid. This policy of sending materials and money but not soldiers was known as the Nixon Doctrine.

Nixon was scarcely able to enjoy the triumph of ending the war in Vietnam, for by 1973 he was deeply involved in the controversy that ultimately forced him to resign his position as president. Beginning in 1971, Nixon had authorized members of his administration to spy on his political enemies. In the run-up to the presidential elections in 1972, several of his spies, nicknamed the Plumbers, were caught by the Washington, D.C., police breaking into rooms at the Watergate Hotel where the headquarters of the Democratic National Committee was located. Nixon used the power of his office to obscure his connection to the break-ins, and he won reelection in 1972. In the years afterward, however, the truth about his relationship to the Watergate burglars emerged amid intense investigations. Nixon resigned his office on August 9, 1974, facing certain impeachment (removal from office for misconduct) by Congress.

The conservative legacy

The success of the conservative movements led by Barry Goldwater and George Wallace, as well as the emergence of radical right-wing organizations, reshaped the Republican Party in ways that continued to be felt through the end of the twentieth century. The key issues promoted by conservatives in the 1960s—reducing the size of the federal government, promoting conservative social values, and fighting Communism—were adopted by Ronald Reagan (1911–2004; served 1981–89), who was elected president in 1980 and again in 1984. Reagan's popularity helped elect more conservative Congress members, and in 1994 House Republicans, led by Speaker of the House Newt Gingrich (1943–), campaigned for a statement of policy they called the "Contract with America," which recommitted them to political programs outlined nearly three decades before in the Sharon Statement. Though it took several decades, the issues first championed by people considered to be on the conservative fringe in the late 1950s had become central to the Republican Party in the 1980s and beyond.

For More Information

Books

Andrew, John A. III. *The Other Side of the Sixties: Young Americans for Freedom and the Rise of Conservative Politics.* New Brunswick, NJ: Rutgers University Press, 1997.

Bruun, Erik, and Jay Crosby, eds. *Our Nation's Archive: The History of the United States in Documents.* New York: Black Dog & Leventhal, 1999.

Carter, Dan T. *The Politics of Rage: George Wallace, the Origins of the New Conservatism, and the Transformation of American Politics.* New York: Simon & Schuster, 1995.

Edwards, Lee. *Goldwater: The Man Who Made a Revolution.* Washington, DC: Regnery, 1995.

Farber, David, and Beth Bailey, with others. *The Columbia Guide to America in the 1960s*. New York: Columbia University Press, 2001.

Goldberg, Robert Alan. *Barry Goldwater*. New Haven, CT: Yale University Press, 1995.

Goldwater, Barry. *The Conscience of a Conservative*. Shepherdsville, KY: Victor Publishing Co., 1960.

Goldwater, Barry Morris. *With No Apologies: The Personal and Political Memoirs of United States Senator Barry M. Goldwater*, New York: William Morrow, 1979.

Lesher, Stephan. *George Wallace: American Populist*. Reading, MA: Addison-Wesley, 1994.

Perlstein, Rick. *Before the Storm: Barry Goldwater and the Unmaking of the American Consensus*. New York: Hill and Wang, 2001.

Schneider, Gregory L. *Cadres for Conservatism: Young Americans for Freedom and the Rise of the Contemporary Right*. New York: New York University Press, 1999.

Schneider, Gregory L., ed. *Conservatism in America since 1930*. New York: New York University Press, 2003.

Web sites

"Alabama Governors: George Corley Wallace." *ADAH: Alabama Department of Archives and History*. www.archives.state.al.us/govs_list/g_wallac.html (accessed on June 1, 2004).

"George Wallace: Settin' the Woods on Fire." *American Experience*. www.pbs.org/wgbh/amex/wallace/ (accessed on June 1, 2004).

Young Americans for Freedom. www.yaf.com (accessed on June 30, 2004).

The Agony of Vietnam

5

The Vietnam War (1954–75) was a war like no other in American history. It was America's longest war: military advisors were in the country from 1954 until 1975, and actual combat troops were in the country from 1965 to 1975. For those government and military strategists who designed U.S. Cold War policy, defending South Vietnam was crucial. According to their thinking, South Vietnam was the first in a strategic line of dominoes (a metaphor that referred to the game in which the first falling domino triggers a long line of collapsing dominoes). In their thinking, should Vietnam fall to Communism, it might trigger a similar political shift in other small Asian nations. Yet from the time that combat troops landed at the South Vietnamese port of Da Nang, American policy was directly challenged and questioned by the largest and most dramatic antiwar protest movement in American history. This movement questioned the ethics of Cold War international politics, and the movement contributed directly to the political downfall of the American president most closely associated with waging the war, Lyndon B. Johnson (1908–1973; served 1963–69). The politics in-

In Vietnam, U.S. troops fought a war unlike any they had fought in the past. Although American soldiers had the advantage of superior technology, they often had difficulty determining who was the enemy. *AP/Wide World Photos. Reproduced by permission.*

volved in fighting and protesting the Vietnam War made it one of the most agonizing conflicts in American history, and the arguments over how, why, and who "lost" the war in Vietnam continued to influence American politics into the twenty-first century.

The Vietnam War was agonizing in other ways as well. It involved American soldiers in some of the most terrifying and demoralizing conditions known in modern warfare. Told that they were traveling to a country to protect friendly people desperate to be saved from communist oppressors, soldiers found that the South Vietnamese people hated their own government because it was generally brutal to them. Many South Vietnamese sided with the communist North Vietnamese, not out of political convictions about the superiority of Communism over democracy, but because the communists professed respect for the peasant farmers who made up the majority of the Vietnamese population. Thus American soldiers found themselves fighting both against a known enemy (the North Vietnamese army) and a shadowy enemy called the Vietcong (South Vietnamese people who supported the communist cause). The problem was that American soldiers could not distinguish enemies from friends in a tropical jungle nation where the very people who welcomed them to their villages during the day might fire upon them at night. Compound these difficulties with the lack of clear military objectives, and the stage was set for an ongoing string of disasters that left many soldiers bitter and disgusted with their own government.

A common term used to describe the Vietnam War is "quagmire"—a difficult, precarious, or entrapping position, according to the *Merriam-Webster Dictionary*. It was certainly that. The United States got involved in the Vietnam civil war with the relatively uncomplicated goal of protecting South Vietnam from becoming Communist. But the realities of fighting a war against Communism in a distant land and with uncertain support from the South Vietnamese people put the entire mission at risk. Eventually, the United States withdrew and allowed the South Vietnamese government to fight its own war. Some called this withdrawal an honorable conclusion to a difficult situation; others called it the first military defeat in U.S. history.

Prelude to war

U.S. involvement in Vietnam can only be understood within the context of the Cold War (1945–91), the great ideological conflict between the United States and Soviet Union over whether Communism or democracy is the most effective form of government. At the end of World War II (1939–45), the United States and the Soviet Union emerged as the two most powerful countries in the world. Though the two had been allies during the war, they had very different political and social systems. The United States was committed to democratic political systems, free-market economies, and freedom of religion and expression. The Soviet Union, on the other hand, had a totalitarian political system (one in which powerful leaders made the important decisions without consulting citizens) and a communist economy. Communist Party leaders controlled all elements of Soviet life. Both the

United States and the Soviet Union possessed nuclear weapons, with the capacity to destroy each other and possibly the entire world if they ever went to war. Both sides were interested in extending what political theorists called their "sphere of influence," the number of countries who could be counted on to be loyal allies in economic and military affairs, and also in containing the spread of the other's sphere of influence. Each side was deeply, sometimes dangerously, suspicious of the other. Their decades-long battle to establish dominance saw some of its most dramatic episodes in the 1960s, including the diplomatic clash over the installation of Soviet missiles in Cuba, the construction of a wall in the divided German city of Berlin, and—most importantly—the Vietnam War.

Vietnam became a Cold War battlefield through a twisting series of events that included a century of French colonization, brief Japanese control, and a communist leader who quoted the American Declaration of Independence. France had first established a colony in the Southeast Asian region known as Indochina in 1858, and by 1893 it had extended its control over all of French Indochina, an area that was later identified as the countries of Vietnam, Cambodia, and Laos. Following the collapse of the French government at the beginning of World War II, Japan easily gained control of French Indochina. Yet Japanese control ended with the war, and on September 2, 1945, Vietnamese nationalist Ho Chi Minh (c. 1890–1969), who had led his people in fighting against the Japanese, declared the formation of the Democratic Republic of Vietnam in language that quoted directly from the American Declaration of Independence. He used this language because he sought the support of the United States for the newly founded nation. The French, however, had different ideas.

In theory, the United States might have supported Ho Chi Minh and his party, the Vietminh, in its attempts to establish Vietnamese independence. The United States supported the efforts of oppressed peoples in small countries to select their own forms of government. It also hoped that the war would bring an end to European colonization of distant countries (colonization involved establishing control over a distant country in order to extract natural resources and benefit the colonizing country), which it saw as hurtful to world peace. The United States followed its own principles when it granted independence to its former colony, the Philippines, on July 4, 1946. But the pressures of the Cold War kept the United States from supporting Ho Chi Minh and the Vietminh. France wanted to regain control of its former colony, and France was an important U.S. ally in Europe. Therefore, when the French established a puppet government (one that supported French interests over South Vietnamese interests) and pointed to Ho Chi Minh's close ties to communist groups in the Soviet Union and (later) in China, the United States was only too happy to support what it characterized as the French fight against Communism in Asia. In the end, anti-Communism was more important than self-determination when it came to U.S. support for the Vietminh.

From 1945 to 1954, the French and their allies, supported by U.S. funds, fought a costly war against Vietminh forces for control of Vietnam. By 1954, however, the war was at a standstill, and the opposing forces signed an agreement at the Geneva Conference that divided the country in two, into the Democratic Republic of Vietnam (DRV), or North Vietnam, and the Republic of Vietnam (RVN), or South Vietnam. The agreement called for an election within two years to reunify the country under one government. But there was to be no election; instead, opposing groups concentrated on either side of the line dividing Vietnam. Pro-Communist forces gathered in the North behind Ho Chi Minh and pro-Western forces joined in the South behind the government of Ngo Dinh Diem (1901–1963).

For the next ten years, from 1954 to 1964, the opposing forces within Vietnam fought for control. From 1954, it was clear that the South Vietnamese government of Diem could not count on popular support. Diem was a Catholic in a nation dominated by Buddhism, and he placed harsh sanctions on Buddhist religious practices. He was also cruel to his political opponents, using torture and murder to achieve his ends. Though it had little public support, the South Vietnamese government had one great advantage: it was backed by the United States, which sent an ever-increasing flow of money and military advisors to stabilize South Vietnam. The North Vietnamese government possessed several advantages. Though it was less well equipped than its rival, it had a larger population and a larger army,. More important, it had the

Atrocities: The My Lai and Hue Massacres

War is dehumanizing: when men take up guns to kill other men, they begin to close themselves to the emotional horror of the act and become desensitized. In some cases, soldiers ignore the "rules" of warfare that bar soldiers from killing civilians, raping women, and destroying property unnecessarily. These war crimes, called atrocities, became particularly numerous in Vietnam. During the war there were countless stories of Vietcong and North Vietnamese fighters rounding up and killing South Vietnamese civilians who did not support their cause, of South Vietnamese officials brutally torturing and killing suspected communists, and of American soldiers shooting women and children in what were called "free-fire zones," battle areas where soldiers were told they could shoot anything that moved. Two atrocities, however, stand out from the Vietnam War.

On March 16, 1968, a platoon of American soldiers led by Lt. William Calley was sent on a search-and-destroy mission near the South Vietnamese village of My Lai. Soldiers in the area had been sniped at, booby-trapped, and harassed by Vietcong fighters for days and were on edge when they entered the village. Though the village contained no enemy soldiers, the Americans went on a rampage, killing between 175 and 400 unarmed women and children, raping several women, and burning the village. Dennis Conti, a member of the company, recalled the orders he received from Lt. Calley in *The Vietnam War: A History in Documents*: "[Calley] said: 'Take care of them.' So we said: 'Okay.' And we sat there and watched them like we usually do. And [Calley] came back again, and he said: ...'I mean kill them.'" Conti told of a fellow soldier gunning down women and children, tears flowing from his eyes. The massacre was hushed up for nearly a year, but a letter sent by Vietnam veteran Ronald Ridenhour led to a Congressional investiga-

sympathy of the people, not just in the North but also in the South, where peasants joined in a secret organization called the National Liberation Front (NLF) to help destabilize the Diem government and speed Vietnamese unification. After 1960, the NLF developed into an armed force, which the South Vietnamese government and the Americans called the Vietcong. By late 1963, North Vietnamese forces, aided by the Vietcong, had grown quite strong, and South Vietnam seemed destined soon to fall.

By 1963, it had become clear to strategists in the administration of President John F. Kennedy (1917–1963) that

South Vietnamese villagers crouch in muddy water to avoid a firefight. *National Archives.*

tion and a highly publicized set of indictments and trials. In the end, only Lt. Calley was convicted of war crimes. Some felt that Calley was a vicious criminal, but many within the military thought that Cal-

ley had been made a scapegoat for poor leadership and a war in which U.S. soldiers could not avoid committing atrocities.

The worst known North Vietnamese/Vietcong atrocity occurred during the Tet Offensive. On January 31, 1968, NVA and Vietcong forces entered the sizable city of Hue, formerly the nation's capital. The communist forces began a systematic roundup of anyone believed to have ties to the South Vietnamese government or U.S. forces, including government officials, Roman Catholic priests, teachers, civil servants, women, and children. When U.S. and South Vietnamese forces retook the city a month later, they discovered mass graves containing the bodies of 2,800 people, some of whom had been buried alive. They also learned of 3,000 civilians who were never located.

the Diem administration was so brutal to the people of South Vietnam that they would soon rise up and reunify the nation under communist rule. In early November 1963, the Central Intelligence Agency (CIA) helped sponsor a coup (violent overthrow of the government; pronounced "koo") against Diem. Counter to U.S. intentions, Diem and his brother were killed, and a string of unsuccessful governments followed until two military officers, Nguyen Van Theiu and Nguyen Cao Ky, took power in 1965. With South Vietnam destabilized by the coup, and the U.S. undergoing a transfer of power following Kennedy's assassination on November 22,

1963, North Vietnam applied even greater military pressure throughout the South. President Johnson, eager to keep South Vietnam from falling to the communists, looked for ways to prop up the precarious and shifting regime.

Americans fight in Vietnam: A slowly escalating war

In early August of 1964, Johnson saw an opportunity to display America's continued commitment to supporting a pro-Western government in South Vietnam. American ships patrolling in the Gulf of Tonkin, off the coast of North Vietnam, alleged that they had been fired upon by North Vietnamese torpedoes (whether missiles were actually fired has never been determined). This "attack," claimed Johnson, gave the United States a clear rationale for increasing American power in the region. President Johnson asked Congress for authorization to "take all necessary measures to repel any armed attack against the forces of the United States and to prevent further aggression." In a very nearly unanimous show of support, on August 7, 1964, Congress passed the Gulf of Tonkin Resolution and the United States found itself in a declared war against North Vietnam.

The war began slowly. It was not until February 6, 1965, when Vietcong forces attacked an American barracks in Pleiku, that American military forces first acted, sending air strikes on military bases in the north. Following another guerilla assault, Johnson ordered a military operation called Rolling Thunder, which called for successively stronger bombing raids to follow each North Vietnamese or Vietcong attack. These air strikes, and later the escalations in the number of ground troops sent into Vietnam, were part of a general policy of "sustained reprisal" that marked U.S. military engagement through 1968. This policy, first articulated by Johnson advisor McGeorge Bundy (1919–1996) in February of 1965, stated that every hostile action should be countered by a proportionately larger reaction. Bundy and others believed that this would deter further aggression and allow the United States to "save" South Vietnam without undue military action. They were wrong.

From the beginning, the policy of sustained reprisal had little effect on enemy activities. North Vietnamese army and Vietcong attacks only increased. The attacks were not di-

rect frontal battles between organized armies. Instead, small groups of Vietcong soldiers typically sneaked into a South Vietnamese village, attacked their targets (perhaps a few American warplanes or South Vietnamese army officers), and disappeared into the night. Strategists did not know where to find and defeat the enemy, because the enemy did not gather in traditional mass camps. In order to deter enemy attacks, Americans dropped more bombs and sent more soldiers. By war's end, the Americans had dropped seven million tons of bombs on Vietnam (surpassing by far the two million tons of bombs dropped in World War II). The United States also increased the number of combat troops dramatically. From 23,000 American troops in Vietnam in 1964 (and most of these in an advisory capacity), troop strength grew to 184,000 by the end of 1965; 385,000 by the end of 1966; 486,000 by the end of 1967; and 536,000 by the end of 1968.

In the end, these increases reflected the core beliefs of the American military. What the Americans wanted was to

American women were among those sent to care for the wounded in Vietnam. Here, U.S. Army nurses await transportation to Nha Trang, where they will work in a field hospital. *AP/Wide World Photos. Reproduced by permission.*

General William C. Westmoreland addresses his subordinates in 1967.
National Archives.

punish the North Vietnamese enough to convince them to stop the attacks on South Vietnamese territory and to gain permanent recognition of the legitimacy of the South Vietnamese government. They believed they could achieve this by pursuing a policy of attrition, through which the North Vietnamese and their sympathizers would be worn down by the superiority of American firepower. Armed with body counts—the number of combatants killed in military encounters—that showed (sometimes falsely, it was later learned) that the communists were absorbing huge losses to relatively few losses for the South Vietnamese and Americans, American generals reassured politicians and the public that it was only a matter of time before communist attacks halted. The end, U.S. commanding general William Westmoreland (1914–) assured the president, was just around the corner; late in 1967, President Johnson assured Americans that he could see "the light at the end of the tunnel," as quoted in *Lyndon Johnson's War.*

The Tet Offensive

In late January of 1968, civilians and soldiers across North and South Vietnam enjoyed the peace and quiet of a cease-fire called in observation of the Vietnamese New Year. Then, on January 31, 1968, while those in the South still rested, the North Vietnamese and their Vietcong allies launched the largest assault of the entire war. On that day, about 84,000 North Vietnamese Army (NVA) and Vietcong troops launched simultaneous attacks on enemy positions across South Vietnam. According to *Historical Atlas of the Vietnam War* by Harry G. Summers Jr., the attacks were launched on 36 of 44 provincial capitals, 5 of the 6 major cities, 64 of the 242 district capitals, and another 50 hamlets (small villages).

The hope of the North Vietnamese was that this major strike would so demoralize the South Vietnamese that their soldiers would abandon their armies and their civilians would rise up against their government. They hoped that this attack might bring the war to a speedy end and reunify Vietnam under communist rule.

In the end, Tet proved to be a major military defeat for the NVA and the Vietcong. The combined communist forces saw nearly one-third of their soldiers—45,000 men—killed in the various battles of the Tet Offensive, which lasted through March of 1968; the Americans lost just over 1,100 men. The campaign virtually destroyed the Vietcong as a fighting force. So thorough was the slaughter of the Vietcong that some historians have wondered whether the government of North Vietnam intended their slaughter so as to eliminate a potential political rival in the event of a unified Vietnam. Ironically, what might have been counted as a major South Vietnamese/American victory proved instead to

Thousands of homes were destroyed in Saigon during the Tet Offensive of 1968. Many residents were left homeless as a result.
© Bettmann/Corbis.

The Agony of Vietnam | 75

President Richard Nixon visits members of the 1st Infantry Division near Saigon in July 1969.
AP/Wide World Photos. Reproduced by permission.

be the stimulus for the United States to alter its policy toward the war. Thanks to Tet, policymakers who had believed that the North was near defeat, including General Westmoreland and President Johnson, had to acknowledge that the war was nowhere near over. According to Summers, the Tet Offensive "put an end to the illusion that U.S. intervention could result in an independent South Vietnam free of Communist aggression and was the beginning of the end of U.S. involvement."

The realization that the North was more than willing to continue to wage an offensive battle, combined with massive public protests in the United States against the war, led to major changes in U.S. policy. (For full coverage of the antiwar movement, see Chapter 6.) General Westmoreland asked for more American troops, but his request was denied, and he was ordered back to the United States. The policy of escalation ended, and beginning in 1968 the number of American troops in Vietnam began to decline, though bombing continued at an elevated rate. One political casualty of the Tet Offensive was the career of Lyndon Johnson. On March 31, 1968, Johnson announced that he would not seek reelection as president.

Vietnamization

Republican Richard M. Nixon (1913–1994; served 1969–74) won a hard fought and extremely close presidential election in 1968, and he brought with him real changes in American policy toward Vietnam. Nixon had campaigned on the promise that he would seek an honorable end to the war. Once he took office in January of 1969, he announced that he would pursue a policy he called "Vietnamization," which meant that he would let the Vietnamese fight the war. Under this policy, U.S. troops would be withdrawn. Nixon ordered 25,000 troops home in June of 1969 alone to prove his point. By the end of 1969, U.S. troops in Vietnam numbered 475,200; by the end of 1970, they stood at 334,600, declining to 156,800 by the end of 1971, 24,200 by the end of 1972, and just 50 troops in 1973 and 1974.

Vietnamization did not mean the end of U.S. involvement in Vietnam, however. Through 1969 and 1970, American troops remained engaged in intense battles to protect South Vietnamese territory from North Vietnamese attacks. Slowly, however, American troops were kept away from areas of intense fighting and concentrated on training and supplying South Vietnamese forces. North Vietnamese attacks slowed from 1969 through 1971, perhaps as the North waited for American troop strength to decline further.

Withdrawing troops solved one problem for the Nixon administration: it quieted those in the United States who questioned the value of sending American soldiers to die for a cause that looked increasingly desperate, and it soothed the increasingly vocal antiwar movement. But it also posed a problem, for Nixon feared that the communists would believe that the troop withdrawal indicated a lack of American resolve. To combat this potential problem, Nixon adopted a daring and, critics charged, dangerous strategy: he ordered the secret bombing of the neutral nation of Cambodia, which lay just to the west of South Vietnam. Vietcong and NVA troops had long used Cambodia as a refuge

A Soldier's War: The Difficulties of Fighting in Vietnam

In every war, soldiers must confront the horrors of facing death in a battle against a determined enemy. But the nature of the war in Vietnam—the lack of clear objectives and identifiable enemies, the youth and inexperience of the soldiers, the tactics of the enemy, and the difficult terrain—made this war particularly difficult for American soldiers.

When the first American combat soldiers crossed the Pacific to fight in Vietnam, many of them did so with the belief that they were fighting to combat the spread of Communism. That feeling of a patriotic mission kept morale high among many soldiers for the first real year of fighting, 1965, and combat missions remained relatively straightforward during that year. Soon, however, both the mission's definition and the actual fighting grew far more complicated. By 1966 the antiwar movement had succeeded in casting real doubt on U.S. motivations for going to war. Antiwar protestors argued that the U.S. was supporting a corrupt South Vietnamese regime and suppressing the will of the Vietnamese people. Many U.S. soldiers could see for themselves the truth of these claims: they saw how incompetent the South Vietnamese army was, and they knew that many South Vietnamese vil-

lagers resented the U.S. presence. In fact, because the enemy Vietcong recruited directly from the South Vietnamese population that the United States was charged with protecting, it became very difficult to distinguish the enemy from a friend.

Soldiers fighting in Vietnam were young. In World War II the average age of the U.S. soldier was twenty-six; in Vietnam, the average age was nineteen. Of the combat deaths among marines in Vietnam, 40 percent were teenagers. These inexperienced soldiers were often led by officers who themselves had little or no combat experience. As combat missions became increasingly dangerous, soldiers panicked in battle. Statistics compiled in the *Columbia Guide to America in the 1960s* show that of the 45,941 combat deaths recorded during the war, 40 percent occurred in the first three months of a one-year tour of duty, when soldiers were still "green." Only 6 percent of soldiers died in their last three months of a tour of duty.

The kinds of fighting faced by U.S. soldiers were stressful. In Vietnam, U.S. soldiers did not attack defined enemy positions with massive shows of force. Instead, they were forced to search out small bands of enemy soldiers in difficult terrain, including high grass, swamps, and thick jungles.

and a travel route to reach South Vietnamese battlefields, and Nixon believed he could show U.S. resolve by bombing these positions. In fact, information lated revealed by Nixon's aides revealed that this secret bombing and back-

The average age of the U.S. soldier in Vietnam was younger than those who fought in World War II. *AP/Wide World Photos. Reproduced by permission.*

A typical mission consisted of a small band of men, perhaps six to ten, sent out to flush out Vietcong and NVA soldiers. Soldiers called this work "humping the boonies." According to Richard L. Wormser, author of *Three Faces of Vietnam:* "[Soldiers] swept the countryside on search-and-destroy missions, set up ambushes, sought contact with the Vietcong.... The Vietcong would strike out of nowhere and then return into nowhere. They planted land mines and antipersonnel bombs that would explode without warning, killing men, blowing off their legs, sending shrapnel through their flesh. A man might see the head of his best friend blown off next to him or the soldier beside him lose his legs." Many soldiers grew to distrust the officers who sent them out on such suicidal missions, and the number of officers killed or wounded by their own men ("fragged" was the soldiers' term) in the Vietnam war was 1,017. American soldiers also turned to drugs in high numbers. Department of Defense figures indicate that 58.5 percent of American soldiers used marijuana; 22.68 percent heroin; 19.59 percent opium; and high percentages used drugs such as LSD, amphetamines, and barbiturates.

After the intensified fighting of 1967, accounts from soldiers indicate that many were more concerned with simply surviving the war than with accomplishing the objectives of their leaders. Desertion rates jumped from 14.7 per one thousand in 1966 to 73.5 per one thousand in 1971. Many of the soldiers who returned from Vietnam began to voice their opposition to the war and to tell stories of the atrocities they had seen. Some even joined veterans' groups opposed to the war, including the best-known group, Vietnam Veterans Against the War.

channel threats (secret messages sent to the North Vietnamese by foreign diplomats) to use nuclear weapons were part of Nixon's "madman" theory, which held that Nixon was so insanely determined to defeat the North Vietnamese

he was capable of nearly anything, including starting a nuclear war.

The Paris Peace Accords

When the secret bombing of Cambodia became
known in 1970 it prompted another upsurge in antiwar
protests across the United States. In one of the most tragic
occurrences of the period, four students were killed by National Guard soldiers during antiwar protests at Kent State
University in May of 1970. But Nixon's use of aerial bombing
continued until it reached his objective, which was to force
the North Vietnamese to negotiate an end to the war. A negotiated settlement was not a new idea; Americans and Vietnamese on both sides had made attempts to negotiate since
the beginning of the war, and Nixon had been pushing hard
for a negotiated settlement since he took office. It was increasing desperation on both sides that finally brought them
to the bargaining table. But that did not happen until after
Nixon ordered the heaviest bombing attack of the entire war,
when American planes dropped 20,000 tons of bombs on
North Vietnam between December 18 and 29, 1972, in what
are known as the Christmas Bombings.

On January 27, 1973, representatives from the United
States, North Vietnam, South Vietnam, and the Vietcong sat
at a table in Paris, France, and signed the document that
ended U.S. involvement in Vietnam. The document, titled the
"Agreement on Ending the War and Restoring the Peace in
Vietnam" but generally known as the Paris Peace Accords,
called for the withdrawal of all U.S. troops within sixty days,
the return of all U.S. prisoners, and the reunification of North
and South Vietnam through peaceful means. The first two
provisions of the Accords were observed: American troops and
prisoners left the country, and Nixon declared that he had
achieved "peace with honor," for there was still an intact pro-
Western government in place in South Vietnam. In the United States, the troops were welcomed home amid general pleasure that the long war in Vietnam was finally over.

For the Vietnamese, however, the war was far from
over. The Peace Accords had left 160,000 North Vietnamese
troops in the South, and South Vietnamese president Nguyen

Van Theiu, who had led the government since 1967, announced that the Accords were "tantamount to surrender" for South Vietnam, according to Summers. The United States had promised to protect the South should North Vietnamese troops launch further attacks, but when those attacks came in the spring of 1975, the United States looked the other way. When the capital city of Saigon fell to the communists in April of 1975, frightened South Vietnamese refugees clung to the skids of the last helicopter that evacuated the American embassy. Saigon was soon renamed Ho Chi Minh City, after the beloved communist leader of the North Vietnamese who had died in 1969, and the country was finally united under communist rule.

Judging the war

When President Nixon declared that the United States had attained "peace with honor" upon its withdrawal from Vietnam in 1973, he was careful not to declare victory. But for Nixon, for Americans at the time, and for historians in the decades that followed, the question was how to judge the American experience in Vietnam. Arguments raged over every element of American policy and action with regard to Vietnam. Some of the arguments concerned the larger strategic questions posed by the Cold War: How did the United States judge which steps it should take to contain the spread of Communism? Did America compromise its ideals when it supported South Vietnamese governments that were clearly corrupt and brutal? What was the appropriate stance for the United States to take toward popularly based nationalist movements that happened to be communist?

Other controversies surround the way the United States waged the war in Vietnam. From the very beginning of U.S. involvement in the country, it was clear that strategists saw the situation in unrealistic terms. For American planners, Vietnam was a test case for the idea that Communism must be stopped. Vietnam was one domino in a great political game, not a complex country filled with people who desperately wished to determine their own national destiny. As historian David Farber noted in *The Age of Great Dreams*, "Vietnam was less a war to be won than a demonstration project illustrating how the United States could shape a Third World revolutionary struggle." To wage all-out war in Vietnam would have been to risk a direct confrontation with the Chinese supporters of North Vietnam and potentially a nuclear war. Thus military planners used just enough American force to prop up the South Vietnamese government, but never enough to win the war. The results were disastrous for the country of Vietnam, for the moderate levels of American involvement likely made the war last far longer than it would have otherwise. They were also a disaster for American soldiers, who either lost their lives in a brutal war that lacked clear objectives or who returned to a country where their service was not appreciated.

For More Information

Books

Anderson, David L. *The Columbia Guide to the Vietnam War*. New York: Columbia University Press, 2002.

Berman, Larry. *Lyndon Johnson's War: The Road to Stalemate in Vietnam*. New York: Norton, 1989.

Detzer, David. *An Asian Tragedy: America and Vietnam*. Brookfield, CT: Millbrook Press, 1992.

Farber, David. *The Age of Great Dreams: America in the 1960s*. New York: Hill and Wang, 1994.

Farber, David, and Beth Bailey, with others. *The Columbia Guide to America in the 1960s*. New York: Columbia University Press, 2001.

Karnow, Stanley. *Vietnam: A History*. 2nd ed. New York: Penguin, 1997.

Lens, Sidney. *Vietnam: A War on Two Fronts*. New York: Lodestar Books, 1990.

Summers, Harry G. Jr. *Historical Atlas of the Vietnam War*. New York: Houghton Mifflin, 1995.

Tucker, Spencer C. *Encyclopedia of the Vietnam War: A Political, Social, and Military History*. 3 vols. Santa Barbara, CA: ABC-CLIO, 1998.

Wormser, Richard. *Three Faces of Vietnam*. New York: F. Watts, 1993.

Young, Marilyn B., John J. Fitzgerald, and A. Tom Grunfeld. *The Vietnam War: A History in Documents*. New York: Oxford University Press, 2002.

Web sites

Recalling the Vietnam War. http://globetrotter.berkeley.edu/PubEd/research/vietnam.html (accessed on June 22, 2004).

"Sixties Project: Primary Document Archive," *The Sixties Project.* http://lists.village.virginia.edu/sixties/HTML_docs/Resources/Primary.html (accessed on April 1, 2004).

Vietnam Online. www.pbs.org/wgbh/amex/vietnam/ (accessed on June 20, 2004).

Vietnam Veterans Against the War. www.vvaw.org (accessed on April 2, 2004).

Vietnam Veterans of America. www.vva.org (accessed on June 22, 2004).

Vietnam: Yesterday and Today. http://servercc.oakton.edu/~wittman/ (accessed on June 19, 2004).

6 The Antiwar Movement

Along with the civil rights movement, the movement to protest American involvement in the war in Vietnam provided some of the defining cultural experiences of the 1960s. From their origins in student protest in the first years of the 1960s, through the nonviolent protests of 1965, and on to the violent disruptions at the Democratic Convention in Chicago in 1968 and the National Guard shooting of students at Kent State University in 1970, the antiwar movement helped to sway public opinion both for and against American participation in the Vietnam War (1954–75). With acts ranging from prayer vigils to noisy demonstrations in American cities, from mailing in draft registration cards to self-immolation (the act of burning oneself to death), antiwar protestors drew great public attention to their cause, forcing the nation to question the legitimacy of its military actions, the honesty of its elected officials, and the consistency of its democratic values and institutions. Nearly four decades after the first American combat troops entered Vietnam, that war and the protests against it remained a source of deep division within American society.

Fertile ground for protest

In the first week of August 1964, President Lyndon B. Johnson (1908–1973; served 1963–69) asked for and received authorization to send combat troops to protect U.S. interests and support the government of South Vietnam in its ongoing civil war against communist North Vietnam. Only six months later, tens of thousands of people across the nation had organized themselves to begin the first of the antiwar teach-ins and protests, and within a few years protestors numbered in the hundreds of thousands. How did this movement coalesce so quickly? The truth was that for several years the conditions had been ripe for the formation of a broad coalition of liberal political groups. The emergence of New Left student political groups on college campuses, fed by rapidly growing numbers of impressionable college students; the existence of a thriving civil rights movement already committed to protesting social injustices; and the receptiveness of an older generation of liberal activists to the antiwar cause all provided fertile ground for the rapid formation of a fully formed antiwar movement in the mid-1960s.

The most important factor in the antiwar movement was the Students for a Democratic Society (SDS). Founded in 1960, the SDS was a small student group based at the University of Michigan, in Ann Arbor, a college town west of Detroit. The SDS emerged from a group known as the Student League for Industrial Democracy (SLID), which had sponsored discussion groups on college campuses. SLID had been in existence for some time, a part of what came to be called the "Old Left," a name given to left-wing political activists who supported communist and socialist causes in the 1920s and 1930s, before involvement with such causes was seen as dangerous during the Cold War (a long-running conflict that pitted the U.S.–dominated democratic West against the communist Soviet countries and People's Republic of China, 1945–91). As the SDS formed, its founders claimed that they were part of a "New Left." This New Left was concerned with civil rights, nuclear disarmament (stopping the production and stockpiling of nuclear weapons), and something they called "participatory democracy," an idea that called for governments and bureaucracies to be more responsive to the needs of citizens.

In June of 1962 the SDS, which had chapters on a number of college campuses across the nation, held a con-

Stokely Carmichael addresses members of the Students for a Democratic Society (SDS) at the University of California about issues pertaining to civil rights. *AP/Wide World Photos. Reproduced by permission.*

vention in Port Huron, Michigan. Following several days of discussion, the SDS issued the "Port Huron Statement," a lengthy and powerful declaration of political principles primarily authored by University of Michigan student Tom Hayden (1939–). The "Port Huron Statement" was publicized across the country, and it drew thousands of supporters both within and outside universities and colleges. For a time, the SDS focused its efforts on building membership on college campuses, where enrollments were growing steadily and where many young adults had been thrilled by the idealism of President John F. Kennedy (1917–1963; served 1961–63). But by the mid-1960s SDS members were still looking for a cause they could rally behind.

The civil rights movement also provided many volunteers for the antiwar movement. Both white and black civil rights workers joined the antiwar movement. For many whites, the civil rights movement had become less welcoming by the mid-1960s. Groups like the Student Nonviolent

Coordinating Committee (SNCC), which had once accepted white assistance, began to turn away white volunteers. Committed to social activism, many of these white pro-civil rights people turned their efforts to the antiwar movement. In increasing numbers as the war went on, black civil rights leaders and workers also came to support the antiwar cause. They made much of the fact that the percentage of combat soldiers who were black greatly exceeded the percentage of people in the United States who were black. African Americans, they argued, were being sent to die for a nation that was not yet willing to grant them full civil rights. Some radical black activists identified more with the Vietnamese than they did with U.S. military planners.

Finally, a number of older political activists became involved in the antiwar movement. These older leftist organizers, especially publisher I. F. Stone (1907–1989), helped youthful movement leaders handle the difficulties involved in coordinating large protests, though many members of this older generation urged a caution that was out of tune with the movement as a whole. Other antiwar protestors came from across the American spectrum—from Catholic and Quaker peace activists, from drug-taking hippies, and—late in the war—from U.S. combat veterans who had seen firsthand the horrors of the war in Vietnam. By 1968, this powerful and diverse movement had a real impact on American policymaking.

The antiwar movement begins

The antiwar movement in the United States was not sparked by the U.S. declaration of war, called the Gulf of Tonkin Resolution, issued in August of 1964. Even following this declaration, President Johnson assured Americans that the goal of the United States in Vietnam was limited to supporting the South Vietnamese government as it tried to stop a pro-communist uprising. As reporting on the distant conflict increased in late 1964, however, it became clear to many that the South Vietnamese government treated its citizens with great brutality and was very unpopular. Americans began to question whether the United States should support such a regime, let alone send American soldiers to fight in support of it. Then, in early 1965, the war grew more intense.

Resisting the Draft

One dramatic and highly symbolic act used by demonstrators to protest the Vietnam War was the destruction of draft cards or the refusal to accept being drafted into the military. The draft, administered by the U.S. Selective Service System, was a government program that chose men between the ages of eighteen and twenty-six to take part in compulsory (required) military service. In theory, the draft selected randomly from among all Americans. In practice, however, it selected men from working-class white and African-American populations out of proportion to their numbers in the general population. As the number of people drafted every month reached 30,000 in 1966, Americans began to protest against the draft in a variety of ways.

The most dramatic form of draft resistance involved destroying one's draft card (cards that contained a number that would be drawn by the Selective Service), often by burning. In April 1967 some 150 to 200 young men from Cornell University burned their draft cards in New York's Central Park, drawing national media attention. Other draft resisters simply turned in their draft cards or never registered for the draft. The most famous person who resisted the draft was boxer Muhammad Ali, who famously claimed "I ain't got no quarrel with the Vietcong." An estimated 300,000 American men resisted the draft in some way during the Vietnam War.

Other ways to avoid military service in the Vietnam War were through deferments, alternative service, or applying for conscientious objector status. Deferments were exemptions from the draft, usually for medical or psychological reasons. Football star Joe Namath received a deferment for his damaged knee, though he was fit enough to play in the National Football League. A common form of alternative service was to join the National Guard. George W. Bush (1946–), who later

The Vietcong (the name for the loosely organized communist army within South Vietnam) attacked American military advisors located at a South Vietnamese outpost named Pleiku, killing eight Americans and destroying ten aircraft. This and several smaller attacks prompted President Johnson and his military staff on March 2, 1965, to initiate Operation Rolling Thunder, an aerial bombing campaign against North Vietnam. The attack also led indirectly to the U.S. policy known as "sustained reprisal," which stated that any attack on American troops would be met with sustained and forceful military responses. It was the first stage in what would be-

A young man burns his draft card to show his opposition to being sent to fight in Vietnam. *AP/Wide World Photos. Reproduced by permission.*

became president in 2001, was assigned to the Texas National Guard. Finally, members of some religious groups, especially Quakers, could claim conscientious objector status, which meant that they held moral ob-

jections to war. Some conscientious objectors performed forms of alternative service, such as work in military medical facilities.

Draft resisters and draft card burners received harsh criticism from the federal government. Selective Service System head General Lewis B. Hershey (1893– 1977) wanted to use his power to immediately draft those who destroyed or turned in their draft cards (a proposal that was not carried out), and he also proposed drafting people who participated in antiwar demonstrations. In the end, as many as 50,000 people fled the country to avoid being drafted, and another several thousand draft resisters were prosecuted and forced to serve prison sentences. In 1977 President Jimmy Carter (1924–; served 1977–81) granted amnesty (freedom from prosecution) to the 11,000 draft resisters who had not yet returned to the country, but the issue of whether one served in Vietnam remained a hot issue among politicians running for national office.

come a steady pattern of escalation, or increase, of U.S. military engagement in the war.

Almost immediately antiwar activists responded to the escalation in American military action. On March 24, 1965, several hundred faculty members and several thousand students at the University of Michigan conducted a "teach-in," an informal all-night discussion forum concerning the events in Vietnam. Within weeks, similar teach-ins were conducted at campuses across the nation. Out of these teach-ins came the ideas for the first organized protests.

The first mass protest against the Vietnam War was held on April 17, 1965, and was organized by the SDS. Though SDS members had expected a few thousand protestors at the March on Washington to End the War in Vietnam, on the day of the event many thousands of people poured into the nation's capital. At least 15,000 neatly dressed and well-behaved people attended the march and listened to the speeches, though some reports indicate that as many as 25,000 people may have attended. The highlight of the event was a speech by Paul Potter, then president of the SDS. "The incredible war in Vietnam has provided the razor, the terrifying sharp cutting edge that has finally severed the last vestige of illusion that morality and democracy are the guiding principles of American foreign policy," Potter told his audience, as quoted in *Takin' It to the Streets*. Imploring the crowd to question the government that was leading the nation into a wide war, Potter asked: "What kind of system is it that justifies...seizing the destinies of the Vietnamese people and using them callously for its own purpose? What kind of system is it that disenfranchises people in the South, leaves millions upon millions of people throughout the country impoverished,...that consistently puts material values before humane values—and still persists in calling itself free and still persists in finding itself fit to police the world?"

Potter's speech, like many antiwar speeches to come, contrasted U.S. actions in Vietnam with American ideals. Though many people would call the antiwar movement unpatriotic, protestors felt that they were exhibiting a higher form of patriotism by asking the nation to live up to its ideals and insist on a foreign policy that reflected American beliefs. It was this idealism that drove the movement forward in the years to come and that made the collapse of the movement late in the decade so disheartening for many involved in it.

Expanded war, expanded protest

The initial buildup of mid-1965 was a first step in what became a regular pattern of U.S. military behavior in Vietnam. General William Westmoreland (1914–), the commander of U.S. forces in Vietnam from 1964 to 1968, and Secretary of Defense Robert McNamara (1916–) were the key architects of U.S. policy. They both believed in the inherent superiority of American soldiers. They convinced President Johnson that American victory would occur quickly, if only he would commit a few more American soldiers for combat. Westmoreland, quoted in David Farber's *The Age of Great Dreams: America in the 1960s,* said in 1965: "We're going to out-guerrilla the guerilla and out-ambush the ambush... because we're smarter, we have greater mobility and firepower; we have endurance and more to fight for...and we've got more guts." (Guerillas were fighters who used irregular tactics, such as harassment and sabotage, to wage war.) These policies drew troop strength in Vietnam from around 23,000 in 1964, to 184,000 troops in 1965; 385,000 in 1966; 486,000 in 1967; and 536,000 in 1968 (all figures are for the end of the calendar year). Troop strength increased, as did the numbers of dead and wounded on both sides.

The commitment and strength of the antiwar movement grew in proportion to the fighting in Vietnam. In addition to increases in the membership of established antiwar groups, including SDS and the War Resisters League (formed in 1923), more than thirty new antiwar organizations were formed in 1965 alone, including the National Coordinating Committee to End the War in Vietnam, based in Madison, Wisconsin; the Clergy and Laity Concerned About Vietnam (CALCAV), an interdenominational church group; the Catholic Peace Fellowship; the Emergency Citizens' Group Concerned About Vietnam; and many others.

Beginning in 1965, a number of antiwar organizations began to organize protests. The protests themselves grew in frequency and size through 1966 and 1967. On April 15, 1967, a group calling itself the Spring Mobilization Committee to End the War in Vietnam drew 125,000 protestors to a demonstration in New York City and 70,000 to one in San Francisco, California. Near the end of October, protestors staged what was the largest and most dramatic demonstration of the entire decade. Organized by the National Mobilization Committee to End the War in Vietnam (nicknamed "the MOBE") the multi-day protest drew some 250,000 people to Washington, D.C. The protest came to a climax when 50,000 demonstrators marched across the Arlington Memorial Bridge to surround the Pentagon, the headquarters of the American military. U.S. Army troops, called upon to keep

Hippies at an antiwar protest at the Pentagon in 1967 offer the military police a flower to emphasize the idea of peace. *National Archives.*

protestors from entering the building, surrounded the structure, and a diverse array of protestors—including hippies with long hair and college students wearing ties and suit jackets—pressed close around them. The entire scene—with folksingers singing, professors delivering lectures against the war, and hippies placing flowers in the gun barrels of the stone-faced soldiers—was captured by many television cameras and broadcast to the nation.

1968: The Tet Offensive

Antiwar protests grew dramatically through 1966 and 1967, as did media coverage of both the war and the protests. Yet polls (opinion surveys that capture viewpoints at a moment in time) showed that in 1967 the majority of Americans supported the efforts of the federal government to halt the spread of Communism in Asia. President Johnson and others in the government assured Americans that the war in Vietnam was going well. Johnson even pronounced that he could see "the light at the end of the tunnel," as quoted in *Lyndon Johnson's War*. Polls showed Americans felt that the protestors represented just a small minority of complainers who were out of touch with mainstream values, and many people within the government remained supportive of the war. The events of 1968, however, shattered this fragile shell of public support for the war and invigorated the antiwar movement.

Military events in distant Vietnam were crucial to the changed tone of the movement in 1968. In January of that year, the North Vietnamese and the Vietcong had launched their biggest military offensive ever, called the Tet Offensive, after the name of the ongoing Vietnamese new year celebration. Initially stunned by the ferocity of the attacks staged across South Vietnam, U.S. and South Vietnamese forces eventually turned back all attacks and ended up declaring a military victory. Nonetheless Tet revealed that American victory was not "just around the corner," as Westmoreland had told people for months. Television images of the conflict in fact showed that the war was getting worse, not better.

The antiwar movement capitalized on the events of the spring of 1968, staging numbers of demonstrations across the country. Notable among the demonstrations were a string of protests held on the campus of New York's Columbia University. In late April and early May, a group of more than 1,000 radical students occupied five buildings on the college campus and issued a proclamation calling for an end to the war in Vietnam (among other demands). The students held the buildings for eight days before hundreds of armed police stormed the buildings, swinging clubs and arresting 692 people.

Not only students expressed opposition to the war in the spring of 1968. Many mainstream politicians, business-

Protesting Corporate Involvement in the War

While big protests like those at Columbia University in New York and at the Pentagon in Washington, D.C., brought national visibility to the antiwar movement, there were also hundreds of smaller marches and demonstrations held across the nation. In terms of directly affecting U.S. policy, these smaller protests were sometimes quite effective.

The Dow Chemical Company, a large U.S. chemical corporation, had developed a good reputation by selling chemicals to other companies and for making some common household products, most notably Saran Wrap. In the mid-1960s, however, the company came under harsh criticism for supplying the U.S. military with a product known as napalm. Napalm was a highly explosive flammable gasoline gel that was dropped from U.S. bombers in Vietnam. Napalm was designed to stick to its victims and burn them. It worked very well, as was revealed in photographs and television clips coming out of Vietnam. For antiwar activists, napalm—clinging fire dropped from the sky, sometimes on civilians in villages—came to symbolize the inhumanity of U.S. conduct in the war.

On May 28, 1966, one hundred people paraded around Dow's facility in Torrance, California, protesting its making of napalm. Other protestors marched in front of Dow's New York offices, chanting slogans such as, "Napalm burns babies, Dow makes money." Soon it was not just napalm that was a target of protestors, but the Dow company, which had become a symbol of the way American corporations fueled the U.S. war machine. In 1967, stu-

The destructive capabilities of napalm are seen in this 1966 photo. Here, U.S. troops on patrol run as a napalm strike is launched in South Vietnam. *AP/Wide World Photos. Reproduced by permission.*

dents at the University of Wisconsin-Madison asked university administrators to ban Dow job recruiters from their campus. When the request was refused, students surrounded the Dow recruiters. Called in to break up the demonstration, police began clubbing and kicking demonstrators; several protestors were seriously injured. The student body, outraged at the attacks on peaceful demonstrators, rose up in unified anger. Students held a strike that shut down the university for two days and eventually brought the resignation of the university chancellor. From the beginning of the protests, Dow had defended its production of napalm. It claimed that it just supplied a product and was not responsible for how the product was used. However, when it came time for the government to renew its contract to purchase napalm, Dow allowed the contract to go to another supplier.

men, and news commentators began to express their doubts about the American strategy. Politicians from within Johnson's own Democratic Party began to make plans to run against him in the fall's presidential elections. One by one, candidates expressed their reservations about the war. None was more dramatic than Senator Eugene McCarthy (1916–), who declared, according to Todd Gitlin's *The Sixties: Years of Hope, Days of Rage*: "In 1963, we were told we were winning the war. In 1964, we were told the corner was being turned. In 1965, we were told the enemy was being brought to its knees. In 1966, 1967, and now again in 1968, we hear the same hollow claims of victory. For the fact is that the enemy is bolder than ever while we must enlarge our own commitment." Johnson was disturbed by the conflict in his own party, but he was truly alarmed when, on February 27, 1968, *CBS Evening News* anchorman Walter Cronkite, a highly trusted journalist, expressed the opinion that "...it seems now more certain than ever that the bloody experience of Viet-

A student sit-in at a Columbia University building in April 1968. More than 1,000 students took over several buildings for eight days before the police were called in.
© *Bettmann/Corbis.*

nam is to end in a stalemate." Johnson is said to have remarked: "If I have lost Walter Cronkite, I have lost Mr. Average American Citizen." On March 31, 1968, Johnson acknowledged the great unpopularity of the war when he announced that he would not run for reelection.

1968: The Democratic Convention in Chicago

With Johnson out of the presidential race, antiwar protestors focused on creating pressure to gain the nomination of an antiwar candidate at the Democratic National Convention, to be held in August of 1968 in Chicago. However, already that year two of the leading individuals of the antiwar movement had been assassinated: Martin Luther King Jr. (1929–1968), the civil rights leader who had taken up the antiwar cause, was killed on April 4, 1968, and Robert "Bobby" Kennedy (1925–1968), the popular younger brother of the slain president who inspired young people with his calls to end war and poverty, was gunned down on June 5, 1968, while campaigning for the presidency. As protestors began to converge on Chicago, Mayor Richard Daley (1902–1976) issued public warnings that his police would not put up with trouble in the streets, and he called in the National Guard to back his threats. With angry, disillusioned protestors, a rigid mayor, a police force with a reputation for brutality, and a swarm of news reporters, the stage was set for a major event.

As the convention drew near, protest groups from across the country gathered in Chicago. The protestors represented the full range of antiwar groups: there were convention delegates who supported antiwar candidates Eugene McCarthy (1916–) and George McGovern (1922–); SDS members led by founder Tom Hayden (1939–); Black Panthers led by the militant separatist Bobby Seale (1936–); peaceful members of church-based groups; and a strange and colorful group called the Yippies, led by hippie pranksters Jerry Rubin (1938–1994) and Abbie Hoffman (1936–1989). Denied permits to demonstrate or march, the protestors moved ahead with their plans anyway. For five days, protestors were viciously beaten and attacked by 12,000 armed members of the Chicago police force.

According to Richard L. Wormser, author of *Three Faces of Vietnam,* "[Police] used clubs, fists, blackjacks, and brass knuckles. They punched and kicked women and children. They swept through gatherings of people chanting, 'kill! kill! kill!', clubbing demonstrators, bystanders, and journalists." At one point, police crowded into a hotel near the convention center and beat delegates who supported the McCarthy campaign. People watching the horrible events chanted out "The whole world is watching!" and indeed it was, for the events of Chicago were later televised to national and international audiences. The whole world could see that people in the United States were deeply divided over the war in Vietnam.

Nixon, Kent State, and the shattering of the movement

Not only was the nation deeply divided over the issue of Vietnam by 1968—when polls showed that approximately

In the wake of the protests that occurred during the Democratic National Convention in Chicago in 1968, various individuals were brought to trial for their role in the demonstrations. Among them were the Chicago Seven, who were tried on conspiracy charges and for inciting others to riot. From top left: David Dellinger, Thomas Hayden, Lee Weiner, John R. Froines. Bottom from left: Jerry Rubin, Rennard Davis, Abbie Hoffman. *AP/Wide World Photos. Reproduced by permission.*

Kent State students surround a student slain by National Guard soldiers, May 2, 1970.
© Bettmann/Corbis.

35 percent of the people supported the war by the fall—they were also seriously divided over who would be their next president. The candidates were Vice President Hubert Humphrey (1911–1978), Republican candidate Richard M. Nixon (1913–1994; served 1969–74), and independent candidate George Wallace (1919–1998). In the end, Nixon won with just 43.4 percent of the vote to Humphrey's 42.7 percent. The difference may have been Nixon's frequent campaign pledge to bring an "honorable end" to the war. For several months following Nixon's inauguration in January of 1969, antiwar demonstrators gave the new president a chance to make good on his promises. But soon it became clear that Nixon had planned few changes to military policy, had increased bombing, and had declared his determination not to be swayed by protestors whom he held in contempt.

By mid-1969, the antiwar movement was back in full swing. There remained large-scale, peaceful protests led by national organizations like the Vietnam Moratorium Committee and the New Mobilization Committee to End the War in Vietnam (New MOBE). These groups organized a series of protests across the nation in October of 1969 and encouraged such actions as taking a day off work or driving with headlights on in the daylight to show symbolic opposition to the war. On Moratorium Day—October 15—100,000 people gathered in Boston, Massachusetts, and the mayor of New York City declared a day of mourning. In November, as news of the My Lai Massacre (an event in which American soldiers slaughtered innocent South Vietnamese civilians) reached the nation, protests increased, and they did so again in the spring of 1970, after Nixon announced that he had begun bombing Cambodia, a neighbor of South Vietnam known to harbor enemy soldiers.

Nixon's announcement of the bombing of Cambodia brought renewed demonstrations at campuses across the country. On May 2, 1970, students at the normally quiet and conservative campus of Kent State University in Ohio burned down the Reserve Officers' Training Corps (ROTC) building on campus, prompting the governor to call in the National Guard to quell (quiet or pacify) what had been several days of demonstrations. On May 4, protests continued and the National Guard shot tear gas into the crowd. Then, without warning, the soldiers opened fire, killing four students and wounding at least nine others. Some of the victims, crossing campus far from the demonstration, were hit by stray bullets. The nation reacted in shock, and demonstrations raged on more than 70 percent of college campuses.

The Kent State shootings marked the high point in the American antiwar movement. Though demonstrations continued following the shootings, they were less frequent and drew less attention. In fact, it is likely that the real turning point in the movement came with the election of Nixon. There were several reasons for the decline of the movement at this point. First, the various groups that had supported and organized demonstrations were coming apart. Internal fighting over tactics and the desire on the part of some demonstrators to pursue more radical and violent forms of protest split groups into factions and limited their effectiveness. A case in point is the SDS. By late 1968 some of the more influential members wanted to adopt revolutionary Communism (the overthrow of the U.S. government, to be replaced with Communism) as the group's political platform. Eventually, these members broke off to form the Weathermen in 1969. The Weathermen wanted to "bring the war home" to the United States with bombings and guerrilla attacks on American targets. They staged several attacks, though their most famous bombing in 1970 in fact took the lives of three of their own members and no others. In the SDS and in other antiwar organizations, few participants were willing to follow a path that led to revolutionary violence against the government and the organizations rapidly fell apart.

Another reason for the collapse of the movement was American military policy itself. Nixon did follow through on his promise to reduce the number of American troops, lowering troop levels to 475,000 at the end of 1969; to 334,600 at the end of 1970; to 156,800 in 1971; 24,200 in 1972; and finally to just 50 in 1973 and 1974. This reduction of American troop commitment was known as "Vietnamization," meaning that the U.S. would return control of the war to the South Vietnamese, though the United States did continue to drop massive amounts of bombs on North Vietnamese and Vietcong targets through 1972. The result, of course, was the eventual collapse of South Vietnam and its unification under communist rule in 1975. (For full coverage of the war, see Chapter 5.)

In many ways, antiwar sentiment simply became more mainstream after 1968. The violent protests of that year, combined with the revelations of atrocities (extremely brutal or cruel acts) by U.S. soldiers and deceit by U.S. military officials helped convince many moderate Americans to embrace antiwar sentiments. More and more members of Congress were willing to speak out against the war or to recommend ways to bring the war to an end. Television programs and popular singers increasing adopted antiwar attitudes. It also helped that an increasing number of combat veterans participated in antiwar demonstrations. The most notable of these was the Vietnam Veterans Against the War (see sidebar). Many other veterans spoke out individually against the war.

Assessing the impact of the antiwar movement

Both during the 1960s and afterward, cultural commentators and historians have pondered whether the antiwar move-

A crowd of pro-Vietnam demonstrators in support of U.S. policy in Vietnam, Wakefield, Massachusetts, October 29, 1967. *AP/Wide World Photos. Reproduced by permission.*

ment had any effect on the way the United States waged war in Vietnam. Some argue that the antiwar movement, by drawing constant and noisy public attention to the missteps and lies of the U.S. military and federal government and to the immorality of U.S. presence in Vietnam, forced the government to change its policies. By making forceful antiwar arguments, the movement made it possible for politicians to embrace moderate antiwar views and draw more mainstream support. This growing mainstream support drove Johnson from office and forced Nixon to lead the withdrawal of troops. Proponents of this argument believe that the antiwar movement was a positive force in American political and cultural life in the decade.

Others have insisted that while the movement did have an impact on U.S. involvement in Vietnam, that impact was primarily negative. Many people at the time deeply resented the criticisms being leveled at the U.S. government. They considered them unpatriotic and held counterprotests of their own, shouting "America, love it or

Vietnam Veterans Against the War

Of all the groups to speak out against the Vietnam War, few had the credibility of the Vietnam Veterans Against the War (VVAW). The group was formed in 1967 by six Vietnam veterans who had met at a protest march in New York City. The group soon expanded to include hundreds and later thousands of war veterans. By early 1971 the VVAW had decided to become more public with veterans' concerns about the war. For three days in January, the group held hearings at which soldiers testified about the cruel and barbaric acts they had seen while stationed in Vietnam. The conclusion they reached at these hearings, called the Winter Soldier Investigations, was that the war in Vietnam was unjust and against their higher ideals as Americans.

In April 1971 the VVAW organized a demonstration in Washington, D.C., that they called Operation Dewey Canyon III, named after an actual military operation held in Vietnam earlier that year. They held a mass march of veterans and mothers of fallen soldiers, and on the final day of protests seven hundred veterans threw their military medals and ribbons over a barricade onto the Capitol steps. That day, twenty-seven-year-old U.S. Navy lieutenant John Kerry (1944–) delivered powerful testimony before the Senate Foreign Relations Committee. At the end of his moving testimony, quoted from *Takin' It to the Streets,* Kerry asked: "We are asking Americans to think about that because how do you ask a man to be the last man to die in Vietnam? How do you ask a man to be the last man to die for a mistake?…We are here to ask, and we are here to ask vehemently, where are the leaders of our country? Where is the leadership?"

leave it," and "My country, right or wrong." Detractors of the movement claim that its frequent criticisms handcuffed U.S. military strategists from waging war the right way and believe that if the U.S. Army had been given freedom to fight it could have easily defeated the North Vietnamese. Movement opponents claim that the importance of the movement was drastically overstated by excess media attention, and they argue that the distrust that the movement encouraged has continued to undermine the federal government's ability to lead.

Some people feel that the impact of the antiwar movement was overstated from the beginning. Though acknowledging that the protests were dramatic and drew media attention, people at the time charged that these protests were the expression of a tiny minority of spoiled college kids with too much time on their hands and disgruntled liberals who quickly became distracted by internal arguments over politics. Supporters of this position claim that the antiwar movement did little to affect military policy. They point to frequent comments by politicians that they were not affected by protests and to debate within the government about how to wage the war without involving China and the Soviet Union, as evidence that essential decisions were made without regard to the protesting in the streets. For believers in this position, the antiwar movement was a distracting sideshow that did not have real impact.

Despite such diversity in evaluations of the impact of the movement on the outcome of the war, many people agree that the antiwar movement of the 1960s had a huge impact on American culture. There never before had been such a sustained, long-term effort on behalf of Americans to express displeasure with U.S. foreign policy. Antiwar demonstrations brought together people from a wide variety of other social movements—including the civil rights movement, the feminist movement, and the hippie counterculture—and gave them a common cause. The participation of young people in all of these movements, and the generalized resistance of those of their parents' generation, helped convey the idea that there was a "generation gap"—or a fundamental difference of opinion—that existed between older and younger Americans. Also the antiwar movement helped to encourage a widespread distrust in government (a distrust that, ironically, was also encouraged by the conservative political movement that criticized protest but wanted smaller government). For better or worse, the antiwar movement helped define the 1960s and continued to have an impact in American society throughout the twentieth century.

For More Information

Books

Berman, Larry. *Lyndon Johnson's War: The Road to Stalemate in Vietnam.* New York: Norton, 1989.

Bloom, Alexander, and Wini Breines, eds. *"Takin' It to the Streets": A Sixties Reader.* New York: Oxford University Press, 2003.

DeBenedetti, Charles, with Charles Chatfield. *An American Ordeal: The Antiwar Movement of the Vietnam Era*. Syracuse, NY: Syracuse University Press, 1990.

Dudley, William, ed. *The 1960s*. San Diego, CA: Greenhaven, 2000.

Farber, David. *The Age of Great Dreams: America in the 1960s*. New York: Hill and Wang, 1994.

Farber, David, and Beth Bailey, with others. *The Columbia Guide to America in the 1960s*. New York: Columbia University Press, 2001.

Galt, Margot Fortunato. *Stop This War!: American Protest of the Conflict in Vietnam*. Minneapolis, MN: Lerner, 2000.

Gitlin, Todd. *The Sixties: Years of Hope, Days of Rage*. New York: Bantam, 1987; revised, 1993.

Hunt, Andrew. *The Turning: A History of Vietnam Veterans Against the War*. New York: New York University Press, 1999.

Isserman, Maurice, and Michael Kazin. *America Divided: The Civil War of the 1960s*. New York: Oxford University Press, 2000.

Kallen, Stuart A., ed. *Sixties Counterculture*. San Diego, CA: Greenhaven Press, 2001.

Lens, Sidney. *Vietnam: A War on Two Fronts*. New York: Lodestar Books, 1990.

McCormick, Anita Louisa. *The Vietnam Antiwar Movement in American History*. Berkeley Heights, NJ: Enslow Publishers, 2000.

Miller, Jim. *Democracy Is in the Streets: From Port Huron to the Siege of Chicago*. Cambridge, MA: Harvard University Press, 1994.

Nicosia, Gerald. *Home to War: A History of the Vietnam Veterans' Movement*. New York: Crown, 2001.

Stacewicz, Richard. *Winter Soldiers: An Oral History of the Vietnam Veterans Against the War*. New York: Twayne, 1997.

Tucker, Spencer C. *Encyclopedia of the Vietnam War: A Political, Social, and Military History*. 3 vols. Santa Barbara, CA: ABC-CLIO, 1998.

Wells, Tom. *The War Within: America's Battle Over Vietnam*. Berkeley: University of California Press, 1994.

Westheider, James E. *Fighting on Two Fronts: African Americans and the Vietnam War*. New York: New York University Press, 1997.

Wormser, Richard. *Three Faces of Vietnam*. New York: F. Watts, 1993.

Web sites

"Sixties Project: Primary Document Archive," *The Sixties Project*. http://lists.village.virginia.edu/sixties/HTML_docs/Resources/Primary.html (accessed on June 1, 2004).

Vietnam Online. www.pbs.org/wgbh/amex/vietnam/ (accessed on June 20, 2004).

Vietnam Veterans Against the War. www.vvaw.org (accessed on June 2, 2004).

Vietnam: Yesterday and Today. http://servercc.oakton.edu/~wittman/ (accessed on June 19, 2004).

The American Economy: Leading the World

7

In 1960, the United States was the most prosperous nation in the world, and it was still growing fast. The nation's prosperity had come on quickly; in the fifteen years since the end of World War II (1939–45), the gross national product (GNP), or the value of all the goods produced in the nation, had shot up by 250 percent. Then, in the first half of the 1960s, GNP grew another 36 percent. Altogether, in the 1960s the United States experienced its longest uninterrupted economic expansion to date in American history (a record for consecutive months of growth unmatched until the 1990s).

This economic boom was fueled by thriving American businesses. By 1962, 66 percent of American manufacturing assets were controlled by the 500 largest companies. Some American corporations grew into global giants. General Motors, IBM, and Coca-Cola, among others, extended their businesses throughout the world. Growing companies brought jobs—many more well-paying, white-collar jobs (that is, salaried jobs that do not involve manual labor) than ever before—and unemployment levels shrank. More and better jobs offered workers more money. The median family income (the income level at which

Workers at General Motors' Fleetwood plant in Detroit, Michigan, walk the picket line in 1964 after United Auto Workers (UAW) and GM fail to reach an agreement on a new contract. *© Bettmann/Corbis.*

half of all incomes lay above and half lay below) in the United States rose from $3,319 in 1950 to $5,620 in 1960 to $9,867 in 1970, according to the U.S. Census Bureau. (Measured in constant 1993 dollars, which allow direct comparison, these figures become $19,900 in 1950, $27,435 in 1960, and $36,747 in 1970.) No matter how people measured it, the amount of money circulating through American households increased dramatically from 1950 to 1970.

Manufacturing facilities—producing such goods as televisions, cars, furniture, and other goods—in particular provided workers with the highest wages in the world. As American business expanded into international markets and increasing sales fueled record high profits, labor unions pressed companies into offering high salaries and substantial benefit packages, including health and life insurance. To secure these generous contracts, unions staged some of the biggest, longest strikes in history. The United Steel Workers held the industry's longest steel strike between July 1959 and January 1960; an airline workers' strike grounded five airlines for six days in 1961; dock workers struck for a month in 1963; and the United Auto Workers halted production at General Motors for nearly two months in 1964. The settlement of strikes and other labor negotiations usually ended with costly labor contracts that specified the wages and benefits of workers. Companies simply passed the extra expense of these agreements directly on to the consumer. For example, U.S. Steel raised its prices after signing a new union contract in 1962, and just five days after signing a three-year contract with the United Rubber Workers union in 1967, Firestone raised its tire prices.

Highs and lows in a thriving economy

For white Americans in the nation's urban centers, opportunity seemed endless in the 1960s. Jobs were plentiful, wages were high, and businesses offered consumers more goods than ever before in an expanding number of malls and retail outlets. Especially for those who had lived through the economic hardships of the Great Depression (1929–39) and the rationing, or limiting of certain goods, of World War II (1939-45), when hard work earned low wages, the economic boom of the 1950s and 1960s seemed like a marvelous reward. With higher wages and access to easy credit (see sidebar), Americans began living more luxurious lifestyles. More and more people came to own their own home, a car (or two), and a television. By the end of the decade, the one million telephones in the United States comprised half of the total number of phones in the world. American homes abounded with technological innovations, including refrigerators, clothes washers and dryers, radios, and other gadgets.

Buy Now, Pay Later: The Rise of the Credit Card

As American businesses recorded higher profits and offered workers higher wages, they also sought ways to encourage Americans to buy more things. One way to do this was to offer credit, allowing people to buy now and pay later. Many companies—especially those selling large-price items such as cars or refrigerators—had extended credit to consumers for decades. In the 1960s, many more banks and finance companies offered credit cards that enabled people to enjoy the wide variety of consumer goods offered by merchants.

Credit purchases in the decades before the 1960s were rather limited, because companies offered credit for purchases only at their establishments or for single large purchases. Credit that could be used at many different merchants was introduced in 1949 when the Diners Club company issued its first cards. The Diners Club company required cardholders to pay off their balances each month but made money by charging consumers a monthly fee for using the Diners Club card and merchants a fee for using the credit service.

By the 1960s, however, credit became easy to get and even easier to use. A handful of credit companies had begun offering universal credit cards (those that could be used at a variety of different places) in the late 1950s. Some of these cards had revolving credit, meaning that card carriers only had to pay a minimum fee each month instead of paying off the total amount of the bill charged to their card accounts. By the mid-1960s two companies, Bank of America and a conglomer-

U.S. prosperity allowed Americans to buy more products and enjoy more expensive forms of leisure. Americans took more vacations—traveling to national parks or flying to foreign countries—watched more ballgames, and enjoyed leisure activities ranging from bowling to boating, and much more.

The general prosperity in the country lifted up nearly all Americans. Every segment of the American population realized some improvement in its living conditions, at least relative to past conditions. Even in Appalachia, a region in the United States in the Appalachian Mountains stretching from New York south to Alabama and the poorest U.S. region, with unemployment rates of 25 percent in 1959, living conditions improved in the 1960s. Harlan County, Kentucky, was the poorest county in this region and in the country as a whole.

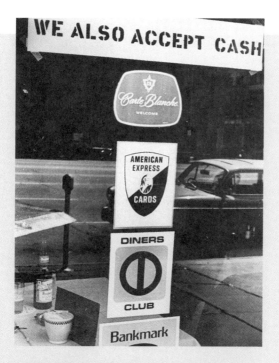

In the 1960s retailers began accepting credit cards, such as these listed on a restaurant window in St. Louis, Missouri, in 1968.
© Bettmann/Corbis.

ation of large banks called Interbank Card Association, offered universal, revolving credit cards to consumers across the country. The cards issued by these two companies came to be known as VISA (in 1976) and MasterCard (in 1980), respectively. Buying on credit quickly became a way of life in United States. Bank of America serviced two million consumer credit cards in 1966 to 64,000 merchants. Within two years the company had doubled the number of cards to four million and increased the number of merchants to 316,000. By 1970 a full 16 percent of American families had at least one credit card and the number continued to rise to over 50 percent in the coming decades. As the number of credit cards increased, so did the level of Americans' consumer debt. But with optimism that the economy would remain strong, Americans did not worry about their growing credit card debt.

A depressed coal mining industry had reduced a huge portion of the residents' income to below the poverty level, yet 67 percent of the households had a television and 59 percent of the families owned a car, according to David Farber in *The Age of Great Dreams*. Thus even America's poorest were richer than people in other countries.

However, comparing American wealth to the financial state in other countries offered no consolation to poor U.S. citizens, and the comparison did not satisfy U.S. policy makers who were convinced that American wealth should be spread more widely. Many Americans became aware of poverty in their prosperous nation following the publication of Michael Harrington's 1962 book, *The Other America*. Harrington argued that poor Americans were invisible, hidden from media attention and from the view of wealthy Americans who were living in the suburbs. But he pointed out—and census figures confirm—that poverty was a real problem in the United States.

Statistics paint a clear picture of the nature of poverty in the United States. Despite the general improvement in Americans' lives, about 20 percent of Americans lived in poverty in the early 1960s. More African Americans experienced poverty in America; while they constituted only 10 percent of the population, they represented over 30 percent of the poor in 1960. And in 1963, fully 50 percent of blacks lived below the poverty line, according to statistics taken by *USA Today*. Poverty for blacks stemmed from extreme and frequent racism, which kept African Americans from gaining access to higher-paying jobs and from the education needed to get those jobs. Pushed from southern farm work as advances in machinery replaced their jobs, many blacks moved to northern cities looking for work with only meager formal education and skills often limited to rural work. Poor blacks were often younger and were concentrated in urban ghettos characterized by their substandard housing and high rates of crime. The condition of these urban poor was in stark contrast to the abundance and prosperity enjoyed by white people in the suburbs. Though blacks constituted a higher percentage of the poor, the total number of poor whites was in fact higher. Poor whites were generally old and lived in out-of-the-way rural areas. Though their numbers were larger, these poor Americans were not as visible as those in more populated, urban areas.

There were a number of conditions that trapped African Americans in poverty. For example, corporations regularly and legally discriminated against people based on race and gender in all parts of the country, limiting their access to jobs or providing lower rates of pay. Suburban housing developers discouraged blacks from even trying to buy their houses. Such discrimination was exposed by the civil rights movement and the women's movement, which got stronger during the 1960s. Some people thought that continued improvements in the economy would naturally lead to the end of poverty and that making laws against discrimination would allow blacks full access to better jobs and housing. But many Americans believed that they should use the nation's vast wealth to actively combat the problems. They thought that economic strength could be used as a tool to bring social justice.

Does prosperity bring responsibility?

While prosperous Americans were happy about their ability to enjoy luxuries, they worried about the greater purpose of the nation's immense prosperity. The success of capitalism seemed apparent; it had made other countries envy the United States. Politicians frequently said that capitalism worked well, and they held up American prosperity as proof that Communism, such as that in the Soviet Union and the People's Republic of China, did not. But other Americans wondered if U.S. wealth could not be used more wisely to lift more Americans out of poverty.

President Lyndon Johnson (1908–1973; served 1963–69) saw U.S. prosperity as an invitation to the federal government to take care of its citizens. In 1964, the first full year of his presidency, he argued that the United States could become a "Great Society," and he proposed a set of government programs that would help realize this goal. White House staff assistant Joseph Califano described the underlying reasons for the Great Society: "We simply could not accept poverty, ignorance, and hunger as intractable, permanent features of American society. There was no child we could not feed, no adult we could not put to work, no disease we could not cure, no toy, food or appliance we could not make safer, no air or water we could not clean," as quoted by Farber. With the rising tax money, which came from Americans who made higher wages, Johnson hoped that the federal government would help reduce inequalities, lift up poor people, and in this way spread the promise of the American system to every citizen. While American business focused on producing profits and jobs, the government would focus on helping those in need.

Although Johnson's Great Society programs were intended to improve every social level of American society, the poorest Americans received special attention. Johnson declared a "War on Poverty" in 1964. He did not want to just give money to poor people; instead, he wanted the federal government to give poor people the tools they needed to lift

President Lyndon Johnson and Lady Bird Johnson visit homes in Appalachia, a poor region of the United States, in 1964 in conjunction with Johnson's War on Poverty program.
AP/Wide World Photos.
Reproduced by permission.

themselves out of poverty, including federally funded education and job training, among other support. By the end of the decade, dozens of legislative bills aimed at relieving poor people's conditions had passed through Congress, including preschool programs, housing acts, and medical assistance. Food stamps and free and reduced school meal programs greatly reduced the number of hungry Americans and the 1965 passage of the Medicaid and Medicare programs offered free or reduced-cost medical care to the nation's poor and elderly. Although the healthcare programs begun during the 1960s cost billions of dollars, they extended the lives and improved the quality of life for the poor.

Overall, poverty did decrease throughout the 1960s. The percentage of Americans who were poor fell from just over 20 percent in 1959 to 12 percent in 1969. Yet many believed that the War on Poverty was not a success. Many worried about the increasing size of the federal government and about the dependency of the poor upon the government. The percentage of government spending on social welfare programs increased from $52.3 billion in 1960 to $113.6 billion in 1968. One example of this increase in spending is the increase in welfare provided by the Aid to Families with Dependent Children program (AFDC). AFDC offered money to more and more families during the decade: the number increased more than five times between 1960 and 1975, according to Farber. The sharp jump in AFDC participants came from several factors: political activism that forced the government to make applying for AFDC aid easier and a shift in the poor people's expectations about federal aid. By the end of the decade, many poor people had come to consider federal aid something they deserved from a society and government that had discriminated against them. The shift in their attitudes can be seen from the numbers of eligible participants in the AFDC program. While only one-third of those who qualified for federal aid applied for help at the beginning of the decade, that number reached nearly 90 percent by the end of the decade, according to Farber.

Domestic spending on anti-poverty programs was not the only drain on the economy as the decade progressed. By the end of the decade the high costs of an expanding war in Vietnam weakened Johnson's ability to pursue his vision for the Great Society. Though he introduced more than a dozen pieces of legislation and new federal programs designed to create jobs, provide training, improve housing, offer basic education, and provide food to the poor, the increasing costs of the war drew criticism and reduced support for the costly federal programs needed to create the Great Society.

Although the American economy remained strong at the end of the decade, it faced new foreign competitors, especially companies from Germany and Japan. With the arrival of foreign products, American businesses focused on becoming more competitive, spending money on research for improved quality and developing more efficient processes. The unions that had forced companies into providing generous benefits and wages to workers lost power by the end of the decade, especially when more conservative politicians began winning seats in Congress after 1968. In the 1970s American businesses struggled to keep up in a far more competitive international market.

For More Information

Books

Cooke, Tim, et al, eds. *The U.S. Economy and the World.* Vol. 4, *Economics.* Danbury, CT: Grolier Educational, 2000.

Farber, David. *The Age of Great Dreams: America in the 1960s.* New York: Hill and Wang, 1994.

Farber, David, and Beth Bailey, with others. *The Columbia Guide to America in the 1960s.* New York: Columbia University Press, 2001.

Gitlin, Todd. *The Sixties: Years of Hope, Days of Rage.* New York: Bantam, 1987; revised, 1993.

Harrington, Michael. *The Other America: Poverty in the United States.* New York: Macmillan, 1962.

Hurley, Jennifer A. *The 1960s.* San Diego, CA: Greenhaven Press, 2000.

Isserman, Maurice, and Michael Kazin. *America Divided: The Civil War of the 1960s.* New York: Oxford University Press, 2000.

Northrup, Cynthia Clark, ed. *The American Economy : A Historical Encyclopedia.* Santa Barbara, CA: ABC-CLIO, 2003.

Web sites

"The Face of Black America." *USA Today.* www.usatoday.com/news/nation/2003-08-22-march-table.htm (accessed on June 3, 2004).

U.S. Census Bureau. www.census.gov (accessed on June 3, 2004).

Civil Rights

8

In 1960, when the civil rights movement first began to gain national attention, African Americans had been working to gain political and economic rights for nearly a century. Blacks had made some progress, but the laws that many southern state legislatures had written to prevent blacks and whites from living as equals—called Jim Crow laws—continued to separate the races in restaurants, schools, theaters, parks, and other public facilities in many states in the South. Those blacks who had migrated to northern and western states in an attempt to escape the legal restrictions of Jim Crow laws found that life in these new locations had similar restrictions because of customs based on racial prejudice, or a judgment or opinion based on a preconceived notions about race. Blacks in the North and West faced discrimination, or poor treatment based on race, in housing and the job market, among other areas. Police and citizens alike enforced the separation of races vigorously. Blacks who tried to mix with whites were arrested, beaten, or killed. Penalties for violence were rarely enforced when the crimes were acted out against blacks.

Early civil rights efforts

Given the dangers involved in seeking to improve their place in American society, blacks' civil rights efforts before the 1960s often consisted of small, nonviolent action and relatively quiet challenges in courts of law. The National Association for the Advancement of Colored People (NAACP) was created in 1909 to work toward political and civil liberties for blacks. Large group protests, which many associate with the 1960s, actually first gained attention during World War II (1939–45). In 1941 President Franklin D. Roosevelt (1882–1945; served 1933–45) gave in to pressure from 100,000 African Americans threatening to march on Washington, D.C., by signing an executive order that banned racial discrimination in government jobs and training programs and in the defense industries that supplied the war effort.

In the 1950s blacks won national attention when the U.S. Supreme Court overturned its 1896 ruling in *Plessy v. Ferguson* that had judged laws made to separate the races acceptable under the Constitution. The Court's 1954 ruling in the *Brown v. Board of Education* case reversed the former opinion, making separation of the races in public schools illegal across the nation. But the Court's ruling was rejected by many white southerners who resisted strongly the idea of mixing between races. To protest the segregation of races on Montgomery, Alabama, city buses, blacks and sympathetic whites refused to ride the city buses ,for nearly a year. The following struggles between southern blacks and whites as the federal government enforced this ruling set the stage for the mass protests of the 1960s.

Greensboro sit-ins

On February 1, 1960, four young black college students staged a quiet protest at a whites-only lunch counter at a Woolworth's store in Greensboro, North Carolina. The four seated themselves at the counter and politely requested service. When management refused service, the men simply remained seated, calmly asking to purchase a cup of coffee until the store closed for the day. The students returned the next day with nearly thirty more students. All protestors sat at the lunch counter requesting service for about two hours. Their second-day efforts attracted the attention of local news

reporters. The following day, sixty-six protestors returned to the lunch counter and filled nearly every seat. The students continued their calm, peaceful protests for a week without once being served. In an attempt to stop the protests, the Woolworth's manager decided to close the store temporarily. But the protest spread, as students at other colleges became inspired to organize their own sit-ins.

The efforts of these students caught the attention of the nation, but especially that of seasoned civil rights activists such as Ella Baker (1903-1986), who had been working for civil rights since the 1920s. Baker organized a conference that took place on April 16, 1960, at Shaw University in Raleigh, North Carolina,. The result of the conference was the formation of the Student Nonviolent Coordinating Committee (SNCC, pronounced "snick"). One of the founding principles of the organization was nonviolence. Members agreed that in order to win the support of non-blacks, they must never respond with acts of violence, even if attacked.

College students participate in a sit-in at a Woolworth's lunch counter reserved for white customers, Greensboro, North Carolina, February 2, 1960. © *Bettmann/Corbis.*

By the end of April, more than 50,000 protestors, mostly students, had staged nonviolent sit-ins in every southern state. During the first half of the 1960s, SNCC members strictly followed their doctrine of nonviolence. Some members were beaten; others shot. And when these attacks hit newsstands and aired on television, SNCC won supporters.

SNCC sparks civil rights activities

A ripple effect triggered other protests throughout the South. Blacks boycotted stores that did not hire blacks and theaters that forced blacks to sit in the balcony. Activists organized voter registration drives and counseled blacks about how to deal with the unfair practices, such as literacy tests and poll taxes, designed to keep them from voting. While most of these protests were small, local events, some, especially those where peaceful demonstrators were attacked by those who opposed them, drew national attention. One example came in 1961 when the Committee on Racial Equality (CORE), a nonviolent civil rights group formed in 1942, organized "Freedom Rides" to protest southern refusal to enforce the 1960 Supreme Court ruling in *Boynton v. Virginia* that prohibited segregated interstate travel. On May 4, 1961, seven white and six black "Freedom Riders" boarded two buses in Washington, D.C., and started their trip into the South, hoping to make it through Alabama and Mississippi. The Freedom Riders encountered hostility at each stop the first week, but by the second week angry people began attacking the buses in earnest. One of the buses was fire-bombed and the riders were beaten in Alabama. The violent attack on the Freedom Riders in Birmingham, Alabama, where police chief Eugene "Bull" Connor (1897–1973) had agreed to ignore white supremacist Ku Klux Klan members who mobbed the bus, made international news. The U.S. Justice Department helped remove some of the riders to safety, but others remained, determined to complete the Freedom Ride into Mississippi. The Freedom Riders recruited more volunteers to join them in Birmingham and continued on to Montgomery, where a mob of nearly one thousand attacked the buses, and further to Mississippi, where they were arrested and put in jail. Soon more demonstrators began taking Freedom Rides across the South to continue the protest.

The next two years saw an increase in violence directed against blacks and sympathetic whites seeking integration. In 1962 President John F. Kennedy (1917–1963; served 1961–63) sent 5,000 army troops to secure a single black student's enrollment at the University of Mississippi, after 160 of the 500 federal marshals ordered to escort James Meredith (1933–) onto the university were wounded by an angry mob. In 1963 the Southern Christian Leadership Conference (SCLC), which had formed in the aftermath of the 1955 Montgomery bus boycott, organized several protests in Birmingham, Alabama. Martin Luther King Jr. (1929–1968), who had become well known during the bus boycott, served as the main spokesperson for the SCLC. Arrested during the 1963 Birmingham protest, King wrote a letter from his jail cell calling for other clergymen to organize against racism. The letter was smuggled out and served as inspiration to protestors who continued to hold peaceful demonstrations in Birmingham. King's plea for a peaceful, determined protest to

Flames shoot out from the bus that Freedom Riders were using to travel on their quest for civil rights in the early 1960s in Alabama. *AP/Wide World Photos. Reproduced by permission.*

end racism, coupled with a violent attack on protestors in Birmingham just days after King's release from jail, helped the civil rights movement. Television cameras captured the all-white Birmingham police force beating peaceful demonstrators, many of whom were women and children, with clubs and knocking them down with blasts from fire hoses. The images shaped public opinion, either for or against integration. Civil rights had become an issue on which people would take a stand; no longer could white Americans passively ignore the issue of race.

Throughout 1963 civil rights activists staged more than seven hundred protests throughout the country. Several civil rights groups cooperated to organize a massive March on Washington, D.C., to publicize their cause. On August 28, 1963, approximately 250,000 demonstrators gathered in the nation's capital to listen to speeches from leaders of civil rights organizations, including CORE, NAACP, SCLC, and SNCC. The rally ended with King's "I have a dream" speech, in which King described a peaceful nation characterized by racial equality and tolerance. King cited the Declaration of Independence to support reasons for the civil rights movement, calling upon the nation to "rise up and live out the true meaning of its creed—we hold these truths to be self-evident, that all men are created equal." More than the thousands of demonstrators heard the rallying speeches calling for racial equality; the entire protest was broadcast by the three national television networks to millions of viewers across the country. In the months that followed, protestors continued their push for civil rights.

Shock and grief gripped the nation on November 22, 1963, when President Kennedy died from gunshot wounds in Dallas, Texas. Kennedy had been considered the first president since Harry Truman to champion blacks' civil rights. But his successor, Lyndon Baines Johnson (1908-1973; served 1963–69), quickly soothed the fears of civil rights activists that they had lost the support of the federal government. Using his considerable political know-how and playing off the memory of the slain president, Johnson lobbied congressmen to gather the needed votes to pass the Civil Rights Act of 1964 through both the House and the Senate. Johnson signed it into law on July 2, 1964. The act banned discrimination and segregation based on race, color, religion, national origin, or gender throughout the nation. It also prohibited federal funding of any discriminatory national, state, or local program. The federal government created the Equal Employment Opportunity Commission to watch how people obey the law.

Voting rights

With the passage of the Civil Rights Act, civil rights organizations shifted their focus to voting rights. A law passed in 1960 had granted blacks the right to vote, but loopholes, or ambiguities or omissions, in the text of the law made it possible for blacks to be blocked from voting. Voter-registration officials in southern states insisted that blacks pass literacy tests or recite the Constitution before being allowed to register to vote. Many civil rights organizations had tried to increase the number of blacks registered to vote, but the first big effort was launched in 1964. SNCC leaders organized Freedom Summer that year. Hundreds of SNCC volunteers bravely set about registering blacks in rural areas of the South, where white resistance was vicious. Within a day of the campaign's beginning three workers had been killed, but the volunteers continued their work. By the end of the summer three more volunteers had been killed and a thousand had spent time in jail. Many others suffered beatings and bombings. SCLC, on the other hand, concentrated on urban areas, drawing the attention of the nation. In 1965 SCLC volunteers led demonstrators on a march from Selma to Montgomery, Alabama, in an attempt to draw attention to the voting rights issue. Just outside the Selma city limits on March 7, marching protestors were attacked with clubs and tear gas by police officers. Rather than discouraging the protestors, the event, which came to be known as Bloody Sunday, drew more volunteers to march to Montgomery. Two days later, Martin Luther King Jr. arrived from Atlanta to lead another group to the Pettus Bridge, the scene of the attack just days earlier, where police blocked their passage. King turned the protestors back.

That night, a group of angry white men from Selma killed Reverend James Reeb, a white minister who had joined the march. His death, in contrast to the death of black protestor Jimmy Lee Jackson a few weeks earlier, brought quick national support for the marchers. By March 21 the protestors

State troopers beat down peaceful marchers who were walking to Selma, Alabama, in support of civil rights on March 7, 1965.
AP/Wide World Photos. Reproduced by permission.

had gained a court order to complete their march from Selma to Montgomery. The march took five days, and by the time the protestors reached Montgomery their group numbered 25,000. At the state capitol King handed a petition requesting voting rights for blacks to Alabama state governor George Wallace (1919–1998). Demonstrators rejoiced at their victory that day but that night were sadly reminded that their journey was not complete when news of the murder of one of the march's demonstrators reached them. Viola Liuzzo, a white homemaker from Detroit, had been driving the demonstration's volunteers to the airport with Leroy Moton, a black volunteer, when she was shot and killed by Ku Klux Klansmen. Despite hardships and loss of lives, the passage of the Voting Rights Act of 1965 signaled the success of this protest.

The violence enacted during the voter registration drives of 1964's Freedom Summer marked a turning point in the minds of many civil rights protestors, especially those trying to register voters in rural Mississippi. Volunteers both black and white were threatened, beaten, and jailed; some were killed. Many activists were upset that blacks were often attacked more harshly than whites, but the death of white volunteers drew more public sympathy than the death of blacks. Equally frustrating was the failure of the Mississippi Freedom Democratic Party to win recognition at the Democratic presidential nomination convention in 1964. The Mississippi Freedom Democratic Party (MFDP) had been formed in 1963 to allow blacks an opportunity to vote at the official Democratic Party convention, a privilege that had long been denied them. Hearings to determine whether the MFDP delegates could participate at the convention were broadcast to the nation. MFDP delegate Fannie Lou Hamer (1917–1977) testified to being beaten several times while in jail for attempting to organize black voters. President Johnson interrupted a broadcast of the hearings with a press conference in an attempt to arrange a compromise in the party. The compromise, which denied MFDP delegates entrance into the convention, proved to many civil rights activists that they could no longer seek answers to their concerns within the established government. Freedom Summer was the last year during the decade that a broad coalition, or joint effort, of black and white activists would work together.

A violent turn

This growing feeling of discontent within the black community marked a shift in the civil rights movement toward what came to be known as Black Power. Though blacks won legal recognition of their rights, they continued to battle the lingering effects of the Jim Crow laws and the attitudes that those laws caused. Even without the legal framework of racial segregation, racial prejudice remained a powerful force in American society. In both the North and South, many white people put social limits on blacks, keeping them from the living in the best neighborhoods, earning higher degrees of education, being hired for better paying jobs, or in countless other ways experiencing the American dream of freedom and prosperity. While the early years of the 1960s had succeeded in winning and enforcing the political rights of blacks, the later years became marked by blacks' determination to rid their lives of these lingering social restric-

National Guard members patrol the streets of Detroit, Michigan, during the July 1967 riots, to discourage people from further rioting. © Bettmann/Corbis.

tions as well. The social limitations placed on blacks by racial prejudices pitted blacks against whites.

The anger welling up inside black communities burst into riots. Just five days after Johnson signed into law the Voting Rights Act of 1965, the Watts district of Los Angeles erupted in violence. On August 11, 1965, news of a young black man's brutal treatment by police triggered an urban riot. For five days, rioters looted stores, set fires, and attacked white motorists passing through the area. The riot left thirty-four people dead and more than one thousand wounded. It took more than 15,000 police and National Guardsmen making nearly four thousand arrests to stop the violence.

Similar riots occurred in over one hundred cities between 1965 and 1968; these riots shocked the nation, especially white Americans. One example of the gap that developed between once sympathetic white Americans and blacks occurred in Detroit, Michigan. Identified as a model city for Johnson's War on Poverty, Detroit offered poor residents more support than many other places, but racially discriminatory practices in housing and employment opportunities continued to exist in the city. The tensions within the black community erupted into a riot in the earlier hours of July 23, 1967. The Detroit riot shut the city down for seventy-two hours. Phones were dead, mail undelivered, garbage uncollected. Banks, shops, and offices closed. Army troops and National Guardsmen used tanks and machine guns to stop the fire-bombing rioters. The riot left forty-three people dead, two thousand injured, and nearly five thousand homeless, and it had done $40 million worth of damage to businesses and residential neighborhoods.

Blacks had been granted their legal rights, but many blacks realized this step was not enough. Blacks living in the north had to contend with de facto (a reality that is not legally recognized or enforced) racial segregation that left their schools inadequately funded, their homes substandard, and their job opportunities limited. At a time when the country was more prosperous than ever before, blacks in inner cities suffered double-digit, amounting to 10 percent or more, unemployment levels. Many realized that the civil rights legislation passed in the early years of the 1960s did not improve their lives. American society, they came to believe, was keeping them in poverty. The demographics, or statistical data about populations, of poverty within American society revealed how unequal opportunities for jobs, housing, and medical care were between blacks and other minorities and whites.

Moreover, many white Americans blamed black people for their poverty. To many whites, blacks had been granted more than enough rights and offered adequate federal support to make a decent life for themselves. Blacks had won their civil rights. Blacks could vote. The social programs of the Great Society, such as welfare and affirmative action, offered blacks a helping hand to right the wrongs of the past. In 1968 the National Advisory Commission on Civil Disorders, which President Johnson had created to investigate the urban uprisings that began with Watts, issued a report that identified a tendency on the part of whites to not accept responsibility for the poverty of blacks. "What white Americans have never fully understood—but what the Negro can never forget—is that white society is deeply implicated in the

The Great Society: A Helping Hand or a Handout?

President Johnson tried to remedy the problems of poverty and racial inequality in his plan for the "Great Society." In 1964 Johnson laid out his plan to enlarge the government in order to improve the quality of life and economic opportunities for all Americans. Through his vision for the Great Society, Johnson and his supporters waged a war on poverty, offering preschool children the Head Start program, young adults between the ages of sixteen and twenty-two job opportunities through the Job Corps, and poor communities a variety of self-help opportunities through the Community Action Program. The Volunteers in Service to America (VISTA) became a domestic version of John F. Kennedy's Peace Corps, providing help in America's poor neighborhoods. For many of the country's poorest citizens, the Great Society offered financial support by raising the minimum wage and expanding welfare to make the Food Stamp and Aid to Families with Dependent Children programs available to more people. Housing subsidies and urban renewal projects also increased the quality of life for many of America's poor by offering low-cost housing to the poor and making improvements to run-down urban residential areas. The Great Society also started Medicaid to offer free medical care to poor Americans, and Medicare to help pay for medical attention for the elderly. By the end of the 1960s, the poverty rate in America had dropped to 12 percent, down from 22 percent in the 1950s.

By 1967, however, Johnson's Great Society seemed likely to fall from the controversy it generated. The Great Society did a great deal to reduce racial injustice in housing, health care, and employment, lifting minorities out of grinding poverty and offering educational opportunities to take them further than ever before. But the growing expense of its programs burdened the government. Given the cost of the expanding war in Vietnam, the Great Society was doomed to failure. Though some of the programs continued into the early 2000s, most of them were scaled back or eliminated by the more conservative administrations of Richard Nixon and, later, Ronald Reagan (1911–2004; served 1981–89). Johnson was deeply upset by the failure of the Great Society and expressed his frustration at the end of the 1960s with his characteristically coarse language in his now famous quote: "That bitch of a war [destroyed] the woman I really loved—the Great Society."

ghetto. White institutions created it, white institutions maintain it, and white society condones it," according to the commission. Whites did not fully accept or understand how the established economics, politics, and social institutions in America had shaped the formation of the ghetto, or poor, mostly black urban neighborhoods. In the second half of the 1960s, the crusade for civil rights focused on eliminating injustice and inequality. But disagreement over what steps were needed to reach these goals led to breakups in groups formed to address civil rights issues.

Black nationalism

While Martin Luther King Jr. and others maintained that nonviolence was the only route to achieving true equality in the United States, a movement embracing violent rebellion began to draw support in the mid-1960s. The emerging movement came to be known as Black Power. Blacks who supported this movement rejected earlier attempts to integrate into American society. Instead, activists embraced all the qualities that made blacks different from whites. Many began to dress in African-inspired clothes such as brightly colored cotton shirts called dashikis, to wear their hair in naturally curly styles, and to study their African heritage. Some of the established civil rights groups kicked out white members, refusing any form of support from whites at all. Creating a separate black nation became a hot topic of discussion.

Growing weary of the slow progress made by nonviolent methods of protest, formerly nonviolent groups changed their approach to pursuing civil rights. The Student Nonviolent Coordinating Committee, whose peaceful sit-ins at the beginning of the decade ushered in the civil rights movement, was among those groups that changed tactics (they also changed their name, replacing the term "Nonviolent" with "National"). Stokely Carmichael (1941–1998), who had participated in the Freedom Rides of 1961 and the voter registration drives in Mississippi in 1963, became chairman of SNCC in 1966. Speaking in Greenwood, Mississippi, in 1966,

Both Martin Luther King Jr. (left) and Malcolm X (right) were leaders in the fight for civil rights and both were assassinated in the 1960s. *AP/Wide World Photos. Reproduced by permission.*

Inspiring Others:
The Women's, Chicanos', and American Indians' Movements

The rapid succession of legal changes brought by the civil rights movement inspired other groups to organize with the hope that they could make a real difference in American society. Women, Chicanos, and American Indians (now referred to as Native Americans) formed groups who successfully organized to improve their lives. Women, including many who had participated in the civil rights movement, started to organize in 1966 once they discovered that laws against gender discrimination created by the Civil Rights Act of 1964 were not being adequately enforced. The first women's organization, the National Organization for Women (NOW), was led by the decade's best-selling author, Betty Friedan (1921–). Friedan is credited with starting the women's movement when she published her book *The Feminine Mystique* in 1963, in which she described the oppressed and stifling lives of homemakers. Friedan's book called attention to how limiting America's cultural expectations were for women. By the end of the 1960s, the women's movement had grown dramatically, effecting permanent changes in the lives of American women.

Mexican Americans, or Chicanos, also banded together to gain social justice. The Chicano movement focused on eliminating discrimination in education, housing, and jobs. César Chávez (1927–1993) emerged as a leader of the movement in 1965 when he led a nonviolent strike of the United Farm Workers (UFW, a union he had organized in California). He created a national boycott of grapes and lettuce during the five-year strike, which ended with the UFW winning for its members an acceptable labor agreement with growers. Like blacks, Chicanos also pushed for inclusion of their culture in education. By the

Carmichael announced: "The only way we gonna stop them white men from whuppin' us is to take over. We've been saying *freedom* for six years—and we ain't got nothin'. What we gonna start saying now is 'Black Power,'" according to *The Columbia Guide to America in the 1960s*. Under Carmichael's leadership, SNCC turned from nonviolent methods of protests and embraced the more militant aspects of Black Power. An even more radical leader, H. Rap Brown (1943–), took control of SNCC in 1967 and continued the group's emphasis on violent rebellion. That year SNCC members voted to oust all whites from their group. SNCC had dissolved by 1971, when Brown began serving a five-year prison sentence for robbery.

César Chávez. *Library of Congress.*

end of the 1960s many universities taught black and Chicano cultural history.

The success of the minority movements inspired Native Americans, or American Indians, to improve their position in the country as well. Native Americans, according to the *Columbia Guide to America in the 1960s,* were "the poorest, least healthy, and worst educated minority group in the nation." Native American activists occupied significant places as an attention-grabbing tactic. Activists took over Alcatraz Island near San Francisco, California, in 1969, a Bureau of Indian Affairs office in 1972, and a trading post at Wounded Knee, South Dakota, in 1973. While these tactics won their cause national attention, other activists lobbied the federal government for new laws that would grant Native Americans more control over their own lives. By the mid-1970s these efforts had paid off. The federal government returned millions of acres, and the Indian Self-Determination and Educational Assistance Act of 1975 granted more control to Native Americans over their own governance—or political institutions—and education.

Groups such as the Black Muslims and the Black Panthers also grew in membership. The Black Muslims, a group formed in Detroit in the 1930s, offered members a religious organization that promoted black dignity and self-respect. The Black Muslims also encouraged separation from white people, an idea called black nationalism. One influential minister of the Black Muslims, Malcolm X (1925–1965), attracted many to the organization during the 1960s. By 1963, however, Malcolm X developed a new philosophy toward gaining civil rights that clashed with the Black Muslims' ideas of separatism. So Malcolm X formed a new group called the Organization of Afro-Americans in 1963 and set about stirring blacks to use armed conflict to improve their position in the United States. Malcolm X's speeches drew crowds of supporters, but his leadership was cut short by the bullet of an assassin in February of 1965.

Another separatist group, the Black Panthers, formed in 1966. Huey P. Newton (1942–1989) and Bobby Seale (1936–), who had worked in Chicago and other cities to defend blacks against police brutality and other forms of racial aggression, founded the Black Panthers in California. Black Panthers dressed in black military outfits and carried weapons. To encourage blacks to liberate themselves through violent confrontation with whites, Black Panthers recommended "picking up the gun." The threat posed by the Black Panthers led to an FBI raid in 1969 that resulted in the death of twenty-eight of the group's members and the arrest of many more.

The violent protests that marked the second half of the decade contrasted dramatically with the peaceful demonstrations of the first half. While the peaceful protests succeeded in causing the passage of legal remedies for black's political and economic positions in America, the violent protests helped shock Americans into understanding that blacks were no longer willing to accept discrimination based on the color of their skin. The unpredictable nature of the violent protest and a general crackdown on crime, rioting, and protest following the presidential election of Richard Nixon (1913–1994; served 1969–74) in 1968 brought an end to many rebellious groups by the mid-1970s. Nevertheless, Nixon continued to support many civil rights programs begun by Johnson. Nixon approved a federal affirmative action plan (a federal program that grants minority groups special employment and educational opportunities in an effort to right past inequalities) and even tried to offer Americans a guaranteed minimum income, or a limited amount of money on which to live, though this last proposal was defeated in the Senate.

Although de facto (socially practiced, but not legally constituted) segregation and racial discrimination continued in the United States, the civil rights movement had a lasting positive impact on the country. The protests inspired many other groups, including women, Chicanos, Native Americans, and environmentalists, to form groups to promote social change. In the early 2000s, black political candidates represented voters across the country. Blacks were appointed to high positions within local, state, and federal government. Blacks also gained access to high levels of education. The pervasive racism of the not-so-distant past had largely disappeared, and the income levels of blacks were slowly gaining ground compared to whites. In the minds of many, however, true equality had not yet been attained.

For More Information

Books

Altman, Linda Jacobs. *The American Civil Rights Movement: The African-American Struggle for Equality.* Berkeley Heights, NJ: Enslow, 2004.

Bloom, Alexander, and Wini Breines, eds. *"Takin' It to the Streets": A Sixties Reader.* New York: Oxford University Press, 2003.

Carson, Clayborne, and Kris Shepard, eds. *A Call to Conscience.* New York: Warner Books, 2001.

Dudley, William, ed. *The 1960s.* San Diego, CA: Greenhaven, 2000.

Farber, David. *The Age of Great Dreams: America in the 1960s.* New York: Hill and Wang, 1994.

Farber, David, and Beth Bailey, with others. *The Columbia Guide to America in the 1960s.* New York: Columbia University Press, 2001.

Gitlin, Todd. *The Sixties: Years of Hope, Days of Rage.* New York: Bantam, 1987; revised, 1993.

Holland, Gini. *The 1960s.* San Diego, CA: Lucent, 1999.

Report of the National Advisory Commission on Civil Disorders. New York: Ballantine, 1968.

Treanor, Nick, ed. *The Civil Rights Movement.* San Diego, CA: Greenhaven Press, 2003.

Uschan, Michael V. *Life on the Front Lines: The Fight for Civil Rights.* San Diego, CA: Lucent Books, 2004.

Weber, Michael. *Causes and Consequences of the African American Civil Rights Movement.* Austin, TX: Raintree Steck-Vaughn, 1998.

Web sites

Civil Rights Heritage Center. www.iusb.edu/~civilrts (accessed on June 23, 2004).

National Civil Rights Museum. www.civilrightsmuseum.org (accessed on June 23, 2004).

Voices of Civil Rights: Ordinary People, Extraordinary Stories. www.voicesof civilrights.org (accessed on June 23, 2004).

We Shall Overcome: Historic Places of the Civil Rights Movement. www.cr. nps.gov/nr/travel/civilrights/ (accessed on June 23, 2004).

Feminism and the Sexual Revolution

9

The women's movement of the 1960s was actually a revival, often called the second wave, of an earlier movement for women's rights that resulted in women's universal suffrage, or voting rights throughout the country, with the ratification of the Nineteenth Amendment on August 26, 1920. But the momentum of the earlier women's movement dwindled as the political, social, and economic hardships of the Great Depression (1929–41) and World War II (1939–45) came to dominate life in America. The stability and prosperity of the postwar years enabled long-standing social problems to gain more attention. By the late 1960s many women joined together to create the second wave of the women's movement in order to push for more equality in their lives. In part inspired by the civil rights movement of the late 1950s and 1960s, which drew attention to gaining rights for African Americans, women advocated for equal rights under the law and in the workplace and also for the liberation of women from stifling stereotypes in domestic and other cultural situations.

Some women's concerns about legal and workplace discrimination could be traced back to World War II, which had brought with it increased employment opportunities for women. By creating a campaign to get women to take traditionally male jobs, the U.S. government enticed women to join the war effort; a famous example of the campaign was the Rosie the Riveter poster, which read: "We can do it." As men went off to war, women by the thousands dropped their children off with family or at the newly created federal childcare facilities and spent their days as policewomen, firefighters, and factory workers, among other things. By doing "man's work," women enjoyed the increased responsibility and higher pay offered in these traditionally male positions. When veterans returned after the war, however, women were forced out of those jobs that had historically been reserved for men. The federal government closed the federal childcare facilities and encouraged women to return home, even though a 1944 Women's Bureau study reported that 80 percent of working women would have liked to keep their wartime positions. While many women returned to lives as homemakers, devoting themselves full time to being wives and giving birth to a generation of children known as "the baby boomers," those who remained in the workforce saw their employment opportunities limited to less well paying jobs historically reserved for females, such as secretarial or teaching positions. Professionally trained women who remained in traditionally male positions earned less than their male co-workers. By the 1960s, women began to pressure employers and the government for equal treatment and pay.

The social stigma facing women had deep roots in the early nineteenth century, but in the 1950s in particular American society developed a cultural reverence of the family that placed restrictions on family members. Television, magazines, religious leaders, and politicians all celebrated an idealized middle-class domestic life, one composed of the breadwinner husband, the stay-at-home wife, and their children, all snug in their house. In 1950 only 16.2 percent of married women with children under six years old worked outside the home. In 1960, however, the statistics were changing: 34.8 percent of all women older than sixteen held a job outside the home; 18.6 percent of them were married with children under age six. By 1970, the percentage of working women rose to 42.6 By the

Television shows of the 1950s like *Leave It to Beaver* presented idealized women who were the perfect wives and mothers, not those who were contemplating careers or protesting in support of gender equality. *The Kobal Collection. Reproduced by permission.*

end of the 1960s, many women lived lives dramatically different from the idealized notion of the previous decade. In addition to an increase in the number of women working outside the home, the American family unit had begun to change. Divorce occurred more frequently, leaving women oftentimes to work and raise children alone. Historian Annegret Ogden reported that the number of female heads of households rose by 1.1 million between 1960 and 1970.

Wife and mother ... or more?: The women's rights movement

Although 96 percent of the respondents in a 1962 Gallup poll indicated that being a housewife was satisfying, the American cultural expectation that women become housewives and mothers caused a growing number of women to feel resentful. Betty Friedan captured these women's sense of frustration and constraint in her book, *The Feminine Mystique.* Published in 1963, Friedan's book identified the difficulties many women experienced in their pursuit of the traditional family life in which the roles of wife and mother defined women by their relationship to others rather than as individuals. Friedan compiled her information from questionnaires that she had sent to her classmates in the 1942 graduating class from Smith College. She learned that many women shared her view that the traditional family roles for women were too limiting. Her classmates who had become stay-at-home mothers desired meaningful, well-paying work outside the home. But she found that those who had become professional women had complaints too; while they enjoyed broader opportunities than housewives, they reported that their job privileges and opportunities were far fewer than those of their male co-workers. Friedan's book sold more than one million copies and triggered an awareness among women that things needed to change.

In 1966 Friedan, along with three hundred women and men, formed the National Organization for Women (NOW) with the intention of achieving equal rights for women. The group organized after becoming frustrated at a National Conference of the Commission on the Status of Women in Washington, D.C., that year, where they had been unable to pass resolutions that would require the Equal Employment Opportunity Commission (EEOC) to acknowledge its legal mandate to end sex discrimination under the Civil Rights Act of 1964. NOW members placed an Equal Rights Amendment to the U.S. Constitution, that would ensure the equal treatment of women under the law, high on the organization's list of political goals. In its efforts to gain support for the amendment, NOW drew attention to the fact that women only made fifty-nine cents for every dollar that men earned in the 1960s and early 1970s. Its efforts also drew attention to the gender discrimination women faced in the job market, including loss of employment because of pregnancy, legal limitations to the weight of objects women were allowed to lift on the job, and the inaccessibility to traditionally male jobs, among other things. Membership in the organization grew quickly, making NOW the largest women's organization in the country.

NOW promoted its causes by conducting political lobbying, by bringing lawsuits, and by organizing mass marches, rallies, and nonviolent civil disobedience protests. NOW's lobbying efforts helped to pass many gender-equalizing pieces of legislation into law, including maternity leave legislation that ensured that women could give birth without losing their jobs, legal prohibitions against ads in newspapers qualifying employment opportunities as either "male" or "female" positions, and welfare reform that provided job training. By bringing lawsuits to courts throughout the country, NOW helped secure the enforcement of many laws. The *Weeks v. Southern Bell* court case, which NOW's southern regional director Sylvia Roberts argued in the fifth district federal court in 1969, offered the first court ruling to enforce the sexual discrimination clause in the Civil Rights Act of 1964. The federal ruling enabled women to apply for and hold jobs that involved lifting more than thirty pounds. Though the Equal Employment Opportunity Commission ruled in 1968 that help-wanted ads in newspapers could not be categorized by gender, most newspapers continued to post separate male and female job ads until NOW succeeded in arguing the issue to the Supreme Court; the court's 1973 ruling made it possible for women to apply for and hold any job based solely upon skill.

NOW also helped to raise the debate about the Equal Rights Amendment to a national level. It staged marches and other events that drew hundreds of thousands of participants in various states. When Congress did pass the equal rights amendment and sent it to the states for ratification in 1972, NOW continued its massive campaigning efforts—including a 100,000-person march on the nation's capital in 1978. Magazines and newspapers ran stories about the implications of the ERA, and tracked the progress of the ratification campaign. Despite these efforts, the amendment failed to gain the necessary state approval by the deadline for ratification

A group of women rally at the Statue of Liberty in support of the Equal Rights Amendment, August 1970. *© Bettmann/Corbis.*

in 1981. Although the attention granted the ERA has since dwindled, NOW continues to work toward equal rights for women into the 2000s.

As membership within NOW grew, from 1,200 in 1967 to nearly 48,000 by 1970, several other groups formed with the similar intention of drawing attention to women's issues by working to change the legal and political systems in America. The Women's Equity Action League (WEAL) formed in 1968 to end sex discrimination in employment. The National Women's Political Caucus formed in 1971 to increase the number of women politicians and appointed officials. Other organizations formed to address the issues of black and other racial or ethnic groups of women, lesbians, impoverished women, business owners, professional women, and female politicians, among others. These organizations did extensive electoral and lobbying work and brought lawsuits to effect change. In the 1960s and early 1970s, these groups were made up of older women, many of whom had professional experience, but later came to include women of all ages.

The other side of the coin: The women's liberation movement

While the women's rights movement pushed for legislation through sophisticated political lobbying and traditionally organized action groups (those with elected officers and dues-paying members), a more informal variant of the women's movement also developed, especially among young women. Women organized in informal groups to seek changes in their own lives and in the world around them. Gathering in small, intimate groups for frank discussions about their lives, these women came to understand in new ways the nature of their oppression and with increased understanding they felt hopeful about creating personal change. This process of reviewing one's life from the perspective of sexual inequality was called "consciousness raising." Some of these women concerned themselves with redefining female roles and insisting on more realistic depictions of women in the media, among other issues. This branch of the women's rights movement came to be called the women's liberation movement.

Many women's liberationists had participated in the civil rights protests and hippie movement, either as volunteers in political organizations or as members of hippie communes. While part of these other groups, women discovered that their hard work was not held in the same esteem as that of their male counterparts. Civil rights organizations of the early 1950s and 1960s offered youths an opportunity to work together to change the world. Young men and women, black

A member of the Women's Liberation Party throws her bra in the trash in protest of the Miss America Pageant in 1968. *AP/Wide World Photos. Reproduced by permission.*

and white, assembled to get their messages out. While the work offered these young people a sense of camaraderie, young women found that most of the decisionmaking in these organizations was reserved for the men. Most of the speech givers were men, and the authors of protest pamphlets and papers were men. Women were expected to perform the grunt work of answering phones, making photocopies, and stuffing envelopes, as well as any cooking or cleaning that needed to be done. Hippies too, while espousing a new society, maintained a social hierarchy with men clearly on top. The leadership of communes, for example, was reserved for men, with peripheral support given by women, whom hippies called "chicks" or, if spoken for, "old ladies."

As these young women worked for the civil rights of racial minorities or tried to create a new society from the hippie standpoint, they began to wonder about their own place in American society. While older women concerned themselves with legal issues and discriminatory banking and education issues, younger women sought to change the cultural prejudices that impeded social equality. These younger women sought changes in the private, domestic lives of women. The fundamental change desired by women's liberationists was an end to women's subordination to men. Women began to push for men to help with such tasks as housework, meal preparation, and childcare, for example. Women also began to resist the standards of beauty that reduced women to sex objects.

The New York Radical Women (N.Y.R.W.), a group of women who had been active in the civil rights, the New Left, and the antiwar movements, organized the Miss America Pageant protest against American beauty standards in 1968 and won the women's liberation movement national attention. Nearly four hundred protestors gathered outside the

Miss America pageant proceedings in Atlantic City, New Jersey. Women's liberationists considered the pageant to be a symbol of how American culture glorified women as sexual beings and how little importance or interest America placed on women as intellectual, emotional participants in society. Protestors threw objects, including curlers, girdles, high-heeled shoes, *Playboy* magazines, and even the bras off their own bodies, into what was called the Freedom Trash Can to symbolize their rejection of America's beauty standards.

While this protest and other civil disruptions drew a great deal of attention to the women's liberation movement, activists' most common method of protest was the much smaller, conscious-raising efforts. Groups, including The Women's International Terrorist Conspiracy from Hell (WITCH), The Feminists, and Cell 16, organized to address a variety of women's issues, such as abortion and childcare. Several of the phrases that came to define the women's liberation movement were coined by a group formed in 1969 under the name Redstockings. Some of the most famous include: "The Personal Is Political," "The Politics of Housework," and "Sisterhood Is Powerful." "The Personal Is Political" is perhaps the most famous, and means that personal situations are not just a result of personal choices but are limited and defined by larger political and social restrictions. At consciousness-raising events women came to realize that their personal experiences were not unique and that together with other women—their "sisters"—they could transform the larger political and social setting in America. Although the women's liberation movement began as a separate branch of the women's rights movement, the two efforts complemented one another and eventually merged or began to work together.

Legacy of the women's movement

Women's groups organized and activated their members to improve the lives of American women. While the legal and political changes achieved during the 1960s were rather limited, those that were gained formed a strong foundation on which significant victories were won in the coming years. NOW's advocacy for the enforcement of Title VII of the Civil Rights Act of 1964 started the ball rolling.

How Homosexuality Came Out of the Closet

The women's movement came to include homosexuals as women's organizations formulated plans for action that would address the issues of all women, including lesbians. The step was bold because, at the beginning of the 1960s, homosexuality was a taboo subject for many Americans. Although some homosexuals had joined homophile, or gay, organizations following World War II, the vast majority kept their sexual preferences to themselves for fear of losing their jobs or being shunned socially. Throughout the 1950s, homosexuals were condemned as sinners by many religious leaders, pronounced mentally ill by psychiatric experts, and harassed by police in the many states that had laws against homosexual behavior.

The more permissive attitudes of the 1960s created an atmosphere in which some gays and lesbians began to assert themselves both socially and politically. The hippies' example of sexual experimentation and social nonconformity helped people feel freer to express their sexual preferences, which opened the door for some homosexuals to become more public about their lives. Furthermore, the political organizing that created the civil rights movement and the antiwar movement provided a foundation on which homosexuals could base their own desires for liberation. Many homosexuals joined these early movements, as well as the women's movement that emerged at the end of the 1960s, as sympathizers of persecuted people and as champions of tolerance. Working to ensure a fairer society for blacks and women may have encouraged many homosexuals to think about winning social equality for themselves as well.

The first march for homosexual rights occurred in May of 1965 when ten men and women picketed the White House. Several other small protests followed that year. The next year, the North American Conference of Homophile Organizations tried to begin a larger movement by creating a legal fund, sponsoring protests, and promoting the formation of homophile groups. By the end of the decade, however, membership in these groups had reached only 5,000, indicating the reluctance of homosexuals to announce their sexual preference. It took a violent act of rebellion to start the gay liberation movement in earnest.

The Stonewall Rebellion marked the real start of the gay liberation move-

Title VII prohibited employment discrimination on the basis of race, color, religion, national origin, or sex. But the law's prohibition against sexual discrimination had been ignored until NOW formed and began its lobbying efforts in 1966. NOW and other groups lobbied for legal protection and welfare benefits of particular importance to

The Stonewall Rebellion continues to be celebrated with marches and parades. Here, some 150,000 people commemorated its 20th anniversary in June 1989. *AP/Wide World Photos. Reproduced by permission.*

ment. Until the early morning hours of June 28, 1969, homosexuals had rarely resisted police harassment and tried to "fit in" to American society. But when police raided the Stonewall Inn, a gay bar in Greenwich Village, New York, something unusual happened: instead of allowing the police to shut down the bar, two thousand gays and lesbians rose up in a violent protest that lasted for two days. As the violent clash subsided, gays, lesbians, and others gathered at peaceful protest rallies, prompting many homosexuals to announce their sexual orientation and to join the movement for gay rights. The Gay Liberation Front and the Gay Activist Alliance formed in the aftermath of Stonewall and soon became the most influential gay rights groups, sponsoring picketing of anti-gay establishments, forming alliances with organizations such as the Black Panthers, and setting up "kiss a queer" booths at student functions on college campuses. Other political action groups incorporated lesbian and gay issues into their agendas. In 1971 NOW became the first major national women's organization to support lesbian rights, making lesbians the theme of two national conferences. By the turn of the new millennium, homosexuals had won basic civil rights and job protections, but much work had yet to be done to achieve equality. For example, many states prohibited gay marriage, denying gays the ability to inherit the death benefits or to be protected under the health insurance of their significant others.

women, including equal pay, childcare, education, abortion, and birth control rights. Important early court decisions that have benefited women include the 1971 Supreme Court decision in *Phillips v. Martin Marietta Corporation*, which outlawed the practice of private employers refusing to hire women with preschool children, and the

1973 Supreme Court decision in *Roe v. Wade,* which made abortion legal throughout the nation.

The movement had also succeeded in opening a multitude of opportunities for women, making it possible for women to advance in fulfilling occupations, to ask for and to receive help with domestic chores from their spouses, and to continue to work for real equality in their own home and in the larger society. Many of the original organizations continued to thrive—NOW had membership of more than one million in 2004—and new ones have emerged. The debate about women's roles in American society continues to this day. Some organizations continue to push for more legal, economic, and political rights for women, while others insist that the women's movement has destroyed the American family and advocate for women to return to domestic lives centered on family nurturing. While the movement may have hinged on the question between stay-at-home mothers and working women at first, over the years more complex issues entered the debate, including the disparities of race, wealth, class, and sexual orientation.

Sexual revolution

Many people speak of the sexual revolution that occurred during the 1960s, bringing with it a newfound openness toward sexuality in American culture. But the sexual revolution's definition, origins, and participants are all subjects of great controversy among historians. The one thing that everyone agrees on is that "something" important happened during the decade. It wasn't that there were prohibitions on sex in the United States before the 1960s; after all, the post-World War II baby boom began in the bedroom. But there were real cultural prohibitions on public discussions or displays of sexuality. What was new in the 1960s was the buzz about sex in public conversations, in books, on television, and in movies. The 1960s saw the removal of social and legal impediments to talking about or practicing sex. The introduction of the first oral contraceptive pill in 1960 started the public talking about sex and contraception. In 1964 the Supreme Court ruled that Henry Miller's *Tropic of Cancer* was not obscene, opening the way for books, magazines, and movies to begin referring to and showing sex in explicit ways that were once censored. Without these barriers, sex became a hot topic and people began to talk about the beginning of a "sexual revolution" during the decade.

Developments in the preceding decades built momentum for the changes to American society in the 1960s. Scientific studies revealed the importance and variety of Americans' sexual lives, and the definitions of pornography and obscenity were challenged in courts. The work of two scientists especially influenced the revolution of the 1960s: Wilhelm Reich (1897–1957) and Alfred Kinsey (1894–1956). Starting in the 1920s, psychoanalyst Wilhelm Reich published his sexual theories that questioned the American moral principles that applied more severe standards of sexual behavior to women than to men—allowing men more sexual experiences than woman—and the wisdom of abstinence for adolescents. Reich argued that men and women, young and old, need sexual release to ward off sickness. He also believed that political change could only occur when the repression of human sexuality ended. After moving to the United States in 1939, Reich publicized the need for humans to reach orgasm, or the peak of sexual excitement, publishing more books and developing a metal and wood box called the Orgone Energy Accumulator that supposedly absorbed the necessary energy for the person inside to achieve orgasm. Although U.S. government officials seized and burned his books and boxes and threw Reich in jail, his ideas sparked debates that laid a foundation for the sexual revolution of the 1960s. Biologist Alfred Kinsey's studies of American sexual habits, the *Sexual Behavior in the Human Male* (1948) and the *Sexual Behavior in the Human Female* (1953), revealed the vast difference between

 **The Pill**

The oral contraceptive pill liberated women from the fear of pregnancy, allowing them to engage in sex for pleasure. Single women could have sexual encounters without the threat of unwanted pregnancy and married women could use the pill to help limit the size of their families. The creation of the pill, developed from research in laboratories throughout the world, is credited to Gregory "Goody" Pincus and his assistant M. C. Chang of the Worcester Foundation in Massachusetts, and John Rock of Harvard Medical School. Manufactured and distributed by Searle Pharmaceutical Company, the pill, named Enovid, first hit the market in 1960. Many women were glad to have a product to help them gain more control over their sex lives. By 1963 nearly 2.3 million women took the contraceptive daily, a number that continued to rise into the twenty-first century.

Americans' actual sexual activities and the social expectations about sex. Kinsey studied heterosexual and homosexual behavior, presenting all his findings without placing a value on one type of sexuality over another. His data revealed that women, contrary to popular belief, were interested in sex for pleasure as well as for reproduction. Moreover, his study showed that half of the women surveyed had premarital sex, or sex before marriage, and 25 percent had extramarital affairs, or sexual intercourse between a married person and someone other than his/her spouse. The work of these scientists along with the changing definitions of pornography created an atmosphere in the 1960s that accepted discussion and questioning of sexuality.

New social norms

In 1959, the U.S. Supreme Court decided that the publication of British novelist D.H. Lawrence's novel, *Lady Chatterley's Lover,* a book that had been censored for its description of adultery, was protected by the First Amendment of the United States Constitution. This decision opened the floodgates for many books and movies dealing directly with erotic topics. By the 1960s Americans could read about sex in explicit language in scientific reports, how-to books, and novels, and they could see candid depictions of some sexual activities on film for the first time. Jacqueline Susann's novel *Valley of the Dolls* (1966) included sexually explicit descriptions and Helen Gurley Brown's *Sex and the Single Girl* (1962) offered young women advice on how to develop an active sex life while still unmarried. These and other books and movies shattered the idea that sex should only be practiced within the confines of a traditional marriage. The 1967 movie *The Graduate,* for example, depicted a middle-aged woman seducing her daughter's boyfriend. Sexual explicitness became more common, creating huge profits for publishers, filmmakers, and retailers.

The legal decisions and scientific studies of the earlier decades—together with the social upheavals of the civil rights, antiwar, and women's movements, the increased use of drugs, and the pulsing beats of rock music—ignited a variety of debates among Americans regarding sex. What role did

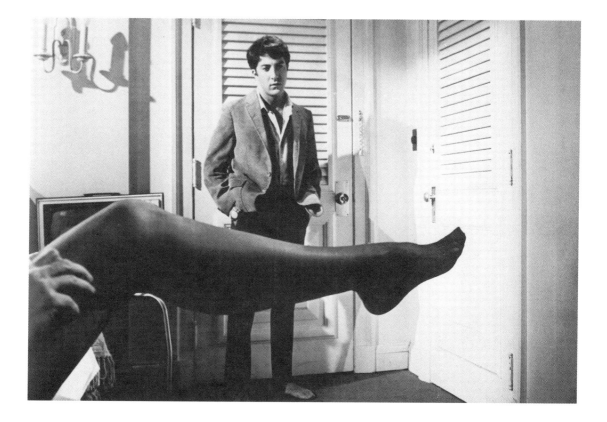

In the 1960s, books and movies that explored sexual themes, such as the 1967 movie *The Graduate*, became more prevalent and socially acceptable. © *Bettmann/Corbis*.

romantic love play in sexual relations? Should men and women be able to fulfill their sexual urges outside marriage? What about interracial and same-sex relationships? These were just a few of the questions the sexual revolution triggered. New moral attitudes about sex also developed, and perhaps the most visible group engaged in developing these new sexual mores were the hippies, drug-taking cultural rebels. Public displays of nudity increased; for example among crowds at rock concerts, some women would bare their breasts. Rock stars sang about sex and some exposed themselves on stage. When popular rock stars such as Janis Joplin sang, "get it while you can" or Crosby, Stills, and Nash sang, "if you can't be with the one you love, honey, love the one you're with," they helped create an air of sexual permissiveness across the country. Promiscuous sexual encounters, or sexual experiences with multiple partners, increased, especially after the introduction of the birth control pill in 1960 freed women from the worry of unwanted pregnancies. Men

Rock singer Janis Joplin sang songs about sex and free love to audiences who stood behind the idea of "make love, not war."
AP/Wide World Photos. Reproduced by permission.

and women began marrying later and having several sexual partners before marriage. Singles bars opened and drew people looking for sexual partners, personal ads with requests for sexual partners appeared in newspapers, and a controversial, highly publicized practice called "swinging," or the practice of couples switching sexual partners, started. Homosexuality also became more accepted and visible to the public.

The debates and sexual experimentation of the 1960s left Americans divided on issues of birth control, homosexuality, marriage and divorce, pornography, premarital sex, and sex education. Some felt that the new social practices freed Americans from cultural limits on their happiness. Others felt the new social permissiveness degraded women, led to juvenile delinquency, and undermined the sanctity of marriage, and would ultimately unravel the fabric of the traditional, family-centered American society. Controversy continued into the early 2000s in lingering battles between conservative and liberal politicians over federal and state funding of abortion, sex education, and healthcare for pregnant women. A potentially deadly legacy of the sexual revolution was the increase in occurrences of sexually transmitted diseases, such as gonorrhea, syphilis, hepatitis B, and herpes. (AIDS was first discovered in 1981.)

For More Information

Books

Douglas, Susan. *Where the Girls Are: Growing Up Female with the Mass Media.* New York: Time Books, 1995.

Dudley, William, ed. *The 1960s.* San Diego, CA: Greenhaven, 2000.

Escoffier, Jeffrey, ed. *Sexual Revolution.* New York: Thunder Mouth's Press, 2003.

Hippies and Sex

In 1965 a group of people living in the Haight-Ashbury district of San Francisco drew the attention of the nation. Living a lifestyle that included drugs and free love and sharing an intense interest in creating a peaceful, tolerant society, the hippies became a highly visible part of what came to be known as the counterculture. These young people had dropped out of mainstream society, as a rebellion against the pressure to conform to the social norms prevalent in the 1950s: mainly the pressure to marry, have children, and get a job. Some also rebelled against the draft and the war in Vietnam. Hippies dressed in colorful homemade or used clothing, rejected nonessential consumer spending, and both men and women wore their hair long. In their attempt to create a new society, hippies often lived in communes, cooperative communities in which people lived and worked together for the common good of the group.

Hippies believed that sexual freedom, including having more than one sexual partner, would spread love throughout the world. Some of the hippies' famous slogans were: "Make love, not war," from an unknown source, and "Love is all you need," from a Beatles song. Nearly 15,000 hippies lived peacefully in the Haight-Ashbury district in 1966, and many hoped their developing culture would change the world.

Hippies believed that love could change the world. *AP/Wide World Photos. Reproduced by permission.*

But the high point of hippie culture came in 1967 with the Summer of Love, when thousands of young people converged on the Haight-Ashbury district. The crowded streets became violent as drug addicts began stealing to support their habits and racial tensions sparked. In October of 1967, realizing that their utopian culture was ending, some hippies in the district paraded a coffin through the streets to symbolize the death of the hippie. Nevertheless, the image of the hippie lived on in songs, movies, and the popular imagination.

Farber, David, and Beth Bailey, with others. *The Columbia Guide to America in the 1960s.* New York: Columbia University Press, 2001.

Harlan, Judith. *Feminism: A Reference Handbook.* Santa Barbara, CA: ABC-CLIO, 1998.

Holland, Gini. *The 1960s*. San Diego, CA: Lucent, 1999.

Hurley, Jennifer A. *Feminism: Opposing Viewpoints*. San Diego, CA: Greenhaven Press, 2001.

Ogden, Annegret. *The Great American Housewife: From Helpmate to Wage Earner, 1776-1986*. Westport, CT: Greenhaven Press, 1986.

Williams, Mary E., ed. *The Sexual Revolution*. San Diego, CA: Greenhaven Press, 2002.

Web sites

Gay and Lesbian Alliance Against Defamation. www.glaad.org (accessed on June 18, 2004).

National Organization for Women. www.now.org (accessed on June 18, 2004).

Sixties Counterculture: The Hippies and Beyond

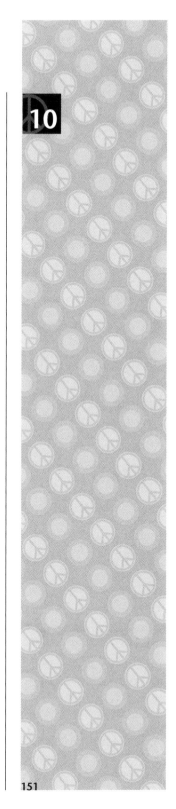

10

When people in the early 2000s think about the 1960s, they might think first about the "hippies." Along with the civil rights movement, antiwar protests, and the Beatles, hippies were one of the most distinctive features of a very colorful decade. Hippies certainly attracted the attention of the media. Their distinctive appearance (bell-bottomed pants, brightly colored shirts, and long loose hair on both men and women), their drug use, and their psychedelic music provided powerful reminders of their rejection of the style and values of their parents. Yet the hippies were important for more than just their lifestyle and fashion choices. As members of a thriving and diverse counterculture, they expressed the deep dissatisfaction many other people felt with American culture in the 1960s. This chapter explores the meaning of the hippies' peculiar brand of cultural dissent.

Streams of cultural dissent

The hippies made up the most colorful, eye-catching, and nonpolitical subgroup of a larger group known as the counterculture. Although some histories use the term counterculture to refer only to the hippies, the counterculture included several distinct groups that criticized developments in American society and advocated for social change in the late 1950s and through the 1960s. One group, called the New Left, consisted of people who were convinced that the American government did not consider the needs of common people and who urged widespread political action by young people, African Americans, and poor people to force the government to address their concerns. The New Left was active in the formation of such groups as the Students for a Democratic Society and the Student Nonviolent Coordinating Committee. Later in the 1960s, members of the New Left dedicated themselves almost solely to the anti-Vietnam War movement. (See Chapter 6 for a complete discussion of the New Left.) Another broad group called for the extension of equal rights and the end to discrimination based on race, ethnicity, and gender. The most visible expression of this group's dissent was the civil rights movement (covered at length in Chapter 8), which called for federal legislation to define and enforce improved conditions for African Americans. There were also significant pressures for full civil rights from Hispanic and Native American groups, and later in the decade a women's rights movement gained strength. Both of these broad groups of dissenters used political means—protests, calls for legislation, and other forms of direct action—to express their dissatisfaction with American culture.

The hippies were the third broad group of dissenters to mainstream American values, though they were also sometimes called the "underground." Like the New Left and the rights-based dissenters, hippies were deeply critical of the society that their parents accepted. The hippies sympathized with the political positions of their fellow dissenters yet rarely used politics as a means of expressing their rejection mainstream values. Politics, they claimed, was the game played by conventional adults, and they wanted no part of elections, lobbying, protests, and other common ways to bring about social change. In fact, they wanted no part of what they called "establishment" culture at all, believing that permanent legal and civil organizations were too concerned with material goods, too competitive, and too dominated by anxiety and corruption. Hippies wanted a new society based on peace, love, and pleasure. Members of the hippie counterculture expressed their dissent through personal expression—they dressed differently, wore their hair differently, listened to different music, talked differently, and used different drugs than their parents. Some hippies formed small groups and lived together in various kinds of small, self-supporting communities called communes.

Before there were hippies…

Some members of the previous generation had a lifestyle that anticipated the 1960s' hippie counterculture. In fact, the members of the Beat Generation of the 1950s—also called simply Beats or Beatniks—made some of the same claims as others made in the 1960s' counterculture. In novels and poems, writers such as Jack Kerouac (1922–1969), Allen Ginsberg (1926–1997), and William Burroughs (1914–1997) announced their generation's dissatisfaction with old-fashioned society. The Beats dropped out of regular society, dressed in jeans and black leather, smoked marijuana though it was illegal, and listened to jazz. In fact, it was the Beats who popularized the word "hip" as a description for something interestingly different, new, and "cool." The Beats themselves adopted many of their traits from the black jazz subculture. Rejected from mainstream society because of their race, black musicians had for years been dressing differently and rejecting white culture. Beatniks and black jazz musicians were thus seen as cultural rebels by young people coming of age in the early 1960s.

It is not uncommon for young people in the United States, or elsewhere, to question and criticize the values of their parents. In fact, rejection of parents' values is widely understood to be an ordinary developmental stage in maturing toward adulthood. But the 1960s countercultural rejection of adult values went well beyond the norm. It was not just the clothing and music of their parents that young people rejected; it was the entire system of values and institutions, which young people called the "establishment." Members of the counterculture criticized schools and colleges that forced students to work for rewards handed down by teachers; an economy that produced and advertised consumer goods as if they could bring happiness and fulfillment; a music industry that cranked out sappy pop songs; a government that sent thousands of young people off to fight a distant war and did not really reflect the interests of the people; and so on. They called this older generation "square," "straight," "uptight," and a variety of other critical names.

In addition to their shared rejection of most mainstream values, many hippies shared a similar social background. Most people who joined the counterculture came from families who had money; the hippies were not members of minority groups who suffered from discrimination. In fact, they were the children of privilege, members of the white middle and upper-middle class. For many, their first stop on the road to the counterculture was college, still a luxury of the well-to-do. Their rejection of mainstream values was surprising because they were the very people who were in position to gain the most—in jobs, political access, and money—from the existing system. That these young people chose to drop out from lives in which they had clear advantages was a sign to many that perhaps something really was wrong with the system.

Haight-Ashbury: Birthplace of the hippies

The countercultural movement and the hippies gradually increased their visibility to the mainstream. The civil rights movement was attracting national attention by the mid-1950s, and the New Left became a factor in American politics in 1962 following the release of its "Port Huron Statement," a stirring announcement of youthful political idealism. But the hippies did not become a recognizable social group until after 1965, the year in which they were named "hippies" in the *San Francisco Chronicle* according to John C. McWilliams, author of *The 1960s Cultural Revolution*. Hippies as a group are hard to define exactly; there were no membership lists and anyone could claim to be a hippie. But once news reports started coming about the cultural revolution going on in the Haight-Ashbury neighborhood of San Francisco, California, most Americans began to understand what a hippie was.

The first real signs of an emerging hippie culture
came in 1963, when a young writer named Ken Kesey (1935–
2001) took the profits earned from the sales of his first book
One Flew Over the Cuckoo's Nest (1962) and bought a log
house in the rural town of La Honda, on the outskirts of San
Francisco. In the late 1950s, Kesey and his friends, many of
them college students at nearby Stanford University, had
taken part in experiments at a local hospital that treated

mental illness. They regularly took hallucinogenic drugs such as LSD, psilocybin, mescaline, and peyote, which caused hallucinations or vivid mental images unconnected to reality. At Kesey's house in La Honda, the friends gathered to experiment with drugs on their own.

Soon more and more people visited the Kesey ranch, "turning on" to, or taking in, the inexpensive drugs and the loud music, then "dropping out," or leaving their jobs, schools, or family, to join the party. Kesey and some of the more adventurous members of the group called themselves the Merry Pranksters. They bought a 1939 school bus, painted it with bright colors, and began driving into San Francisco to organize concerts, street theater, and events they called "Acid Tests." "Acid" is a slang abbreviation for the drug lysergic acid diethylamide, called by its initials for short, LSD. "Acid test," an expression that normally refers to any serious test that proves something definitely, was their name for these events. The hippies' events involved gathering people together to take LSD, smoke marijuana, and listen to rock music. The favorite band at the Acid Tests was the Grateful Dead, led by guitarist Jerry Garcia (1942–1995).

The Pranksters and their increasingly popular Acid Test music and drug festivals found friendly territory in the neighborhood of Haight-Ashbury, near Golden Gate Park and San Francisco State University. Haight-Ashbury was becoming a magnet for college dropouts and thrill seekers looking for cheap drugs and a relaxed lifestyle. It was the perfect place to stage the Merry Pranksters' biggest festival yet, the Trips Festival.

Held in late January of 1966, the Trips Festival was held in several parks and concert halls in the Haight-Ashbury area. According to McWilliams, author of *The 1960s Cultural Revolution*, "there was plenty of LSD, and the festival was a wide-open three-day party drawing 20,000 people who wore Victorian dresses, Civil War uniforms, four-inch heels, Indian headbands, and clown regalia." Kesey and his Pranksters dressed in outrageous costumes—one as a gorilla, another in a spacesuit—and operated a lightshow. Hundreds and hundreds of young people "tripped" or used LSD and puffed on marijuana cigarettes, called joints. Participants slept in the streets and flashed each other a new greeting, a peace sign

made by forming the first two fingers into a "V." Police, who had feared the worst from this event, were amazed at the lack of violence and disruption. This three-day event caused many people to recognize that a new culture was being created: a hippie culture.

Word soon got out about the strange events happening in San Francisco. Among college students and other young people, the hippie scene in Haight-Ashbury became something to explore or "check out" The population of the neighborhood seemed to swell almost overnight; by the summer of 1966, some 15,000 hippies had moved in, many of them "crashing," that is, sleeping together in shared apartments, and some simply living on the street or in local parks. Stores opened to serve hippie needs. McWilliams writes: "The Print Mint sold psychedelic posters, the Weed Patch dispensed drug paraphernalia, and the Blushing Peony had an inventory of 'non-establishment' clothes…. Because hippies preferred marijuana and LSD to alcohol, the Haight had few bars." There were hippie newspapers and even an LSD Rescue Service to help people having bad experiences with drugs. As people flocked to Haight-Ashbury, the neighborhood also came to the attention of the media, both print and television. Soon, the entire United States was learning about these strange people called hippies.

Haight-Ashbury became the colorful, outrageous symbol for a growing hippie movement. It was undoubtedly the national center of psychedelic activity, but there were outposts of hippie culture thriving elsewhere in the country, in New York's East Village neighborhood, in big northern cities like Chicago, Boston, and Detroit, and on college campuses across the nation.

Hippies: Good or bad?

In 1967, historian Arnold Toynbee called hippies "a red warning light for the American way of life," as quoted in *Newsweek*. There were ways in which hippies could be considered a real threat to the social order. The most radical of the hippies called for the end of the American political order and for the introduction of anarchy, the absence of government. In its place they offered vague promises of "peace" and "love." If taken seriously, such goals were far more revolutionary than the changes being sought by antiwar activists or civil rights demonstrators. Few, however, took the hippies that seriously, including the hippies themselves. Even their most openly political actions—such as nominating a pig for president in 1968, a stunt performed by the Yippies, a loosely organized hippie political party—were meant more as

Yippies!: The Political Side of the Hippies

Hippies were not generally known for being political: they were too busy getting high and listening to music to bother with protests and changing the government. But there were a number of hippies who recognized that the hippie mantra of "tune in, turn on, drop out" had radical political significance. These more vocal and motivated hippies—including Timothy Leary, Allen Ginsberg (1926–1997), Paul Krassner (1932–), Abbie Hoffman (1936–1989), and Jerry Rubin (1938–1994)—thought that if they could disrupt the political process and bring the benefits of sex, drugs, and rock'n' roll to the attention of the nation, they might change the nation (and eventually the entire world) for the better. Sometime in 1967 or early 1968, Rubin, Hoffman, and others decided to form a group called the Yippies, with the letters YIP later said to stand for Youth International Party.

The Yippies were not a typical political party: they did not have rules or even a list of members. They did not have political theories, but they did have actions. Their goal was chaos. Groups of self-identified Yippies pulled off guerrilla theater, a term that referred to certain outdoor dramatic events concerning controversial political or social issues, events such as burning money in public, scattering money on the floor of the New York Stock Exchange and laughing while stockbrokers scrambled after it, nominating a pig (named Pigasus, a pun on the mythological winged horse name Pegasus) for president, and disrupting the Democratic presidential nominating convention in Chicago in the summer of 1968. They offered absurd political slogans such as "Rise up and abandon the creeping meatball!"

Without a mass of followers willing to respond to their calls to take to the streets, the Yippies managed to bring about only small and ineffectual protests. In the end, the most they achieved was to provoke laughter and to get themselves arrested. By the early 1970s the Yippies had disbanded altogether.

jokes than as serious political statements. The humor was lost on those who were not sympathetic.

To many others, the hippies were primarily a nuisance. People living near hippies resented their carefree ways, for hippies were notorious for not taking good care of their homes or apartments. Mayors of cities ordered police to chase off those hippies who slept or begged for money on the streets. As one resident of Haight-Ashbury told *America* magazine columnist William W. MacDonald, "If some hippies moved next door to

me I would move out, because I couldn't tolerate the filth." California governor Ronald Reagan captured this perception of hippies when he claimed that a hippie was someone who "dresses like Tarzan, has hair like Jane, and smells like Cheetah," as quoted in *Turbulent Years: The 1960s.*

To the hippies themselves, of course, their lifestyle was quite meaningful—at least for a time. It allowed them to experiment with new ways of living. Some important parts of their lifestyle were drug use, a new form of spirituality, and unconventional music.

Harvard professor Timothy Leary speaks before a packed audience at the University of Wisconsin–Madison in 1967 about LSD. He encouraged students to "turn on, tune in, and drop out." *AP/Wide World Photos. Reproduced by permission.*

Drug use: LSD

The drug use common among hippies was a controversial part of their lifestyle. Many hippies insisted that it was an essential part of their rejection of the "establishment" and no worse, in any case, than the widespread use of tobacco, alcohol, and prescription drugs among mainstream adults. Ironically, the drug so much a part of hippie culture, lysergic acid diethylamide or LSD, was available legally until 1966 in California and until 1967 in the rest of the United States. Invented in 1938 by a Swiss scientist, it was thought to have potential as a treatment for mental illness, and both the federal government and many universities conducted studies with the drug in the 1950s. Participants in these experiments reported on the powerful hallucinations they experienced while on the drug. Others were willing to experiment with a drug that was said to expand a person's consciousness. Consciousness includes mental awareness including thoughts, feelings, and emotions, in addition to awareness of physical sensations.

One of the biggest promoters of the drug was Dr. Timothy Leary (1920–1996), who as a professor of psychology at Harvard University introduced the drug to many of his students and later popularized its use. Interviewed by *Playboy* magazine in 1966, Leary described the experience of taking LSD as involving an "incredible acceleration and intensification of all sense and of all mental processes.... Around a thousand million signals fire off in your brain every second; ... you find yourself tuned in on thousands of these messages that ordinarily you don't register consciously." People who took the drug, or "tripped," which is the slang term for being under its influence, described music taking physical shape and color, and physical touch playing like music in their heads. Some claimed that they saw God. Many users claimed that once a person takes LSD, the person can never go back to seeing the world like a drug-free person or "straight" person sees it.

LSD users said that the drug "blew their mind," and many wanted to constantly return to the altered state that it offered. In Leary's memorable phrase for his *Playboy* interview, they wanted to "turn on, tune in, drop out." Leary and others promoted this "dropping out," or leaving one's job, school, or family, as a positive thing, pointing to the great creativity and happiness of those who took hallucinogenic drugs regularly. LSD use, said Leary, "produced not only a new rhythm in modern music but a new décor for our discotheques, a new form of film making, a new kinetic visual art, a new literature, and has begun to revise our philosophic and psychological thinking." When Leary was forced to leave his academic position (as other academics grew increasingly wary of LSD use), he moved to California, where he became a kind of guru or leader to those wanting to use LSD to form a new society.

Many others, including the lawmakers who made the drug illegal, worried about the negative effects of LSD. The best-known negative effect of the drug for the user was the "bad trip." In a "bad trip," the drug user experiences intense and irrational fear and frightening sensory perceptions, sometimes to the point that the user considers committing suicide to escape. Another danger is the LSD flashback, in which a person re-experiences part of an LSD trip some days or weeks after taking the drug. But in the 1960s it was the way LSD encouraged people to disconnect or "drop out" that scared non-users the most. Parents worried that a young adult taking the drug would immediately "drop out" and join his or her hippie friends living on the street; politicians feared that if too many people dropped out and joined the hippies, they could not maintain social order.

Once LSD was made illegal nationwide in 1967, use of the drug declined dramatically. No longer could hippies take the drug and "trip" in public parks or on city streets. By the end of the 1960s, many thought the risk of being arrested and put in prison, as some hippies were, outweighed the thrill of using the illegal drug.

Hippie spirituality

The counterculture movement was not expressly religious, at least not in conventional terms, but for many of its participants, life as a hippie was in some ways like belonging to a religion. Many people became hippies after having an experience, often under the influence of LSD, that converted them to a new set of beliefs or philosophy of life. Abandoning "straight" society, the hippie joined others who believed in peace, love, and togetherness. Unlike organized religions, there was no central rulemaking body and no book of religious teachings, but many hippies claimed that nature was their church and all the world their holy book.

In the words of Timothy Miller, author of *The Hippies and American Values,* hippies rejected established religions and churches as "self-righteous centers of hypocrisy, stations for the blessing of the Establishment, wealthy organizations mainly interested in preserving themselves, havens for the narrow-minded, [and] anachronisms utterly irrelevant to modern life." An anachronism is anything that is outdated and not suited to or useful in the present. Like many other spiritual seekers during the 1960s, members of the counterculture explored Eastern religions, such as Hinduism and Buddhism, and were intrigued by the teachings of the Maharishi Mahesh Yogi (1911–), who in the mid-1960s brought a technique for concentration and reflection, called Transcendental Meditation, to the United States. Other people joined together and lived in communes, self-supporting rural communities that sometimes had spiritual components. Still others—especially those who were more easily persuaded—joined religious or seemingly religious cults, such as the Hare Krishnas and the Moonies (also called the Unification Church), and a few decided to follow Charles Manson (see sidebar). A cult is a group of people who believe in a religion or set of beliefs that appears to be very different from established religions. Like young people everywhere, hippies sought spiritual answers. Not surprisingly, hippies did so outside the conventional channels of family life and mainstream religions.

Music of the hippies: Psychedelic rock

The hippie movement, unlike the Beat movement, produced no great literature or art. The works of literature that emerged from the hippie subculture were disjointed, rambling, and sometimes incoherent, mirroring the hallucinations that fueled the writing; the art tended to emphasize flowers or bright patterns but showed no groundbreaking talent. By far the greatest creative expression of the hippie movement was its music, which best depicted the rapid shifts of thought and heightened intensity associated with LSD use.

From the beginning of the "Acid Tests" held at the Kesey ranch and in Haight-Ashbury, hippies had been looking for and inventing music that fit their unique approach to life. They were helped by legendary LSD dealer Augustus Owsley Stanley III (1935–). When he bought some musical instruments and gave them to Jerry Garcia and members of his band, known as the Grateful Dead, new music began to emerge. The Dead, as they were known, combined rock, folk, and jazz in long, rambling "jams" that contained wandering instrumental solos and references to drug use. The new style of music that these musicians invented came to be known as psychedelic or acid rock.

The Dead played at parties and festivals throughout San Francisco beginning in 1965, and they became the favorite band of the hippies living in Haight-Ashbury. Soon, however, the musical style called psychedelic rock began to expand. Straight rock'n' roll relied on fairly short songs—three or four minutes—with a verse-chorus-verse structure played by two guitars and a drum set. But psychedelic rock was far more complicated: songs stretched on for ten or twelve minutes; verses might not be repeated at all and became far more poetic and obscure; and bands added all variety of instruments, from fiddles and banjos to Indian sitars, a

The Grateful Dead, pictured here in 1969. Famed guitarist Jerry Garcia, who died in 1995, is pictured at the bottom center. *AP/Wide World Photos. Reproduced by permission.*

long-necked, stringed instrument. American bands and performers including Jefferson Airplane, The Doors, Janis Joplin, and Jimi Hendrix emerged as favorites of hippies, and British bands such as the Yardbirds and the Byrds emerged from England's drug scene with their own distinctive psychedelic music. Caught up in the counterculture enthusiasm for LSD, established bands—notably the Beatles and the Rolling Stones—also began to create psychedelic music. Taken to-

Charles Manson: The Dark Side of the Hippies

Among the many people who flocked to Haight-Ashbury in the summer of 1967 was a career criminal and psychopath, Charles Manson (1934–). Intelligent but mentally disturbed, Manson saw himself as the messiah in a religion that combined the hippie fondness for "peace" and "love" with a strange mixture of biblical prophecy and Scientology. He gathered around himself a group of troubled hippies—runaways, vagrants, and castoffs from broken homes—that he called "The Family." During 1967, "the summer of love," Manson and his hippie Family wandered through California, hunting for food, prostituting the women to raise money, and committing petty crimes. In 1968 they settled down at a friend's ranch outside Hollywood to live communally.

At the ranch, Manson's teachings grew increasingly bizarre, yet his followers grew to nearly fifty people. He prophesied that the world was about to experience a disaster that would kill most humans and that he and the Family would rise up from the desert to rule over the remains of the human race. But first, he said, they must destroy those who stood in their way. In August of 1969 Manson convinced several of his followers to go on a string of killings. Over two nights they murdered seven people, including well-known actress Sharon Tate and coffee magnate Abigail Folger.

The crimes were investigated by district attorney Vincent Bugliosi (1934–),

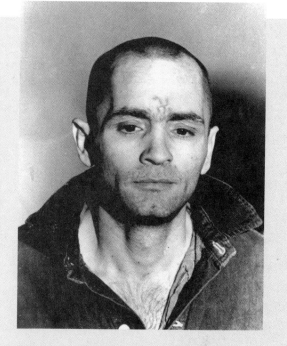

Charles Manson en route to the courtroom during the Sharon Tate murder trial, April 19, 1971, Los Angeles, California. *AP/Wide World Photos. Reproduced by permission.*

who finally revealed the connection between Manson, his Family, and the bloody slayings. The investigation and arrests made the Family the subject of much media attention, as Family members shaved their heads and demonstrated outside the courtroom. Manson and eight Family members were eventually convicted of murder in 1971, and the remaining cult disbanded. As of 2004 Manson remained in prison. The media attention on the case seemed to confirm the worst fears of those who believed that the hippie lifestyle of drugs and sex could easily lead to crime.

gether, the work of these bands constitutes a new chapter in the history of rock'n' roll.

Psychedelic rock music was the first element of hippie culture to be mass marketed to the rest of the United States and then to the world. Thanks perhaps to the influence of the Beatles and their enormous fan base, rock music radio stations played psychedelic music and fans loved it. The music could be played on the radio because the references to drug use were always coded in obscure language. When the Beatles, for example, sang about "Lucy in the Sky with Diamonds," the innocent could enjoy the lovely image while drug users knew that the initials of the song title stood for LSD. Similarly, Jefferson Airplane's song "White Rabbit"— with its lyric "one pill makes you larger, one pill makes you small"—could be an interpretation of the children's story *Alice in Wonderland* or a description of a drug trip. References to drug use were frequent in rock lyrics of the late 1960s and early 1970s, but as long as they were not too direct, radio stations would play the songs.

The "summer of love"

To the extent that a shapeless, unorganized movement like the hippies could be said to have reached a peak, many people think it did so in 1967, in what became known as "the summer of love." Hippies thronged the streets of Haight-Ashbury, psychedelic music poured from radios, LSD was still readily available, and the cops of San Francisco were still willing to turn a blind eye on the whole scene as long as there was no violence. One of the defining moments of the year was the "Human Be-In," a strange festival of the hippie experience.

The "Human Be-In" began on January 14, 1967, a date that signaled the beginning of what a hippie astrologer called the "Age of Aquarius." An announcement of the event, quoted in Jane and Michael Stern's *Sixties People,* read: "Berkeley [California] activists and the love generation of the Haight-Ashbury will join together with members of the new nation who will be coming from every state in the nation, every tribe of the young (the emerging soul of the nation) to powwow, celebrate, and prophesy the epoch of liberation, love, peace, compassion, and unity of mankind." And they did. For several days, hippies wandered the streets of the city, taking LSD, wearing flowers in their hair, loving each other, and cleaning up the whole scene afterward.

The mood of the event carried through the summer, through a series of festivals and peaceful demonstrations attended by hippies with long flowing hair and joyous smiles. In June, 50,000 people gathered at the Monterey International Pop Festival, south of San Francisco, to groove to the sounds of psychedelic rock. It was Monterey that launched the careers of Jimi Hendrix and Janis Joplin. The festival, like so many of the events of that summer, was peaceful and problem-free, seeming to demonstrate to the world that the hippies' message of love and peace was real. Finally, in October of 1967 hippies led by Abbie Hoffman placed flowers in the gun barrels of soldiers guarding the Pentagon in Washington, D.C. This gesture was a powerful symbolic act that seemed to symbolize the victory of love over war.

The end of the dream

No sooner had the hippie movement reached its peak than it began to show signs of collapse and disintegration. The media spotlight that shone on Haight-Ashbury in the spring of 1967 turned the neighborhood into a tourist attraction, with a variety of ill effects. First, the neighborhood began to attract people who were not interested in the hippie lifestyle, with its commitment to peace and love, but only open drug use. Some were just "day hippies," who came to "drop acid," which means to take a dose of LSD, and then return home; others were hard-core drug addicts who turned to crime to support their drug habit. Second, Haight-Ashbury became a stop on passing tours, sandwiched between the Golden Gate Bridge and Fisherman's Wharf. Bus tours cruised through, tourists pressed their noses to the tinted glass while listening to a guide explain: "You are passing through the Bearded Curtain.... Among the favorite pastimes of the hippies, besides taking drugs, are parading and demonstrating; … malingering; plus the ever present preoccupation with the soul, reality, and self-expression, such as strumming guitars, piping flutes, and banging on bongoes," as quoted in *Sixties People*.

By 1968, however, the political climate in the United States began to turn against the counterculture in general.

Singer and poet Jim Morrison of The Doors died mysteriously of heart failure while in France in July 1971. By September of that year, thousands of fans had flocked to his grave in Paris's Pere Lachaise cemetery, showing their devotion in the form of flowers and graffiti.
AP/Wide World Photos. Reproduced by permission.

Once peaceful antiwar protests had grown increasingly violent in the past year, and race riots in some of the nation's major cities in 1967 and 1968 showed the violent side of the civil rights movement. In late 1969, a hippie cult leader named Charles Manson (1934–), who lured hippies to his ranch with promises of free love and drugs, masterminded a string of murders in the foothills of Los Angeles. Mainstream Americans who had once looked on these countercultural movements as fairly benign began to see in them a real threat to the social order.

In 1968 Americans elected for president Republican Richard Nixon (1913–1994), who as a candidate had promised a return to law and order. Across the country, police forces that had once tolerated hippie communities began to make arrests for drug use and vagrancy. According to McWilliams, anti-hippie billboards appeared in New York that stated "Keep America Clean: Take a Bath" and "Keep America Clean: Get a Haircut," and the governor of Tennessee declared: "We want every long-hair in jail or out of the state." Hippies were forced to retreat to rural communes or private homes, thus disrupting the communities that they had built in urban settings. Many simply returned to "straight" life, taking jobs and entering the mainstream. The age of the hippie was in decline.

Hippies live on

In the fall of 1967, some hippies in Haight-Ashbury had celebrated the demise of their culture in a "Death of Hip" ceremony, complete with a coffin bearing the symbolic corpse of the "summer of love." In fact, their predictions of the death of the hippie movement were premature, for major expressions of hippie culture continued to appear in American culture. In fact, the biggest music festival of the decade—the Woodstock Music and Art Fair, held in upstate New York in August of 1969—was noteworthy not just for the stellar lineup of bands but also for the peacefulness with which nearly half a million people conducted themselves for three days of sun, rain, and drug use. Slowly but surely, however, hippie communities disbanded, and hippie musicians turned to new styles, or they died. (Jimi Hendrix, Janis Joplin, and Jim Morrison of The Doors all died within a year of each other in 1970 and 1971, all from drug overdoses.)

As the hippie movement came to an end, its images were assimilated or became part of ordinary life. Hippie music filled the airwaves, and the symbols of hippie pride—flowers and paisley patterns, for example—were plastered over all manner of products, from lunch baskets to children's clothing to fabric that could be used to make curtains. The hippie dress style became popular: mainstream males began to wear bell-bottomed pants and blousy shirts, and females began to wear long, flowing gypsy-style dresses. Ordinary people flashed the peace sign. Popular television shows such as *Rowan and Martin's Laugh-In* and *The Smothers Brothers Comedy Hour* used hippie dress and hippie words as a source of humor, thus reducing their revolutionary significance. In these ways, and many more, the powerful engine of American commercialism cashed in on the once-radical hippie style.

Remnants of hippie culture have echoed through American culture ever since the 1960s ended. For example, bell-bottom pants and long hair on men have gone in and out of style over the years. The hippie belief that if enough people join hands and sing about love, perhaps they can change the world, entered history as a quaint expression of a strangely frivolous, difficult to define, and yet in some ways appealing social movement.

For More Information

Books

Austin, Joe, and Michael Nevin Willard. *Generations of Youth: Youth Cultures and History in Twentieth-Century America*. New York: New York University Press, 1998.

Bugliosi, Vincent, with Curt Gentry. *Helter-Skelter: The True Story of the Manson Murders*. New York: Norton, 1974.

Dudley, William, ed. *The 1960s*. San Diego, CA: Greenhaven Press, 2000.

Farber, David. *The Age of Great Dreams: America in the 1960s*. New York: Hill and Wang, 1994.

Farber, David, and Beth Bailey, with others. *The Columbia Guide to America in the 1960s*. New York: Columbia University Press, 2001.

Kallen, Stuart A., ed. *Sixties Counterculture*. San Diego, CA: Greenhaven Press, 2001.

McDonough, Jack. *San Francisco Rock: The Illustrated History of San Francisco Rock Music*. San Francisco, CA: Chronicle Books, 1985.

McWilliams, John C. *The 1960s Cultural Revolution*. Westport, CT: Greenwood Press, 2000.

Miller, Timothy. *The Hippies and American Values*. Knoxville: University of Tennessee Press, 1991.

O'Neill, William L. *Coming Apart: An Informal History of America in the 1960s*. Chicago, IL: Quadrangle, 1971.

Sloman, Larry. *Steal This Dream: Abbie Hoffman and the Countercultural Revolution in America.* New York: Doubleday, 1998.

Stern, Jane, and Michael Stern. *Sixties People.* New York: Knopf, 1990.

Stevens, Jay. *Storming Heaven: LSD and the American Dream.* New York: Atlantic Monthly Press, 1987.

Turbulent Years: The 1960s. Alexandria, VA: Time-Life Books, 1998.

Periodicals

"The Hippies." *Newsweek* (July 7, 1967): p. 18.

MacDonald, William W. "Life and Death of the Hippies." *America* (September 7, 1968): pp. 150–151.

"*Playboy* Interview: Timothy Leary." *Playboy* (September 1966).

Web Sites

Bove, Tony with Allen Cohen and Raechel Donahue. *Haight-Ashbury in the 1960s: Music and Images.* www.rockument.com/haimg.html (accessed on June 6, 2004).

The Digger Archives. www.diggers.org (accessed on June 6, 2004).

Grateful Dead. www.dead.com (accessed on June 6, 2004).

Hippies on the Web: Haight-Ashbury Music and Culture. www.rockument.com/links.html (accessed on June 6, 2004).

Kesey, Zane. *Ken Kesey Art Show.* www.key-z.com (accessed on June 6, 2004).

Leary. www.leary.com (accessed on June 6, 2004).

Decline or Revival? Changing Currents in the American Religious Experience

As in so many areas of life, Americans in the 1960s questioned past religious practices and searched for authenticity or genuineness in their spiritual experiences, whether in established faiths or in new religious groups that formed as cults or communes. A cult is a group of people who share the same beliefs but whose beliefs and lifestyle are unlike the majority's beliefs; a commune is a group of people who live together cooperatively, sharing work and expenses. Moderate Protestant churches, long the bedrock of American religion, saw declines in membership, while membership increased in smaller, theologically more conservative Protestant sects, with their more fervent and expressive forms of worship. The other mainstream religions—Catholicism and Judaism—also experienced important changes. The Catholic Church modernized some of its key doctrines and celebrated the election of America's first Catholic president, John F. Kennedy (1917–1963; served 1961–63), but at the same time it resisted changing its views regarding human sexuality, which led to a loss of membership. Jewish leaders worried that their religion was weakening as Jews embraced the secular (non-religious) elements of American culture, and they looked for ways to revive a sense of Jewish identity. No matter their religion, many Protestants, Catholics, and Jews filtered their participation in the major social movements of the era—especially the civil rights movement and the antiwar movement—through the lens of their religious perspective.

While shifts in attendance and doctrine within the major established religions probably impacted more Americans, fringe religious issues attracted much public attention and, for many, characterized the religious climate of the 1960s. For example, one of the most notorious figures in the public debate over spirituality was an outspoken atheist, Madalyn Murray O'Hair (1919–1995), who used the publicity she gained from battling against prayer in schools to create the impression of a rising tide of atheism where none really existed. Other minor figures attracted major attention: the Maharishi Mahesh Yogi (1911–) promoted Eastern religions such as Buddhism and Hinduism and was helped along by the highly public support of the Beatles and other celebrities, and the Hare Krishnas seemed far more numerous than they really were because they frequently asked for money in American airports. Along with hippies and their communes, cults and certain individuals who wanted to change mainstream religious practice seemed to define the era, even if they did not.

Questioning the Protestant mainstream

The United States had long prided itself on its religious diversity. Founded as a refuge for those fleeing religious persecution in Europe, the United States had in principle been very tolerant of religious diversity. In practice, however, Protestant churches—especially the mainstream Baptist, Methodist, Episcopalian, Presbyterian, and Lutheran churches—dominated the religious landscape. Other major world religions—especially Catholicism and Judaism—occupied a position decidedly outside the mainstream. Before World War II (1939–45), members of non-Protestant religions had suffered from de facto segregation: Catholics and Jews often found it difficult to gain public office and were often distrusted by the Protestant majority because of their religious views.

Modern-Day Revivalist: Oral Roberts

America's Protestant churches had a long history of revivalism. As early as the colonial era, mainstream Protestant churches had participated in movements to renew religious faith. The first such movement, peaking in the 1740s, was known as the Great Awakening; in the early 1800s a second Great Awakening earned parts of New York the nickname "The Burned Over District" for the intensity of religious revivals that took place there. Another such revival took place in the late 1950s and early 1960s in Pentecostal churches such as the Church of God, the Assemblies of God, and the Full Gospel Church. Once criticized for their strange practices—including speaking in tongues and handling serpents—these churches entered the mainstream thanks to a new generation of media-savvy evangelists such as Oral Roberts.

Born in 1918, Oral Roberts became a minister in the Pentecostal Holiness Church, but by 1947 he had left the church to lead an evangelical crusade of his own. Roberts led dramatic services in which he purported to heal the sick, and his tent revivals drew thousands. Soon, Roberts reached even bigger audiences when he began airing a radio program on more than three hundred radio stations. Roberts asked for contributions to his ministry; in return, he sent such trinkets as pieces of "prayer cloth" which he had personally prayed

over. By the early 1960s he had a faithful audience of many thousands, and he began to deliver his message on television.

Roberts tempered his message as he reached more viewers—he decreased his emphasis on healing and miracles—and by the mid-1960s he took his Pentecostal followers into the mainstream with him. In 1966 he was invited to the International Conference on Evangelicalism, where he befriended America's best-known evangelist, Billy Graham (1918–). Roberts, Graham, and others used modern media to draw adherents to their conservative Protestant views, revitalizing interest in this religious perspective, especially among poor and working-class Americans.

Roberts went on to create a major evangelical empire that included long-running radio and television programs and, in 1965, the creation of Oral Roberts University, the first accredited Pentecostal university, in Tulsa, Oklahoma. In 1978 the university added a medical school, where teachings combined standard medical practices with faith healings. Roberts was widely ridiculed in the late 1980s when he announced, on national TV, that God had threatened to "call him home" unless he raised eight million dollars to maintain his ministry. Roberts was saved from this prophecy by followers who came up with the money, but he lost credibility as a result.

But World War II began to change this dynamic. Justly proud of their role as champions of freedom and appalled by the way German Nazis had dehumanized Jews during the Holocaust, Americans began to grow more tolerant of divergent religious viewpoints.

The postwar years saw an upsurge in church attendance across the religious spectrum. In 1960, 50 percent of Americans reported that they regularly attended a church or synagogue, more than at any time in American history. God was instilled in American life in many ways: the words "under God" had been added to the Pledge of Allegiance in 1954 and the words "In God We Trust" were added to U.S. currency a year later. Politicians regularly attributed America's successes to God's grace, and the American belief in God was one of the key issues used to differentiate Americans from their enemies in the Cold War, the so-called godless communists of the Soviet Union.

However, despite the reassurances of this widespread unanimity, many Americans were dissatisfied with the quality of their spiritual life. Many felt that the established churches had grown complacent and self-satisfied, and these individuals began to leave their houses of worship in growing numbers. For example, membership in the Episcopalian church dropped 17 percent between 1965 and 1975; in the same period, membership in the United Presbyterian Church and the United Church of Christ shrank 12 percent, and in the United Methodist Church it diminished 10 percent. Americans were clearly seeking meaningful religious experiences elsewhere.

Catholics and Jews enter the mainstream

Among the biggest beneficiaries of increased religious tolerance were the Catholic and Jewish faiths. Perhaps the biggest symbol of increased religious tolerance was the election of John F. Kennedy (1917–1963; served 1961–63) as president in 1960. While Catholics had been successfully elected to lower political offices, including Congress, many Protestants believed it was not safe to elect a Catholic president. For many, the fear was that a Catholic president would be forced to choose between his loyalty to the country and his obedience to the pope, the head of the Catholic Church. Campaigning for office in the fall of 1960, Kennedy eased concerns when he told the Houston Ministerial Association:

"The Most Hated Woman in America": Atheist Madalyn Murray O'Hair

Though many Americans questioned their religious faith and searched out more meaningful spiritual experiences in the 1960s, few were willing to publicly declare that they denied the existence of a supernatural being. Madalyn Murray O'Hair was different. This college-educated single mother directly challenged general beliefs in the existence of God when she fought against school prayer in a Baltimore, Maryland, school district. Her court challenge to school policies eventually rose to the level of the Supreme Court, which ruled in 1963 that prayers could not be said in schools. O'Hair's very public campaign against school prayer earned her the nickname "The Most Hated Woman in America."

In the years that followed the Supreme Court decision, O'Hair campaigned to eliminate the words "under God" from the Pledge of Allegiance and the words "In God We Trust" from currency. In the process she created what amounted to an atheist (a person who does not believe in the existence of God) empire: she published atheist periodicals, hosted atheist radio shows, toured in a barnstorming religious debating show, and created a string of atheist organizations. By turns angry, profane, vengeful, and terrifically persuasive, she stirred controversy and attracted attention like few others, then suddenly she disappeared under mysterious circumstances in 1995. It took several years for police to uncover the bizarre kidnapping/murder plot that led to her death.

"I am not the Catholic candidate for President. I am the Democratic Party's candidate for President, who also happens to be Catholic." Kennedy also promised that he would resign the presidency if he was ever forced to "either violate my conscience, or violate the national interest." When his conduct as president showed no specific religious influence it reduced concerns about a Catholic president, so much so that the Catholicism of 2004 presidential candidate John Kerry was accorded no undue attention.

The Catholic Church went through important and dramatic changes of its own in the 1960s. Pope John XXIII, elected to the church's highest office in 1959, believed that the church needed to modernize its services and some of its doctrines. He convened a council in Rome called Vatican II, which lasted from 1962 to 1965, and several American bishops were invited. Vatican II introduced several changes to Catholic worship services: it allowed mass to be said in the native tongue instead of Latin, and it allowed priests to face their congregation from behind the altar instead of facing the altar with their backs toward the congregation. Vatican II also called for Catholics to reach out to other religions in a spirit of tolerance and absolved Jews of any guilt for the death of Jesus. These changes were intended to bring Catholicism in tune with the spirit of the times and to increase church membership. In fact, many Catholics resented the changes or lost faith because some of their beliefs were suddenly revised by the pope. Some thought the changes diminished the authority of the church and made it seem less like a refuge from other religious practices than it had been. Despite Pope John's liberal approach in some areas, though, the church stood fast in its refusal to condone birth control, alienating those who wanted the church to become more progressive on that issue. Overall attendance at Catholic services declined throughout the 1960s, though by the end of the decade the Catholic Church remained the single largest denomination in the United States, with 48 million members in 1970.

When Jewish immigrants began to arrive in the United States in large numbers in the late nineteenth century, they brought with them a distinct culture and set of religious practices that were preserved in tight-knit communities. By the mid-twentieth century, however, Jews had spread throughout the United States and begun to adopt American values and cultural practices. By the 1960s some Jewish leaders feared that the Jewish faith was becoming dangerously diluted as Jews assimilated into American culture, which means they blended with non-Jews. For example, intermarriage among Jews and non-Jews increased rapidly in the 1950s and 1960s, while weekly attendance at synagogue (the Jewish house of worship) declined to just 17 percent of the Jewish population in 1964 (compared to 42 percent among Christians). Jews in general were becoming increasingly secular in their orientation toward life, prompting many to believe that Judaism in the United States would exist more as a culture than as a religion. In 1967, however, events in Israel—the historical homeland of the Jewish faith—sparked a revival of engagement with Jewish issues in the American Jewish community. In the Six Day War between Israel and its Arab neighbors Egypt, Syria, and Jordan, Israel drove Arab forces

Black Muslims

Part religion and part militant political movement, the Black Muslims were feared and misunderstood by outside observers of the 1960s. Black Muslims belonged to a religious group known as the Nation of Islam. Church doctrine declares that a mysterious man named Wallace D. Fard appeared in the black ghetto of Detroit, Michigan, in 1930 and revealed himself as Allah, the Muslim god. His chief disciple was Elijah Poole (1897–1975), who adopted the name Elijah Muhammad and led the religion after Fard's disappearance in 1933.

As interpreted by Muhammad, the Nation of Islam combined traditional Islamic teachings with black separatism (the belief that American blacks should form a separate nation away from white people). Muhammad taught that whites are devils who took control of Earth in order to oppress black people, the true children of Allah. Those who joined the Nation of Islam dropped their former last names—thought to have been brought down to them via the owners of their slave ancestors—in favor of the letter "X" or an Islamic name. With his charismatic teaching style, Muhammad drew many followers to his religion—including prominent black celebrities like boxer Cassius Clay (1942–), who took the name Muhammad Ali upon joining. The Black Muslims' angry anti-white rhetoric scared many, but it appealed to those blacks weary of the slow pace of gains made by the civil rights movement.

The Black Muslims enjoyed their greatest prominence in the early 1960s

from disputed land and claimed the Old City of Jerusalem for Israel. The war sparked great pride among Jews around the world, and Christians in the United States tended to side with Jews instead of Arabs in this conflict.

The evangelical alternative

According to Maurice Isserman and Michael Kazin, authors of *America Divided: The Civil War of the 1960s,* many of those seeking new spiritual guidance turned to evangelical Christian churches. Evangelical churches, wrote Isserman and Kazin, "offered troubled individuals what [mainstream churches] could not: the balm of simple answers to perennial questions of the soul." Evangelical churches stressed the personal relationship between the believer and Jesus and stressed

In 1964 a member of the Black Muslims holds a newspaper noting "A Savior Is Born," marking the anniversary of the birth of the group's founder Wallace Fard. © *Bettmann/Corbis.*

thanks to the teachings of Malcolm X (1925–1965). Malcolm X's dynamic leadership expanded the group dramatically, increasing membership to over 100,000 members, and his speeches drew media attention. For a time Malcolm X was considered a rival to Martin Luther King Jr. (1929–1968), for intellectual leadership of the civil rights movement. Malcolm X and many other members left the Black Muslims in the mid-1960s when it was discovered that Elijah Muhammad and his family had been involved in sexual and financial scandals. Malcolm X was assassinated in 1965, shortly after he left the Black Muslims. The Nation of Islam continued in the early twenty-first century under controversial leader Louis Farrakhan (1933–).

the idea and experience of being "saved" and "born again." More conservative or fundamentalist churches stressed the literal truth of the Bible, and some encouraged people to express their religious ecstasy through practices such as "speaking in tongues" (in which an individual "possessed" by the holy spirit speaks in allegedly ancient languages) or the handling of serpents. Evangelical and fundamentalist churches offered the fire and excitement that many people sought, and attendance in such churches rose dramatically, with many denominations seeing double-digit gains in membership.

One result of the growth of the evangelical movement was an increase in a phenomenon called televangelism—evangelism preached on television programs. Televangelists were dramatic preachers who saw the TV audience as their flock, and they delivered their sermons via weekly or

The Reverend Billy Graham preaches to a packed audience of 8,000 students at the University of California in 1967. The topics of his sermon, in conjunction with the Campus Crusade for Christ, ranged from LSD to Jesus Christ. *AP/Wide World Photos. Reproduced by permission.*

daily programs. Two of the best-known televangelists of the 1960s were Oral Roberts (1918–) and Billy Graham (1918–). Both used their eye-catching charm and powers of persuasion to draw viewers and, especially in the case of Roberts, build religious empires with the money contributed to their cause from audiences. Some criticized televangelists for enriching themselves while promoting false religious ideas, but no one could deny that these preachers drew mass audiences.

One outgrowth of the rise of evangelical churches was the success of the Campus Crusade for Christ. Founded by California businessman Bill Bright (1921–2003) in 1951 and supported by Billy Graham, this evangelical group worked to bring the "good news" of the New Testament of the Bible to students on American college campuses. They found a perfect environment for their message: college enrollments soared in the 1960s, and many young people were leaving the churches of their parents and looking for new ones. Campus Crusade for Christ evangelists were young and hip; they wore casual clothes and spoke like other college students. They made special efforts to convert those who had bad experiences with drugs and sexual permissiveness, offering Jesus Christ as a refuge from the fast-paced youth culture of sex, drugs, and rock'n' roll. By the mid-1970s the Campus Crusade for Christ had a budget of $42 million and 6,500 employees; it retained a presence on college campuses throughout the rest of the twentieth century and into the early 2000s.

Eastern religion, cults, and communes

Spiritual seekers who did not feel comfortable with conventional (or unconventional) Christian, Catholic, or Jewish practices found many alternatives in the 1960s, from established religions imported from other cultures to strange invented religions cobbled together by opportunistic hucksters. Numbers of Americans were drawn to Eastern religions imported from China and India, such as Tibetan Buddhism and Zen Buddhism. Religious teachers from these countries traveled to the United States to help people understand their practices, and a number of books were published that explained aspects of Buddhism, such as reincarnation and meditation. The most famous teacher, or guru, of the era was Maharishi Mahesh Yogi (1911–), the promoter of transcendental meditation, a practice from the Hindu religion that is intended to bring inward enlightenment through a particular technique of quiet contemplation. Maharishi first came to the United States in 1959 and then conducted a world tour in 1967, when he spoke at major American universities such as Yale and the University of California at Berkeley. By the late 1960s Maharishi had gained a following among celebrities such as the Beatles, Jane Fonda, Mia Farrow, philosopher Marshall McLuhan, and football star Joe Namath. Maharishi's books sold thousands of copies, and many people attended seminars to learn to his meditation style.

The Hindu religious teacher, Swami Bhaktivedanta Prabhupada (1896–1977), was responsible for starting perhaps the highest-profile religious cult of the 1960s. Bhaktivedanta settled in New York City in 1965, when he was sixty-nine years old, and he set about to teach young hippies

A group of Hare Krishnas plays music on Hollywood Boulevard in Los Angeles, California, 1969.

© JP Laffont/Sygma/Corbis.

how to devote themselves to the Hindu god Krishna. Hare Krishnas, as followers of Krishna were known, were very disciplined: they renounced many forms of worldly pleasures, including drugs, alcohol, gambling, and recreational sex. In fact, they devoted themselves entirely to the improvement of Krishna consciousness, their religious enlightenment. Hare Krishnas came to widespread attention in the late 1960s and early 1970s when they began to proselytize, which means to attempt to persuade others to convert to their beliefs, and ask for money as donations in airports, bus stations, and on street corners. With their shaved heads and saffron-colored robes, the Hare Krishnas were the decade's most obvious symbol of the growing popularity of Eastern religion.

Many of the unorthodox religious subgroups that formed in the decade bore no relation to historical religious practices. For example, L. Ron Hubbard (1911–1986) established the Church of Scientology in 1954 to practice a religion that he had created from fragments of Eastern religion,

The "God Is Dead" Movement

Scientific advances—such as the theory of human evolution, which was first put forth by Charles Darwin in the mid-1800s, and the "big bang" theory regarding the creation of the universe, which emerged in the 1910s—had been calling into question many of the fundamental teachings of established religions. By the 1960s, some religious thinkers, or theologians, wondered whether the concept of a supernatural God was useful in understanding the world around them. Books such as Gabriel Vahanian's *The Death of God: The Culture of Our Post-Christian Era* (1961) and Thomas J. J. Altizer's *The Gospel of Christian Atheism* (1966) asked readers to consider a religious life divorced from traditional conceptions of God. These ideas reached a mass audience in 1965 when *Time* magazine published a cover story on the "God Is Dead" movement and other mass media outlets followed suit.

The entire issue proved far overblown: the questioning of God was never a widespread movement but rather a reflection of the work of a few religious intellectuals. Most churchgoers rejected any idea that God might be dead, as reflected by the widely quoted data that 90 percent of Americans believed in God. A popular bumper sticker of the time read: "My God is not dead. I talked with Him this morning."

modern psychology, and his own science-fiction writing. The church aggressively recruited new members, who paid steep fees to be brought to enlightenment. Many outside observers charged that Scientology is a cult that enriches its leaders at the expense of gullible or easily manipulated members. Cult Awareness Network director Cynthia Kisser told *Time* magazine report Richard Behar, "Scientology is quite likely the most ruthless, the most classically terroristic, the most litigious and the most lucrative cult the country has ever seen."

Along with these organized and systematic religious organizations, Americans also participated in many less formal spiritual experiences and groups. Many rejected organized religion altogether, engaging instead in self-guided spiritual explorations. Some self-help books with spiritual themes and unconventional mentors and gurus offered advice for such individuals, participants in the classic American quest for self-knowledge. Sometimes these seekers found their way into communes (self-contained communities where work and many other experiences are shared by members), some of

12 Sports and the Changing Tides of American Culture in the 1960s

The 1960s had its share of thrilling athletic events, fiercely contested rivalries, dominant teams, and inspiring sports heroes. The Green Bay Packers, the Boston Celtics, and the New York Yankees dominated professional football, basketball, and baseball, respectively. Yet the decade also saw upstart teams such as baseball's New York Mets and football's New York Jets produce dramatic championship seasons. Long-standing records were shattered in major league baseball, as Roger Maris hit sixty-one home runs in 1961, and Maury Wills stole 104 bases in 1962. College football and basketball remained tremendously popular sports. In 1968 alone, three football teams—the University of Texas, Ohio State University, and Penn State University—all compiled undefeated records. In college basketball, coach John Wooden's University of California, Los Angeles (UCLA) Bruins were kings of the court, winning ten national championships between 1964 and 1975. Athletes and teams in many other sports pushed the boundaries of their field, thrilling fans with their prowess.

Obviously, there are great stories to be told about sports in the 1960s. Yet it was not the athletic contests themselves that defined the changing nature of sports in the 1960s, but rather the way that developments in sports reflected the pressing societal issues of the era, from Cold War politics to civil rights to the widespread commercialization of culture. This chapter discusses the way American sports participated in the sweeping social changes that characterized the decade.

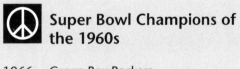

Super Bowl Champions of the 1960s

1966	Green Bay Packers
1967	Green Bay Packers
1968	New York Jets
1969	Kansas City Chiefs

Note: There was no Super Bowl before 1966, just a National Football League (NFL) champ and a American Football League (AFL) champ.

The power of money

Throughout the first half of the twentieth century, amateur sports had been heralded as the ideal form of athletic competition. Amateur sports, it was believed, were pure. Athletes competed for the glory of the game, not for money. They dedicated themselves to the glory of their college or, in the case of the Olympic Games, their nation. Though professional sports had a following—especially professional baseball—paid athletes were generally not held in the same positive light as their amateur counterparts, for it was thought that they were corrupted by their desire for money. But the innocence of the amateur athletic ideal was undermined by commercial pressures during the 1960s.

For more than fifty years, college sports had been the most popular form of athletic entertainment, with allegiances to teams formed on a local or regional basis. Fans supported their local colleges and universities, even if they had not attended those schools themselves, and children grew up wanting to play for school teams near their homes. But television widened fans' local loyalty in college sports. Infusing millions of dollars into university athletic departments and reshaping the way athletics were presented, television networks turned college sports into a big business.

Beginning in the late 1950s and early 1960s, television networks signed contracts to televise college sporting events. Wanting to show fans the best games, they tended to focus on the teams with winning records or large numbers of fans. These teams received additional revenues, and their

World Series Champs of the 1960s

1960	Pittsburgh Pirates
1961	New York Yankees
1962	New York Yankees
1963	Los Angeles Dodgers
1964	St. Louis Cardinals
1965	Los Angeles Dodgers
1966	Baltimore Orioles
1967	St. Louis Cardinals
1968	Detroit Tigers
1969	New York Mets

coaches could develop recruiting networks that fanned out across the nation in search of the best players. Winning schools got more money from television networks, and the richer the school, the better it was able to compete for the best talent. Thus money drove the competition for players to an extreme, as the best programs in college sports competed not only to win games but also to recruit players. It was a vicious cycle that some say thoroughly corrupted college sports, making student athletes into semi-professional players, and making college leagues into a system that prepared players for eventual participation in professional sports, much like the farm system in major league baseball.

Though some regretted the impact of big money on college sports, no one could deny that television was an important way to capture the excitement of college sports such as football and basketball. Sports historians Randy Roberts and James S. Olson point to the introduction of the slow-motion instant replay as one of the factors that made televised sports so exciting. Television cameras could sort through the tangle of twenty-two players on a football field, for example, to zoom in on the key block that allowed the runner to break through. Television cameras could also roam the sidelines, bringing close-ups of player reactions and in-depth interviews. Television made the game seem more vital and exciting, and it made celebrities of the most notable coaches and players.

Sports celebrities

Even before the 1950s, media coverage of athletes had the effect of making heroes, but the nature of the sports hero changed in important ways in the 1950s and 1960s. In the early parts of the century, sports heroes tended to be presented in a positive, one-dimensional light. Radio stories, newspapers, and newsreels (short features shown in theaters

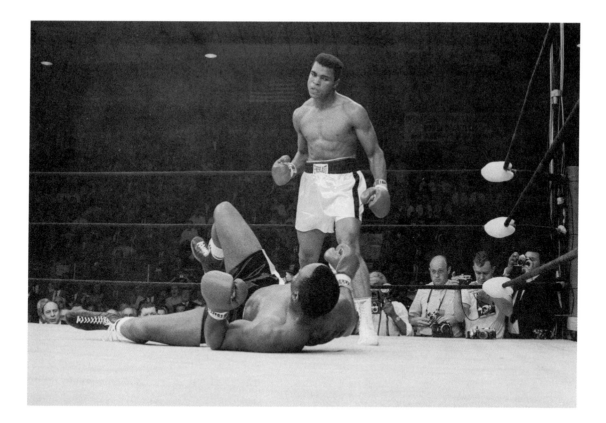

before a full-length film or between two full-length films) stressed only the achievements of athletes and offered fans only a look at the most positive elements of an athlete's personality. Fans did not learn about the personal troubles or political opinions of their idols; in fact, nobody even dreamed that sports figures had political opinions. Such coverage allowed athletes with very troubled lives—such as baseball players Babe Ruth, who drank heavily, and Ty Cobb, who got into vicious fist fights—to be widely perceived as both champions and role models. But the growth of feature-length magazine articles about sports figures in magazines such as *Sports Illustrated* (launched in 1954) and the popularity of televised sports began to change the way Americans came to know their heroes. These new media gave fans an intimate look into the lives of famous athletes, oftentimes exposing their failings and problems. Media coverage of sports heroes in the 1960s did not go as far as it did in the early 2000s—when practically every misstep of athletes was reported—but

Heavyweight boxing champion Cassius Clay stands over his opponent, Sonny Liston, in 1964. The next day, Clay changed his name to Cassius X. Soon after, he changed his name to Muhammad Ali, in recognition of his acceptance of the Muslim religion. *© Bettmann/Corbis.*

Joe Namath was one of the most famous faces in professional football in the 1960s. *AP/Wide World Photos. Reproduced by permission.*

it did remove from athletes the image of perfection they once enjoyed.

Increased television coverage of sports gave athletes a platform on which they could announce their views and opinions. Several of the most famous athletes of the era took advantage of the presence of microphones in pre-event or post-event media coverage. Boxer Cassius Clay (1942–), for example, used the media to intimidate his opponents. Before fighting Sonny Liston in 1964, Clay boasted in verse, as quoted in John Tessitore's *Muhammad Ali: The World's Champion*: "Float like a butterfly. Sting like a bee. Your hands can't hit what your eyes can't see." When Clay's victory made him the heavyweight champion, coverage of his poetic pronouncements only grew. The day after the fight, Clay announced that he was dropping his last name in favor of the letter X, thereby renouncing the name he had inherited from those who had once owned his slave ancestors. Soon after, he changed his name to Muhammad Ali, in recognition of his acceptance of the Muslim religion. He proclaimed to reporters: "I am America. I am the part you won't recognize, but get used to me. Black, confident, cocky—my name, not yours. My religion, not yours. My goals, my own. Get used to me." America not only got used to Ali—who reigned on and off as boxing champion through the 1970s—but they grew to love the smart, boastful boxer who promoted racial advancement alongside his own career.

Professional football provided two of the decade's brightest celebrities, and the two were a study in contrasts. Vince Lombardi (1913–1970), who coached the Green Bay Packers for most of the decade, led his football team to National Football Conference championships in 1961, 1962, 1965, and 1966; in 1967 they won the first-ever Super Bowl. Lombardi was a throwback to the old school of coaching: he hammered his players into learning the fundamental skills and he stressed hard work and execution over fancy plays.

He was revered by many who distrusted the permissive, anything-goes spirit of the 1960s that allowed men to wear long hair and do things like smoke marijuana. Sportswriters liked reprinting his many pronouncements about winning football and building men, but he disclaimed credit for the most famous quote attributed to him: "Winning isn't everything, it's the only thing." By contrast to Lombardi, Joe Namath (1943–), a flashy quarterback who had played college football at the University of Alabama before taking charge of the upstart New York Jets of the American Football Conference, was a notorious womanizer and heavy drinker. Namath defined the brash, devil-may-care attitude that typified a new generation of sports stars. He achieved his greatest fame in 1969 when he predicted that his Jets would upset the Baltimore Colts in the Super Bowl and then followed through by leading his team to a stunning victory.

Billie Jean King dominated the tennis world in the 1960s by winning three straight singles championships at Wimbledon. *AP/Wide World Photos. Reproduced by permission.*

There were many other sports heroes during the 1960s—including baseball stars Sandy Koufax, Mickey Mantle, and Frank Robinson; basketball stars Wilt Chamberlain, Bill Russell, and Lew Alcindor (later known as Kareem Abdul Jabbar); golfers Arnold Palmer and Jack Nicklaus; tennis player Billie Jean King; and numerous others. Thanks to TV and magazines, fans came to know these people who gained the status of movie stars. In the years that followed, press coverage of sports went further into the athletes' private lives, so that by the 1990s few details of an athlete's life remained free of media attention. This publicity brought media-savvy stars great wealth, but it also subjected them to great pressures.

Politics, race, and sports

Some of the most pressing political issues of the 1960s affected the world of sports. Perhaps most pressing was the in-

National Basketball Association Champions of the 1960s

1959-60	Boston Celtics
1960-61	Boston Celtics
1961-62	Boston Celtics
1962-63	Boston Celtics
1963-64	Boston Celtics
1964-65	Boston Celtics
1965-66	Boston Celtics
1966-67	Philadelphia 76ers
1967-68	Boston Celtics
1968-69	Boston Celtics
1969-70	New York Knicks

fluence of the civil rights movement. African Americans had long asserted their equality with whites, and in many cases athletic contests provided an even playing field on which African Americans could prove their case. By the 1960s all of professional and most of college sports were integrated, which meant that black players played on the same teams along with whites. That integration was not yet complete, however. For example, until the late 1960s, racist attitudes kept African American athletes from playing the key positions in football—quarterback and middle linebacker. In 1967 when Bill Russell of the Boston Celtics became the first African American to coach a pro basketball team, few blacks occupied coaching positions and none owned a professional team.

In college basketball, the Southeastern Conference (SEC) remained rigidly segregated through the mid-1960s. SEC teams even refused to play opponents with black players until 1963. In 1966 the whites-only policy was given a decisive test. The undefeated and all-white University of Kentucky basketball team played in the national championship game against the mostly black Texas Western University. The smaller, younger TWU team defeated the powerful Kentucky team with a final score of 72 to 65. Within a few years Kentucky had recruited its first black player, which ended segregation on the Kentucky basketball team.

By the mid-1960s it was no longer rational to deny black equality in athletics. A number of black athletes used the fame they acquired through sports to advance the cause of all African Americans. Boxer Muhammad Ali was perhaps the most vocal champion of black civil rights. In fact, he went ever further in protesting American involvement in the Vietnam War (1954–75) by refusing to be drafted. According to Tessitore, Ali claimed that black people had "no quarrel with the Vietcong," the Vietnamese guerrilla soldiers who fought against the United States. Other black players supported civil rights causes in less vocal ways.

One of the most dramatic statements of support for black civil rights came in the 1968 Olympic Games, held in Mexico City, Mexico. American sprinters Tommie Smith and John Carlos finished first and third, respectively, in the 200-meter dash. When they stepped on the awards podium to accept their medals, the two black athletes bowed their heads and raised their gloved fists in the air in a dramatic salute to "black power," a radical wing of the civil rights movement. Their statement was seen on televisions around the world, and many Americans were embarrassed that their "race problem" had been broadcast to the world. International Olympic Committee chairman Avery Brundage stripped the sprinters of their medals, but the point was made.

In 1967, Bill Russell, right, became the first African American to coach a pro basketball team. *AP/Wide World Photos. Reproduced by permission.*

Politics of another sort crept into the Olympic Games held in 1960, 1964, and 1968: Cold War politics. Ever since the end of World War II (1939–45), the United States and the Soviet Union had been in a pitched battle to establish the dominance of their opposed political and economic systems, American democracy vs. Soviet communism. In each of the Olympic Games staged in the 1960s, the Americans and Soviets used the performance of their athletes as a scorecard for their political contest. Broadcasters in both countries kept close track of the medals won by their respective countries. In both 1960 and 1964, Soviet athletes dominated both the summer and winter competitions. Americans soon complained that the Soviets had cheated. They pointed to the fact that Soviet athletes were paid by the state to compete, which made Soviet athletes professionals, whereas American athletes were not paid and thus were truly amateurs. They also complained that Soviet athletes were turned into athlet-

American sprinters Tommie Smith, center, and John Carlos, right, standing on the awards podium with their fists in the air as a salute to black power during the 1968 Olympic Games. *AP/Wide World Photos. Reproduced by permission.*

ic machines with performance-enhancing drugs. Critics pointed to spectacular gains made by Soviet weightlifters and to the fact that Soviet women had begun to appear distinctly masculine. One drug test revealed that these female athletes had a genetic makeup that did not quite classify them as female; a Hungarian doctor called them "genetic mosaics." By the 1968 summer games, more careful drug testing and superior athletes allowed the Americans to overtake the Soviet

Union for the first time, with 107 total U.S. medals to the Soviet Union's 91.

Each side used the publicity surrounding the Olympic competitions to point out the failures of the other's political system. The Soviet Union, for example, openly criticized the United States for the slow progress that it was making on granting civil rights to its people. The United States countered these embarrassing statements by making public the inferior living standards and restrictive social system of communist countries.

For More Information

Books

Farber, David, and Beth Bailey, with others. *The Columbia Guide to America in the 1960s.* New York: Columbia University Press, 2001.

Fitzpatrick, Frank. *And the Walls Game Tumbling Down: Kentucky, Texas Western, and the Game that Changed American Sports.* New York: Simon & Schuster, 1999.

Jay, Kathryn. *More than just a Game: Sports in American Life since 1945.* New York: Columbia University Press, 2004.

Ritter, Lawrence. *The Story of Baseball.* Rev. ed. New York: Morrow Junior Books, 1999.

Roberts, Randy, and James S. Olson. *Winning Is the Only Thing: Sports in America since 1945.* Baltimore, MD: Johns Hopkins University Press, 1989.

Sanford, William R. *Joe Namath.* New York: Crestwood House, 1993.

Stewart, Mark. *Basketball: A History of Hoops.* New York: Franklin Watts, 1998.

Stewart, Mark. *Football: A History of the Gridiron Game.* New York: Franklin Watts, 1998.

Tessitore, John. *Muhammad Ali: The World's Champion.* New York: Franklin Watts, 1998.

Web sites

Olympic Games. http://www.olympic.org/uk/games/index_uk.asp (accessed on June 25, 2004).

Wide World of Sports Highlights–1960s. http://espn.go.com/abcsports/wwos/milestones/1960s.html (accessed on June 25, 2004).

The Arts in 1960s America

13

The arts—literature, art, dance, and theater—went through a fascinating period of growth and change during the 1960s. New, experimental art forms like pop art and happenings drew new public attention to artistic expression. Literary artists challenged traditional ideas about fiction and poetry. Increased financial support from government as well as private donors opened new museums and regional theaters and helped art exhibitions and dance and musical performances tour the country. The increased publicity of art, theater, dance, and music brought larger audiences to museums and performances than ever before. Young people were especially encouraged to develop their own artistic talents during the 1960s in the workshops, dance schools, and regional theaters that multiplied throughout the country.

Trends in the arts reflected both the turbulent social and political trends of the time and the influence of artists and writers of an earlier generation. By the 1960s, America had been involved in some sort of military conflict for nearly three decades. World War II (1939–45), the Cold War (1945–91), the Korean War (1950–53), and the Vietnam War (1954–75) all had an impact on the way Americans perceived the world, and American writers especially paid attention to the impact of these wars on people's feelings and thoughts. The civil rights movement and the sexual revolution helped to expand participation in the arts, as growing numbers of African Americans and women contributed to artistic production. These new participants brought fresh insights to the art they practiced. Finally, growing commercialism in American society had a deep impact on the arts. Rising prosperity increased audiences for the arts, and widespread television ownership meant that televised productions could be seen by a national audience. But many artists believed that the heightened concern for consumer goods deadened the soul, and they used their art to question and criticize American consumerism.

Experimenting with style and form

More so than ever, artists in the 1960s experimented with new styles and forms. Some used imagery that commented on America's affluent commercial lifestyles. Others developed art that rejected U.S. commercialization. From these artistic experiments there arose several distinctive art movements during the 1960s. The most important were pop art, minimalism, and conceptual art. Photography also developed as a fine art during this time.

Artists noticed that American culture was filled with commercial images: on television and billboards, and in magazines and newspapers, commercial art was used to sell everything from dish scrubbers to soup cans to cars to movie stars and their movies. Pop artists used commercial art techniques to create new artistic forms. At first pop art was called "new realism," because it depicted real-life objects. The best-known pop artist was Andy Warhol (1928–1987). Warhol became famous when he exhibited a series of stylized paintings of Campbell's soup cans. Later, he produced silk-screen pictures of celebrities' faces, including actress Marilyn Monroe (1926–1962) and rock star Elvis Presley (1935–1977). Roy Lichtenstein (1923–1997) became famous for his huge canvases depicting scenes from comic strips. These paintings emphasized the small dots of color that make color by seeming to blend together in the small print of a newspaper page. The works of

Roy Lichtenstein's comic strip art is featured in "Kiss II" from 1962. *AP/Wide World Photos. Reproduced by permission.*

both Warhol and Lichtenstein were widely reproduced in the 1960s, and they forced viewers to consider the fine line that exists (or maybe does not exist) between art and commercial design.

Pop art took many other forms as well. Artist Claes Oldenburg (1929–) turned his New York studio into "The Store" in 1961 when he recreated a neighborhood of small shops with familiar objects made out of plaster. Visitors interacted with the shops and "The Store" became a powerful comment on American consumption. "The Store" was an artistic presentation called a "happening" (see sidebar). By the mid-1960s, Oldenburg and Coosje van Bruggen (1942–) collaborated to create colossal sculptures for several cities; the first was *Lipstick (Ascending) on Caterpillar Tracks*, a twenty-three-foot-tall lipstick mounted on caterpillar tracks (the tracks of a construction vehicle), installed at Yale University in 1969.

Minimalism, another important style of the 1960s, reduced art to simple geometric shapes of uniform color. The style was pioneered by Frank Stella (1936–) with his pin-stripe paintings of 1959 and came to stress form and material. Artists such as Carl Andre (1935–), Donald Judd (1928–), and Robert Morris (1931–) first used the style in sculpture, creating enormous geometric shapes in single, uniform colors. Morris's first minimalist exhibitions, which occurred in 1964 and 1965 in New York City, featured rooms filled with simple wooden boxes. Minimalism was the direct opposite of the abstract expressionism of the 1950s, which celebrated the artist's imagination and feelings with highly abstract images charged with emotional expression. Minimalist sculptures were often industrially fabricated and showed no sign of an artist's hand. Minimalism was not meant to represent anything other than the subject depicted—no emotion, no larger context. The style placed the substance of the art above the artist's skill. Although critics dismissed it as a technique that required no skill, minimalism became very popular during the 1960s.

Photography also developed as a form of fine art during the 1960s. Photographers, such as Diane Arbus (1923–1971) and Henri Cartier-Bresson (1908–), turned photographs of everyday life and portraits of everyday people into high art through their ability to compose their shots and to depict their subjects with compassion. Cartier-Bresson tried to capture what came to be called the "decisive moment" in his snapshots. The term "decisive moment" came from the American translation of his book *Images à la sauvette* in 1952. Taking pictures of everyday people on the streets of cities all over the world, Cartier-Bresson elevated snapshot photography to fine art. During the 1960s, his pictures graced the pages of *Life* magazine, among others, and he also produced documentaries for CBS News. Arbus's portraits of

In 2003 Robert Smithson's *Spiral Jetty,* which was created in Utah's Great Salt Lake more than thirty years earlier, was exposed due to drought conditions. *AP/Wide World Photos. Reproduced by permission.*

children, couples, carnival people, and celebrities revolutionized portrait photography, and she taught her documentary photographic techniques at some of the best art schools in the United States, including Parsons School of Design in New York, from the late 1960s until she ended her life.

By the end of the 1960s, a new trend called conceptual art drew attention not to the artwork itself but to the process by which artists made their work or the ideas behind their work. Conceptual art was one of the most challenging art forms of the period, for it questioned the right of the art establishment—especially wealthy art collectors, gallery owners, and museum curators (people who oversee museum collections)—to define art. Part of the motivation behind conceptual art was political. Inspired by the advances of the civil rights movement and the women's movement, African American and women artists found their work excluded from conventional art museums and galleries. One of the responses of such artists, and the many who sympathized with them, was to take art out of the galleries and into the streets and minds of the people. Conceptual artists displayed unfinished art works, ideas for art works, and live performances that could not be repeated. Critics complained that there were no standards by which to judge such works, but defenders answered that this was the point. From these concerns other intellectual art styles developed. Some examples are Robert Morris's piles of rocks and dirt and Robert Smithson's (1938–1973) *Spiral Jetty* (1970), a 1,500-foot-long mound of earth spiraling into Utah's Great Salt Lake.

The innovative art movements of the decade forever changed the boundaries between fine art and popular art. No longer was a small group of wealthy art critics and collectors the sole judge of artistic merit. The new art styles enabled fine and popular art forms to merge and judged the work of non-elite groups, such as minorities and women, valuable. The fact that art forms could exist only for a short time or were seen only by small audiences gave popular opinion more authority in the art world, and the role of popular opinion continued to expand throughout the end of the twentieth century and into the early 2000s.

Literature of the 1960s

Literature and poetry went through dramatic changes during the 1960s. Early in the decade some of America's most celebrated and influential writers died, including e.e. cummings, William Faulkner, Robert Frost, and Ernest Hemingway. After the deaths of these established figures, younger writers began experimenting with new styles. The new styles reflected writers' desires to capture the atmosphere of the

Art Happenings

In 1959 New York artist Allan Kaprow (1927–) began a trend for artistic presentations called happenings. Happenings invited visitors into a theatrical set in which they interacted with the art; visitors might encounter sculpture, music, theatrical drama, and other artistic forms. Though happenings seemed spontaneous to visitors and were often unpredictable, they were in fact complicated, tightly coordinated events. Unlike regular exhibitions, at which visitors would just view completed pictures or sculpture, happenings enabled visitors to participate in art. Some of them were described as "living sculptures."

The term "happening" came from Kaprow's first event, called *18 Happenings in 6 Parts*, held in 1959 at the Reuben Gallery in New York. For the event, Kaprow set up clear plastic walls to divide the gallery into three rooms. Using strictly choreographed movements, performers offered visitors tickets to the event, directed them to specified seats in particular rooms, and at designated times guided them to another room. In the rooms, visitors viewed a performer squeezing oranges, a person lighting matches, an artist painting, and a group of performers playing toy instruments, among other things. Kaprow's other happenings included *Coca Cola, Shirley Cannonball?* (1960), in which visitors watched an enormous cardboard boot kicking a ball in a gym to the beat of a fife and drum; *Words* (1962), an event offering visitors the chance to rearrange words painted on cardboard on the wall of a gallery; and *Push and Pull: A Furniture Comedy for Hans Hofmann* (1963), which offered visitors the opportunity to rearrange the furniture in two rooms. Other artists who created happenings included Robert Rauschenberg (1925–), Claes Oldenburg (1929–), and Jim Dine (1935–).

Most happenings occurred in art galleries. Some, however, were set out of doors, at artists' studios, in empty lots, or at train stations, among other places. The goal of happenings was to offer visitors the opportunity to question the distinction between types of art and its place in public life. Happenings peaked in popularity in the early 1960s. Although many of the happening artists returned to more traditional forms of artistic expression, their work gave rise to performance art. Performance art came to be a distinctive form of live artistic presentation that could include painting, dance, song, poetry, and other artistic expression. It was distinct from theater, as were happenings, because performance art did not include characters or plot. Both happenings and performance art were considered to be "pure" art because neither could be purchased or traded; they could only be experienced.

changing times. Writers used absurd elements, black comedy, and personal memoirs in their literary experiments. Thomas Pynchon (1937–) experimented with the narrative form of the novel itself. In his novel *V* (1963), Pynchon presented a nonlinear story in which he used descriptive "snapshots" taken between 1898 and 1944 from the lives of the novel's many characters to create a multidimensional image of society. Authors Joseph Heller (1923–1999) and Kurt Vonnegut (1922–) depicted the horror and dehumanization of World War II through parody or black comedy, which treats with humor subjects that are not really funny. In his novel *Catch-22* (1961), Heller used a satiric writing style and the character of Yossarian to criticize medicine, business, religion, government, and the military. In *Slaughterhouse-Five* (1966), Vonnegut used the absurd, or non-rational, to highlight the randomness of war; his character Billy Pilgrim survives the dangers of World War II only to be captured by aliens and taken away in a flying saucer.

Along with experiments in style, literature opened to a wide range of topics. The variety of topics resulted in part from eased censorship rules and an increase in the number of minority and women writers. Tom Wolfe's (1931–) *The Kandy-Kolored Tangerine-Flake Streamline Baby* (1965) shocked some and thrilled others with its use of once-censored language and depictions of the period's psychedelic lifestyles. Two Pulitzer Prize-winning novels of the decade depicted the experiences of ethnic and racial minorities. Shirley Ann Grau's (1929–) *The Keepers of the House,* which won the Pulitzer in 1965, portrayed the social and political struggles of a southern family with a background of interracial marriage; and N. Scott Momaday's (1934–) *House Made of Dawn,* which won the Pulitzer in 1969, told the story of a young Native American man as he tries to reconcile the differences between white society and that of his ancestors. Women writers, including Anne Sexton and Sylvia Plath, wrote powerful poems about the female experience.

In addition, the Black Arts Movement (BAM) of the mid- to late 1960s ushered in a host of works by African Americans; among the most influential were LeRoi Jones (later called Imamu Amiri Baraka), Ed Bullins, Nikki Giovanni, Adrienne Kennedy, and Larry Neal. This movement combined the art of writing with the political purposes of the civil

Playwright LeRoi Jones walks with his wife, Sylvia, and their son as they head for court in conjunction with charges brought against him during the 1967 New Jersey riots. © Bettmann/Corbis.

rights movement. Black artists used their literature and art to lift up and inspire other blacks. The works of many involved in the Black Arts Movement were a new foundation upon which blacks could build a society centered on their unique culture and heritage. Although the BAM dissolved by the 1970s, African Americans continued to produce valuable literary and artistic works throughout the twentieth century and into the 2000s.

On the American stage

On Broadway, the center for mainstream American theater, little changed during the 1960s. Broadway is a street in New York City where America's most influential theaters are located and the term "Broadway" refers to theater productions performed in the theaters on this street. Traditional musicals, including *Hello Dolly!* (1964) and *Fiddler on the Roof* (1964), attracted large audiences. Satirist and playwright Neil Simon (1927–) began a career that was to make him one of America's most successful playwrights with hits during the decade. His mainstream plays *The Odd Couple* (1965), *Sweet Charity* (1966), and *Plaza Suite* (1968) offered audiences humorous peeks into modern, urban lifestyles. But while traditional theater brought in large profits, experimental theater offered audiences unexpected views of life. These new plays were were referred to as "off Broadway" because they were produced in theaters, cafes, or other locations outside the Broadway district and because of the experimental nature of their content.

Developing rapidly during the 1960s, experimental theater shunned traditional theatrical realism that relied heavily on dialogue. The new theatrical forms used surreal— or distorted—imagery, nonverbal sounds, and choreographed—or planned—movements to shape their stories. Theater became increasingly political during the decade, with plays helping to define or interpret the political agendas of ethnic and sexual minorities and women. The playwright David Rabe (1940–) introduced his Vietnam Trilogy that deals with the brutality of war and racial issues. Other playwrights also used the theater to comment on pressing political situations of the decade, such as civil rights and women's equality. For their new theater, playwrights avoided traditional theaters, and instead staged their first performances in small New York cafes.

One of the decade's best new playwrights was Sam Shepard (1943–), who emerged as a great talent during the 1960s with plays that explored the changes occurring in many of America's traditional ways of life, including changes in the Old West and the infiltration of rock 'n' roll music into American culture. Shepard was especially successful producing plays in small theaters. African Americans joined the wave of new experimental theater. Playwrights such as LeRoi Jones (1934–; later known as Imamu Amiri Baraka) brought the politics of racial discrimination to the stage in such plays as *The Toilet* (1965), in which high school boys' bigotry is revealed in a fight in the boys' restroom, and *The Slave* (1966), which features a race riot as a backdrop to a black man's search for personal vengeance against his former white wife who is now married to another man. By the end of the 1960s several theaters featuring the works of African Americans had become established, including the Free Southern Theater, which celebrated the black culture that developed in the South, and the Black Arts Repertory Theatre in Harlem, New York, which concentrated on black experiences.

Musical theater developed during the decade to include a new influential form: the rock musicals *Hair* and *Jesus Christ Superstar* were two of the most influential. *Hair*, which debuted in 1967, presented a view of the lifestyles of hippies, or those who dropped out of mainstream society, and commented on the growing conflicted feelings toward the war in Vietnam in the late 1960s. *Hair* shocked audiences with its controversial political positions, language, and onstage nudity. The trend started by *Hair* was continued by *Jesus Christ Superstar*, which premiered in 1971. *Jesus Christ Superstar* chronicled the last seven days in the life of Jesus of Nazareth as seen through the eyes of his disillusioned disciple, Judas Iscariot. Believing Jesus to be only a mortal man, Judas grows frustrat-

The rock opera *Hair,* as performed here in 1968, shocked audiences with its controversial political positions, language, and onstage nudity. *AP/Wide World Photos. Reproduced by permission.*

ed as Jesus' followers begin hailing him as a god. Judas determines that Jesus must be stopped and gives authorities information leading to the capture of Jesus. Judas quickly realizes that his actions will make Jesus a martyr and hangs himself. Despite criticism from some religious groups, *Jesus Christ Superstar* became a huge box-office hit. It ran for 720 performances on Broadway and later was made into a film.

New money for art

Since the early years of the United States, state and federal government officials and others had occasionally proposed legislation to support the arts. In 1913 a federal charter incorporated the National Institute of Arts and Letters, and in 1916 the American Academy of Arts and Letters was incorporated to support artistic endeavors. During the administration of President Franklin D. Roosevelt in the 1930s, the federal government even employed 40,000 artists.

In the 1960s, major strides were made in arts funding. The National Foundation on the Arts and Humanities Act of 1965 established the National Endowment for the Arts. As a public agency, the National Endowment for the Arts assisted the growth and development of art in America via monetary grants. The president appointed and the Senate approved advisors to the endowment, all of whom were chosen for their expertise in a particular field of the arts or humanities. The endowment's first grant was presented to the American Ballet Theater in 1966. The $100,000 grant brought the Theater back from financial doom. Throughout the decade and afterward, the endowment sought out opportunities to support the arts with federal grants while also encouraging private funding of the arts. Recipients of federal grants during the 1960s include regional dance companies, museums (for the purchase of works by living artists), artists such as Alexander Calder (1898–1976), who erected a sculpture in Grand Rapids, Michigan, in 1968, and Isamu Noguchi (1904–1988), whose sculpture entitled *Black Sun* was dedicated in Seattle, Washington, in 1969. In the early 2000s, the endowment continued to enrich the lives of Americans by supporting the development of the arts and humanities.

A scene from a 1968 New York City Ballet production featuring Patricia McBride and Edward Villella.
AP/Wide World Photos. Reproduced by permission.

The increase in public funding of artistic work especially influenced the development of dance in America. Classical, modern, and ethnic dance troupes received money to develop and present their art. With large grants from the National Endowment for the Arts, George Balanchine (1904–1983) created new ballets, developing the classical style at the American Ballet Theater in New York. Choreographer Jerome Robbins (1918–1998) of the New York City Ballet also benefited from public funds. Martha Graham (1894–1991), a pioneer of modern dance, received a grant to tour the country with her group. Through public funding, the Alvin Ailey American Dance Theater became the first black dance group to represent the United States abroad when it toured the Far East, Southeast Asia, and Australia as part of President John F. Kennedy's "President's Special International Program for Cultural Presentations" in 1962; it also made a ten-country African tour for the State Department in 1967.

The increase of public and private funding for artistic endeavors, the creation of new forms and settings for their art works by visual artists, the inclusion of ethnic and sexual minorities into all of the arts, and many other influences helped open the art world to a much broader audience than ever before. This legacy of the 1960s continued throughout the century and into the 2000s.

For More Information

Books

Archer, Jules. *The Incredible Sixties: The Stormy Years that Changed America*. San Diego, CA: Harcourt Brace Jovanovich, 1986.

Batchelor, David. *Minimalism*. New York: Cambridge University Press, 1997.

Farber, David. *The Age of Great Dreams: America in the 1960s*. New York: Hill and Wang, 1994.

Goldberg, RoseLee. *Performance: Live Art since 1960*. New York: Harry N. Abrams, 1998.

Holland, Gini. *The 1960s*. San Diego, CA: Lucent, 1999.

Mason, Paul. *Pop Artists*. Chicago, IL: Heinemann Library, 2003.

Miller, Denise, et al. *Photography's Multiple Roles: Art, Document, Market, Science*. New York: Museum of Contemporary Photography, Columbia College, 1998.

Reynolds, Nancy, and Malcolm McCormick. *No Fixed Points: Dance in the Twentieth Century*. New Haven, CT: Yale University Press, 2003.

Sandler, Irving. *Art of the Postmodern Era: From the Late 1960s to the Early 1990s*. New York: IconEditions, 1996.

Web sites

Hiltz, Virginia, and Mike Sell. "The Black Arts Movement." *University of Michigan*. www.umich.edu/~eng499/ (accessed on June 26, 2004).

The National Endowment for the Arts. www.arts.endow.gov/ (accessed on June 25, 2004).

Popular Entertainment: Escape and Engagement

14

In film and television it is hard to determine which movie or program best represents American popular culture in the 1960s. Television included such diverse programs as the popular western *Bonanza* (1959–73), with its depiction of life on a nineteenth-century cattle ranch and *The Smothers Brothers Comedy Hour* (1967–70), in which comedians Dick and Tom Smothers pushed the boundaries of social satire, sexual innuendo, and taste. Films of the decade included big-budget spectacles like *Lawrence of Arabia* (1962) and *Cleopatra* (1963), set in ancient times and featuring huge casts and lavish sets, and small independent movies such as *Easy Rider* (1969), which depicts two hippie rebels searching for freedom from the mainstream's restrictive rules as they motorcycle across America. Music was also diverse. It included the socially aware folk songs of Bob Dylan, the surf sounds of the Beach Boys, the romantic crooning of Frank Sinatra, and the late 1960s psychedelic rock of Jimi Hendrix. Even the popular music of the Beatles included very different songs, such as the early happy song "I Want to Hold Your Hand," and the angry later songs such as "Revolution" and "Helter Skelter."

Folk singer Bob Dylan (center) performs with Rick Danko (left) and The Band's Robbie Robertson (right) in a benefit tribute to folk singer-songwriter Woody Guthrie at Carnegie Hall in 1968. *AP/Wide World Photos. Reproduced by permission.*

The truth is, no single TV show, film, or song captured the spirit of the whole decade. In this period of political and social upheaval, American popular entertainment was a study in contrasts. To some extent, television, film, and music all engaged with the pressing issues of the day. In each of these media, there were performers and creators who were deeply engaged with such issues as the civil rights movement, the push to end American involvement in the war in Vietnam, or the quest for individual identity. These works or programs resonated with people who had similar concerns and thus they came to stand as symbols of the decade. In addition, there were a number of performers and producers whose sole intention was to entertain. Their creations, whether they were television programs, films, or songs, allowed viewers and listeners to escape to more lighthearted pleasures. Engaging with and helping people escape from the complex political and social issues of the day, American popular entertainment truly served the interests of all variety of Americans.

Television in the 1960s

By the beginning of the 1960s, television had become perhaps the single most important source of entertainment and news for Americans. It was estimated that in 1960 some 90 percent of American homes had at least one television set, up from 20 percent just ten years before. Though there were many televisions, there were not many TV channels. Most televisions only offered channels 2 through 13, and the three major television networks—ABC, CBS, and NBC—offered the vast majority of programming. TV viewers received their signal from a local broadcasting station, for there was not yet satellite or cable TV.

Critics complained that, with few exceptions, the programming offered on American television was junk. Federal Communications Commission (FCC) chairman Newton Minow (1926–), who took office in 1960 with the Kennedy administration, hoped to use the persuasive power of his position to convince broadcasters to create better programming. In a 1961 speech to broadcasters quoted in his book, *Abandoned in the Wasteland,* Minow proclaimed: "When television is good, nothing … is better. But when television is bad, nothing is worse. I invite you to sit down in front of your television set when your station goes on the air and stay there without a book, magazine, newspaper, profit-and-loss sheet or rating book to distract you—and keep your eyes glued to that set until the station signs off. I can assure you that you will observe a vast wasteland."

Minow's speech attracted much attention—especially his dramatic phrase "vast wasteland"—but it did little to change American television. For better or worse, American television was driven by commercial concerns. Programming was paid for by advertising, and advertisers knew the kinds of programs they preferred: safe, family-oriented shows that would draw the largest audience and offend no one. Increasingly, advertisers and programmers used a rating system devised by Arthur Neilsen to measure which shows people preferred to watch and thus which shows advertisers wanted their ads to appear on. Over time, Nielsen ratings became the standard measure of a show's success.

Driven by ratings and by the needs of advertisers, the networks gave people what they seemed to want: Westerns,

In the 1960s television show *Bewitched* (starring Dick York and Elizabeth Montgomery), a young woman, who happens to be a witch, tries to be an idealized homemaker. Hip and savvy, she frequently uses her special "powers" to help her husband out of a jam with his boss or with his wicked mother-in-law. *AP/Wide World Photos. Reproduced by permission.*

family-based situation comedies, game shows, variety shows, and all manner of light, unchallenging entertainment. In addition to the shows mentioned in the sidebar, popular programs from the decade included one about a talking horse (*Mister Ed*), a beautiful young witch trying to live a normal human life (*Bewitched*), a friendly dolphin (*Flipper*), and seven stranded castaways on an uncharted desert isle (*Gilligan's Island*), among many others. Children were bombarded with cartoons on Saturday mornings, and housewives enjoyed daytime talk shows and soap operas. Not until the late 1960s did Americans begin to experience more diversity in their programming. In 1967 President Lyndon B. Johnson (1908–1973; served 1963–69) introduced the Public Broadcasting System, giving Americans a real alternative to commercial television programming. Also, networks began to introduce somewhat more imaginative and daring programming, encouraged as they were by the success of the racy, political content in the *Smothers Brothers Comedy Hour* and *Rowan and Martin's Laugh-In.*

☮ The Most Popular TV Shows of the 1960s

A sampling of the most popular television shows from 1961, 1965, and 1969 reveals a great deal about America's viewing preferences. First, Americans loved Westerns: *Gunsmoke* was the top-rated show in 1961, followed by *Wagon Train* and *Have Gun Will Travel; Bonanza* took top billing in 1965 and remained near the top for nearly ten years; in 1969, both *Bonanza* and *Gunsmoke* were among the top six shows. These shows were not mere fluff, as some have complained of television in the 1960s. These Westerns dealt with moral issues. Because the shows were set well in the American past, producers and writers could probe such issues without coming too close to the troubling political issues of the day.

Also popular were family-based situation comedies. *The Andy Griffith Show*, its spinoff *Gomer Pyle (U.S.M.C.)*, *The Real McCoys, I Love Lucy, The Dick Van Dyke Show, Mayberry R.F.D., Peyton Place II, Family Affair,* and *The Beverly Hillbillies* all occupied spots in the top ten during the decade.

Ranging from sincere shows illustrating moral lessons (*The Real McCoys*) to the sheer goofiness of a suddenly wealthy family of hillbillies adjusting to their new life in Beverly Hills (*The Beverly Hillbillies*), such shows stayed well away from the serious issues of the day and were great favorites of advertisers.

There was life in TV beyond situation comedies and Westerns. Variety shows sometimes cracked the top ten in ratings, with *The Red Skelton Hour* reaching sixth in 1965 and *Rowan and Martin's Laugh-In* taking the top spot in 1969. These shows combined comedy, music, and improvisational skits. Another favorite of the era was crime dramas; *The Untouchables* reached eighth in 1961, and *The Fugitive* was fifth in 1965. In 1961 a game show, *The Price Is Right*, placed ninth, becoming one of the rare game shows to place in the top ten. The original *Price Is Right* aired from 1957 to 1965; revived in 1972 with Bob Barker (1923?–) as host, the game show continued to run into the new century.

Some of the highest quality television programming in the 1960s was found on the network news programs. The networks had a great deal to cover in the 1960s. From the assassination of President Kennedy in 1963, to the many dramatic events of the civil rights movement, to frontline action in the Vietnam War (1954–75), network news programs offered detailed, compelling coverage that brought these important events into American homes. In fact, many historians believe that national news coverage of the beatings of civil rights marchers by white policemen and of the violence of the Vietnam War helped strengthen public opinion around these issues in ways that could not have happened before the widespread use of television. One example of the power of television news came in 1967, when highly respected American newsman Walter Cronkite (1916–), anchor of *CBS Evening News*, voiced his opinion at the end of one broadcast that the war in Vietnam was a stalemate and that the United States should negotiate a withdrawal. It was suspected that Cronkite's statement and its assumed effect on public opinion was a key factor in President Johnson's decision not to seek reelection in 1968.

Movies in the 1960s

In many ways, the American film industry had lost its way in the 1960s. The rise of television in the 1950s had presented the industry with a huge challenge. Now that most Americans could be entertained at home with their television, moviemakers could not count on the enormous audiences that had made them rich in the 1920s, 1930s, and 1940s. The entire movie industry reorganized in what is widely known as the death of the studio system. Before the 1960s, the studio system described how giant movie companies, or studios, operated. Studios produced and distributed movies, and they managed the careers of most movie stars. By the 1960s, however, most movies were produced independently and sold to the studios for distribution, and it was this arrangement that represented the death of the studio system. Taken together, the death of the studio system and the rise of television were the forces that shaped the movies of the period.

The big movie studios did not withdraw from producing movies altogether. Instead, they focused their efforts on making movies that were clearly different than TV fare: big budget epics. With casts of thousands, lavish sets, distant locations, and the biggest stars, pictures such as *Ben-Hur* (1959), *Lawrence of Arabia* (1962), and *Cleopatra* (1963) were far more spectacular than anything offered on the small screen. They cost a good deal more to make—*Ben-Hur* cost $15 million to make, while *Cleopatra* cost $37 million—but they also brought the kinds of profits that otherwise remained out of the reach of the studios.

Rating the Movies

Movie censorship—rules to forbid certain kinds of material—has a history nearly as long as moviemaking itself. Following a series of scandals and scandalous movies made in Hollywood in the 1920s, the Motion Picture Association of America (MPAA; the film world's governing body) instituted the Production Code, which placed strict limits on the sexuality, violence, and "incorrect" moral lessons that could be shown in movies. By the 1960s, however, the Code had become ineffective. Cultural standards for what was acceptable were changing fast, and people wanted to have access to movies that reflected the way people really lived—including nudity, homosexuality, and violence.

In November of 1968, the MPAA began a voluntary ratings system. Movies could be rated G, for general audiences; M, for mature audiences (this rating was later changed to PG, for parental guidance; the PG-13 rating came in 1984 to indicate to parents that some material was not for children under thirteen); R, for restricted, meaning that anyone under seventeen must be accompanied by an adult; and X, meaning children under seventeen not admitted. Though the system was voluntary, moviemakers of the 1960s felt that they had to submit their film for a rating in order to reach a mass audience. The ratings system continued into the early 2000s. Typically, only foreign films and pornography are released without a rating.

The withdrawal of the big studios from movie production did not mean an end to filmmaking by any means. Instead, it meant that an increasing number of films were made by independent producers who either sought financing from the studios or financed their films on their own. The result was a real diversity in the kinds of films that were made. Some were cheaply produced and designed to appeal to specific limited audiences. American International Pictures, for example, specialized in making "beach films," such as *Beach Party* (1963), *Beach Blanket Bingo* (1965), and *How to Stuff a Wild Bikini* (1965), and horror films, including *Attack of the Giant Leeches* (1959), *Die, Monster, Die!* (1965), and *Queen of Blood* (1966). Inexpensively made and poorly acted, these films nevertheless show eye-catching subjects—like girls in bikinis and scary monsters. Other movies were imported from abroad, including a series of immensely popular movies from England starring the fictional character James Bond.

The Beatles perform in a scene from their 1964 movie *A Hard Day's Night*.
The Kobal Collection. Reproduced by permission.

music. The decade began amid fears that rock'n'roll was dead. This new musical form, born in the 1950s, seemed to be in decline, and more established musical genres like jazz, swing, and pop crooning by the likes of Frank Sinatra and Tony Bennett enjoyed resurgence. But rock's decline was short-lived. Beginning with the dance craze started by Chubby Checker's popular 1960 song "The Twist," rock'n' roll went through a remarkable transformation, splintering off in a dozen different directions. By the end of the decade, rock'n' roll, in its many forms, was by far the most popular music in America.

Rock music was given a tremendous boost beginning in 1963 with the emergence of the Beatles, a British rock group that many consider the greatest band of all time. The Beatles made their first visit to the United States in 1964, thrilling teen audiences with such songs as "Love Me Do," "Please Please Me," "She Loves You," and "I Want to Hold Your Hand." They were simple love songs, expertly performed and artfully arranged, and they launched a revolution in music. The Beatles remained at the top of the American music charts throughout the decade, even as their music became much more complicated and harder edged. They also triggered what became known as the British Invasion, the U.S. introduction of other British rock bands such as the Rolling Stones and the Animals.

The Beatles opened a space in American popular music for innovation, and a number of distinctive sounds developed to fill that space. The Beach Boys from southern California combined beautiful harmonies with catchy rhythms to create such songs as "I Get Around" and "Good Vibrations"; their unique sound helped create a genre of its own known as surf music. In the late 1960s, several bands based in San Francisco, California, began to diverge significantly from the lighter rock sounds of the Beatles and the Beach Boys. Performers such as the Grateful Dead, Jefferson Airplane, and Janis Joplin introduced harder-edged guitar playing, driving beats, and more socially conscious lyrics. Closely associated with the drug-using culture of San Francisco's Haight-Ashbury district, these bands played what was known as psychedelic rock, named after the hallucinogenic drugs favored by hippies. Perhaps the most notable musician of this form of music was Jimi Hendrix, whose guitar playing prowess amazed and delighted many audiences.

Some of the most original and popular music of the 1960s was produced by Motown Records in Detroit, Michigan. Created by African American producer Berry Gordy Jr. (1929–) in 1959, Motown produced fifty-six number-one hits during the decade. Motown's top acts were Stevie Wonder, Diana Ross and the Supremes, Marvin Gaye, the Temptations, the Four Tops, Martha and the Vandellas, and Smokey Robinson. Though very few of the songs produced by Motown commented directly on the evolving civil rights move-

Legendary guitarist Jimi Hendrix performs before huge crowds at Woodstock on August 18, 1969. His life was cut short by a drug overdose in September of 1970. © Henry Diltz/Corbis.

Woodstock and Altamont

Two music festivals held in 1969 at opposite ends of the nation captured the promise and tragedy of the youthful hope that emerged during the 1960s that music could change the world. Woodstock, held in August 1969 in a farm field near Woodstock, New York, was promoted by four young businessmen hoping to host a three-day festival celebrating peace and music. From modest early plans the festival soon ballooned in size and scope. Festival planners booked some of the greatest musical acts of the era, including The Who; Jimi Hendrix; Janis Joplin; Crosby, Stills, Nash, and Young; Joe Cocker; and Santana. But they did not anticipate the size of the crowd that gathered. An estimated 500,000 people descended on the event, quickly overwhelming all plans for traffic, food, and accommodations. For three days, through rain and shine, concertgoers dug the music in a general spirit of happiness and peace. Though conservative observers were horrified at open displays of nudity and drug use, many felt that the concert proved the positive spirit of the age. Woodstock was, in many ways, a symbolic high point of the 1960s.

If Woodstock was the high point, Altamont was the low point. Held just a few months later, on December 6, 1969, at the Altamont Speedway near Livermore, California, the concert was organized by the British rock band the Rolling Stones as a free concert for their fans. The show included many of the bands that had played at

Concertgoers view the Woodstock Music and Arts Fair from the roof of a Volkswagen van, August 1969. *AP/Wide World Photos. Reproduced by permission.*

Woodstock and promised to attract nearly as many peace-loving hippies as the earlier concert. But there was a serious complication: concert organizers had hired the Hell's Angels motorcycle gang to act as security. The Angels, known at the time for their violent and illegal behavior, accepted their payment in beer and soon got out of hand. Concertgoers who ventured too close to the stage were beaten. During the Rolling Stones' set, Hell's Angels stabbed and kicked to death one young man, and the violence grew so intense that the concert came to a halt. Just as Woodstock was seen as a high point, Altamont signaled to many that the era of peace and love was over.

ment, the very existence of a black record company producing hits by black artists helped convince many that African Americans deserved equal status in American society.

Though rock and its variations dominated the radio airwaves during the decade, folk music also enjoyed a surprising popularity. Folk music had existed in the United States since the founding of the nation; in its early forms it was just the simple music made by common people and played on acoustic instruments. The folk revival of the late 1950s and 1960s began when such groups as the Weavers and the Kingston Trio recorded older tunes from the 1930 and 1940s. It was Bob Dylan (1941–) who truly revolutionized the genre, however. Dylan was deeply influenced by Woody Guthrie (1912–1967), whose songs from the 1930s protested living conditions during the Great Depression (a period of economic distress that lasted from 1929 to 1941). Dylan brought direct social commentary back to folk music. In songs such as "Blowin' in the Wind" and "The Times They Are a Changin'," Dylan called for an end to war and discrimination. Dylan eventually created a new form, folk rock, when he used an electric guitar instead of conventional acoustic instruments to play his music. Folk musician Joan Baez (1941–) was the female counterpart to Dylan, and the two toured together on occasion. More than any other genre in the 1960s, folk music was the music of liberal ideals, as folk singers of all sorts supported civil rights and sang out against the Vietnam War.

For More Information

Books

Calabro, Marian. *Zap!: A Brief History of Television*. New York: Four Winds Press, 1992.

Cantwell, Robert. *When We Were Good: The Folk Revival*. Cambridge, MA: Harvard University Press, 1996.

Edelstein, Andrew. *The Pop Sixties*. New York: Ballantine Books, 1985.

Lebrecht, Norman. *The Companion to 20th-Century Music*. New York: Simon & Schuster, 1992.

McNeil, Alex. *Total Television: The Comprehensive Guide to Programming from 1948 to the Present*. New York: Penguin, 1996.

Miller, Jim, ed. *The Rolling Stone Illustrated History of Rock and Roll*. New York: Rolling Stone Press, 1980.

Minow, Newton N., and Craig L. Lamay. *Abandoned in the Wasteland: Children, Television, and the First Amendment.* New York: Harper Collins, 1995.

Pendergast, Tom, and Sara Pendergast, eds. *St. James Encyclopedia of Popular Culture.* Detroit, MI: St. James Press, 1999.

Schwartz, Richard A. *Cold War Culture: Media and the Arts, 1945–1990.* New York: Facts on File, 1997.

The Enduring Legacy
of the 1960s

15

As the 1960s began, Americans were filled with hope and optimism. Their newly elected president, John F. Kennedy (1917–1963; served 1961–63), called on Americans to join him as they ventured into a "New Frontier," one that included the expansion of prosperity at home and democracy around the world and the placing of a man on the moon. Kennedy's optimism, his enthusiastic visions, were emblematic of one side of the 1960s, the side that historian David Farber aptly called "the age of great dreams" in his book of the same title. Others shared Kennedy's tendency to dream: civil rights leader Martin Luther King Jr. called on Americans to live out their commitment to equality for all; President Lyndon B. Johnson created a set of programs known as the Great Society with the goal of wiping out poverty and ensuring equality; antiwar protestors called for a just and moral U.S. foreign policy; hippies dreamed of a world where peace and love were all that mattered.

These dreams, and many others, were powerful goals for action in what turned out to be a tumultuous decade. They led mass numbers of Americans into action. Acting on

their dreams, Democratic presidents dramatically expanded the size of the federal government; civil rights protestors marched and bled in the streets; American soldiers died in Vietnam in order, they were told, to stop the spread of Communism; Hispanic Americans led boycotts in the fields of southern California; Native Americans forcibly occupied land they believed belonged to them; women asserted their equal rights; and peace activists burned their draft cards as a signal of their refusal to fight in the war. There were also quieter ways of living out the American dream. For many—perhaps for what Republican president Richard Nixon called the "silent majority"—living out the American dream meant getting a college education, taking a secure job, and raising a family. American economic prosperity put this dream within reach of more Americans than ever before.

The lives of several political leaders were cut short by assassins in the 1960s. However, their unfinished work and dream of a better America inspired a new generation, which included future U.S. president Bill Clinton (served 1993–2001), who met President Kennedy on the grounds of the White House in July of 1963. *Getty Images. Reproduced by permission.*

By the end of the decade, however, many of the dreams that had so motivated Americans were either shattered or distorted nearly beyond recognition. The dream of an expanded federal government that looked out for the needs of less fortunate Americans, for example, had run aground by 1968. The Democratic politicians who led that dream, especially President Johnson, were forced to direct time and money away from domestic affairs and toward a costly war in Vietnam, and a rising conservative movement began to argue forcefully that government had grown too large and should be limited. The antiwar movement, which began with people united around a common cause, was still capable of staging major protests at the end of the decade, but internal fighting among organization leaders and a tendency for some protestors to use violence kept this movement from attracting the mainstream support it needed to remain a real political force. Even the civil rights movement, arguably the most successful of the social movements of the

1960s, was diminished by the end of the decade. Though it had secured the passage of major legislation, the assassinations of leaders Martin Luther King Jr. and Malcolm X left the movement without stable leadership, and many followers drifted off into involvement with a variety of ineffective and short-lived projects, such as the black separatist movement. The hippie movement had begun in the mid-1960s with visions of peace and togetherness, but by the late 1960s the drug use that first fueled the movement had proved to be its undoing. The social vision of the early years became fuzzy and unclear, and by the end of the decade all that remained were long hair, bell-bottoms, and a few good rock songs.

Just because the grand social dreams of the 1960s did not survive the decade intact, however, does not mean that they did not exert a huge influence on the character of American culture, both during the decade and in the years that followed. In fact, many of the issues that were raised in the 1960s—including the role of the federal government in domestic and foreign policy; the need to extend civil rights to all people regardless of race, ethnicity, and gender; the place of sexuality in society; the commercialism of American culture; and the separation of church and state, to name just a few—remained of fundamental concern to Americans in the twenty-first century. The legacy of the 1960s can be understood by examining those issues that began in that era and continued to resonate with American life in the twenty-first century.

Until the 1960s, Americans generally expressed a great deal of trust and confidence in the federal government. They tended to believe that politicians told the truth and did not actively deceive the American public. But the actions of American politicians during the Vietnam War and the mass protests that followed weakened this essential bond of trust. President Johnson and his leading advisors and generals made a series of statements about U.S. war aims and achievements; when those statements were proven false, many Americans lost faith that politicians were telling the truth. President Nixon increased this lack of trust when he ordered the secret bombing of Cambodia in 1969. The trust level weakened further when people saw Nixon face impeachment for his role in ordering and covering up break-ins at Democratic Party headquarters at Watergate and then resign from office in 1974. After that time, press accusations and congres-

sional investigations of presidential wrongdoings and cover-ups became a common feature of American political life. Every president from Ronald Reagan (1911–2004; served 1981–89) up to and including George W. Bush (1946–; served 2001–) was subject to highly publicized criticism and scandals that eroded public trust.

Prior to the 1960s, organized mass protests were a fairly uncommon experience in American life. The civil rights movement, however, became a pioneer in the creation of public actions designed to sway government policy. With its bus boycotts, lunch counter sit-ins, marches, and mass rallies, the movement demonstrated the political power that lay in a mass of well-organized and disciplined people, and the model that they created for advocacy continued to be used into the early 2000s by women, ethnic minorities, and homosexuals. While rights-based protest brought about significant changes in laws designed to offer equal protection and rights to minority groups, changing deeply imbedded cultur-

al stereotypes and social patterns proved more difficult. Blacks still experienced much higher levels of poverty than whites and had more difficulty getting adequate education and jobs. Homosexuals continued to work in the early 2000s to gain access to full protection of the law in many states and for legal recognition of gay marriages. But the presence of black, gays, and other minorities in sports, television, music, and other areas of culture was breaking down some stereotypes and misunderstandings that cause discrimination (the singling out of minority groups for unfavorable treatment).

Sadly, one of the legacies of the 1960s was an increase in the acceptance of violence. By any measure, the 1960s were violent years: one president (John F. Kennedy), one presidential candidate (Robert Kennedy), and two prominent civil rights leaders (Martin Luther King Jr. and Malcolm X) were assassinated; civil rights activists were regularly attacked, beaten, and sometimes killed by armed police forces and white mobs, most notably in Birmingham, Alabama, in 1963; antiwar pro-

The Enduring Legacy of the 1960s

Clothing styles from the 1960s have continued to come in and out of fashion. Here, model Nadege wears striped bell-bottoms, designed by Valentino, in 1995. © Photo B.D.V./Corbis.

testors experienced similarly violent attacks for voicing their opinions, most notably at the Democratic National Convention in Chicago in 1968 and at Kent State University in 1970; urban riots flared in major cities throughout the mid- and late 1960s, causing death and the destruction of property; and war raged in Vietnam. This violence was brought into American homes by extensive television coverage, which made the beatings and killings seem immediate and close. Television coverage made violence seem normal, and diminishing restrictions on the content of television programming allowed violence to become increasingly a part of American entertainment. It remained so in the early 2000s.

The 1960s also ushered in a number of more lighthearted cultural changes. One of the great changes was a relaxing of standards of dress and personal appearance. In the early 1960s, young people dressed and wore their hair in conservative styles: boys wore suits and crew cuts, and girls wore neat dresses and hairstyles similar to those worn by their mothers. But the student-led protest movements of the early 1960s, the immense popularity of the long-haired British band the Beatles, and the stylistic excesses of the hippies helped bring about a revolution in American style. By the end of the 1960s, long hair for men, blue jeans, and brightly colored clothes were commonly worn by people of all ages. This loosening of acceptable norms for dress extended to other area of personal behavior, including sexuality and drug use. By the end of the 1960s, and continuing into the twenty-first century, youthful experimentation with sexual expression and use of illicit drugs were far more common.

Another legacy from the 1960s was the widespread commercialism that pervaded American culture in the following decades. The movement toward a society that revered consumer goods and celebrities was already underway in the

1950s, but it fully took hold in the 1960s when television ownership skyrocketed and mass-market magazines began to focus on lifestyles based on wealth, consumption, and leisure. Television, movies, and magazines all promoted consumer goods as the ultimate expression of personal identity and indeed of American patriotism. In the long Cold War with the Soviet Union, one of the true markers of American superiority was its ability to provide cars, clothes, high-quality food, and other goods to average Americans. Television, film, and sports stars attracted attention for their glamour and for their wealth, and American professional sports became a huge business in this period. These patterns only increased over time.

The 1960s introduced many issues and events that had long-lasting effects on U.S. culture and American beliefs. Issues connected to the role of the American military in foreign conflicts, the legal separation of church and state, the way that art and literature reflect cultural change, and the way that the Olympic Games have a role in international politics offer significant parallels between the early 2000s and the tumultuous decade of the 1960s. For better or for worse, the decade of the 1960s was a testing ground for some of the most controversial and engaging issues that continued to affect Americans in the twenty-first century.

For More Information

Books

Collier, Christopher, and James Lincoln Collier. *The Changing Face of American Society: 1945-2000.* New York: Benchmark, 2002.

McCormick, Anita Louisa. *The Vietnam Antiwar Movement in American History.* Berkeley Heights, NJ: Enslow Publishers, 2000.

McWilliams, John C. *The 1960s Cultural Revolution.* Westport, CT: Greenwood Press, 2000.

Where to Learn More

Books

Altman, Linda Jacobs. *The American Civil Rights Movement: The African-American Struggle for Equality.* Berkeley Heights, NJ: Enslow, 2004.

Anderson, David L. *The Columbia Guide to the Vietnam War.* New York: Columbia University Press, 2002.

Archer, Jules. *The Incredible Sixties: The Stormy Years that Changed America.* San Diego, CA: Harcourt Brace Jovanovich, 1986.

Austin, Joe, and Michael Nevin Willard. *Generations of Youth: Youth Cultures and History in Twentieth-Century America.* New York: New York University Press, 1998.

Bloom, Alexander, and Wini Breines, eds. *"Takin' It to the Streets": A Sixties Reader.* New York: Oxford University Press, 2003.

Breuer, William B. *Race to the Moon: America's Duel with the Soviets.* Westport, CT: Greenwood Publishing, 1993.

Burner, David. *Making Peace with the 1960s.* Princeton, NJ: Princeton University Press, 1996.

Cantwell, Robert. *When We Were Good: The Folk Revival.* Cambridge, MA: Harvard University Press, 1996.

Collier, Christopher, and James Lincoln Collier. *The Changing Face of American Society: 1945-2000.* New York: Benchmark, 2002.

Dougan, Clark. *A Nation Divided.* Boston: Boston Publishing Co., 1984.

Witcover, Jules. *The Year the Dream Died: Revisiting 1968 in America.* New York: Warner Books, 1997.

Wormser, Richard. *Three Faces of Vietnam.* New York: F. Watts, 1993.

Young, Marilyn B., John J. Fitzgerald, and A. Tom Grunfeld. *The Vietnam War: A History in Documents.* New York: Oxford University Press, 2002.

Web Sites

American Presidents Life Portraits. http://www.americanpresidents.org

"The Cuban Missile Crisis, 1962: The 40th Anniversary." *The National Security Archive.* http://www.gwu.edu/~nsarchiv/nsa/cuba_mis_cri/

Divining America: Religion and the National Culture. http://www.nhc.rtp.nc.us/tserve/divam.htm.

Hippies on the Web: Haight-Ashbury Music and Culture. http://www.rockument.com/links.html

John F. Kennedy Library and Museum. http://www.jfklibrary.org

"The Living Room Candidate: Presidential Campaign Commercials, 1952-2004." *American Museum of the Moving Image.* http://livingroomcandidate.movingimage.us/index.php

Lyndon Baines Johnson Library and Museum. http://www.lbjlib.utexas.edu

National Civil Rights Museum. http://www.civilrightsmuseum.org

"The Presidents of the United States." *The White House.* http://www.whitehouse.gov/history/presidents

The Richard Nixon Library and Birthplace. http://www.nixonfoundation.org

The Sixties Project. http://lists.village.virginia.edu/sixties/

The 1960s—Social Unrest & Counterculture. http://www.historyteacher.net/APUSH-Course/Weblinks/Weblinks27.htm

Vietnam Online. http://www.pbs.org/wgbh/amex/vietnam/

Voices of Civil Rights: Ordinary People, Extraordinary Stories. http://www.voicesofcivilrights.org

Index

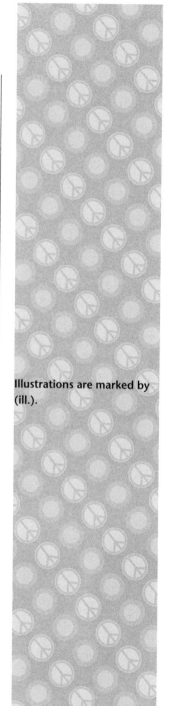

Illustrations are marked by (ill.).

H

Haight-Ashbury district, 154–158, 166–167, 219

Hair (musical), 205, 206 (ill.)

Hamer, Fannie Lou, 123

Happenings, 202

Hare Krishnas, 162, 173, 182, 182 (ill.)

Harrington, Michael, 109

Hayden, Tom, 86, 96, 97 (ill.)

Head Start, 30, 31 (ill.), 126

Heller, Joseph, 203

Hemingway, Ernest, 201

Hendrix, Jimi, 164, 167, 169, 209, 219, 219 (ill.), 220

Hershey, Lewis B., 89

Hinduism, 162, 173, 181–182

Hippies, 1, 5, 43, 92 (ill.), 140, 147, 149, 151–171, 155 (ill.)

Ho Chi Minh, 18, 68, 69

Hoffman, Abbie, 96, 97 (ill.), 159, 167

Hoffman, Dustin, 216

Holland, Gini, 12

Holocaust, 174–175

Homosexuality, 142–143, 148

"Hot lines," 17

Hubbard, L. Ron, 182–183

"Human Be-In" (1967), 166

Human evolution, 183

Humphrey, Hubert H., 13, 43, 44, 98

I

"I Have a Dream" speech (King), 4, 5 (ill.), 29, 120

Indian Self-Determination and Educational Assistance Act of 1975, 129

Interbank Card Association, 109

Isserman, Maurice, 178

J

Jabbar, Kareem Abdul (born Lew Alcindor), 191

Jackson, Jimmy Lee, 121

Jefferson Airplane (musical group), 164, 166, 219

Jesus Christ Superstar (rock opera), 205–206

JFK: The Untold Story (film, 1991), 23

Jim Crow laws, 115, 123

Job Corps, 126

John XXIII, pope, 176–177

John Birch Society, 58

Johnson, Claudia Alta Taylor "Lady Bird," 28 (ill.), 31 (ill.), 112 (ill.)

Johnson, Lyndon B., 3 (ill.), 41 (ill.), 112 (ill.)
  escalation of Vietnam War by, 1, 28, 38–40, 65, 72–77, 85, 90–91
  image of, 40–41
  presidency of, 2, 24, 27–47, 28 (ill.), 77
  presidential campaign of, 31–35, 55
  social politics of, 28–31, 35–38, 111–113, 120–121, 125, 126, 223
  as vice president, 27
  and Warren Commission Report, 23

Jones, LeRoi (later Imamu Amiri Baraka), 203, 204 (ill.), 205

Joplin, Janis, 147, 148 (ill.), 164, 167, 169, 219, 220

Judaism, 172–173, 177–178

Judd, Donald, 199

K

Katzenbach, Nicholas, 56 (ill.)

Kazin, Michael, 178

Kennedy, Adrienne, 203

Kennedy, Jacqueline "Jackie" Bouvier, 11, 11 (ill.), 24, 28 (ill.)

Kennedy, John F., 3 (ill.), 9 (ill.), 224 (ill.)
  assassination of, 2, 22–25, 120, 227
  on civil rights, 20, 50, 119
  domestic policies of, 11, 20–22
  economic policy of, 21–22

Poverty
   in Appalachia, 108–109, 112
      (ill.)
   in U.S., 109–111
   Johnson's war on, 2, 30–31,
      111–113, 125
Powers, Francis Gary, 12
Prayer in school, 33, 173, 176
Prejudice. *See* Racism, against
   African Americans; Segrega-
   tion
Presley, Elvis, 197
Project Apollo (space program), 61
Project Gemini (space program),
   61
Project Mercury (space program),
   21
Project Soyuz, 61
Protestant churches, 172, 173–175
Psychedelic era, 156, 163–166
Psychomimetic drugs, 156,
   160–162
Public Broadcasting System (PBS),
   212
Pynchon, Thomas, 203

R

Rabe, David, 205
Race riots, 1, 4, 43, 124–127, 124
   (ill.)
Racism, against African Ameri-
   cans, 4, 5, 29–30, 110–111,
   115, 116, 123–124
Rauschenberg, Robert, 202
Reagan, Ronald, 63, 126, 160, 226
Redstockings, 141
Reeb, James, 121
Reich, Wilhelm, 145
Religion
   changing American experience
      of, 172–185
   hippie spirituality, 162–163
Religious cults, 162, 163, 172
Republic of Vietnam (RVN), 69
Republican Party, 49, 50, 53–55
Reserve Officers' Training Corps
   (ROTC), 99
Reston, James, 25
Reuss, Henry S., 13
Ridenhour, Ronald, 70

Right wing. *See* Conservative po-
   litical movement
Robbins, Jerome, 207
Roberts, Oral, 174, 180
Roberts, Randy, 188
Roberts, Sylvia, 137
Robinson, Frank, 191
Robinson, Smokey, 219
Rock, John, 145
Rock and roll music, influence of,
   146, 147, 163–166
Rockefeller, Nelson, 55
Rockwell, George Lincoln, 58, 58
   (ill.)
Roe v. Wade, 144
Rolling Stones, The (musical
   group), 164, 220
Roman Catholicism, 8, 172,
   175–177
Roosevelt, Franklin D., 32, 116,
   206
Rosie the Riveter, 134
Ross, Diana, 219
ROTC (Reserve Officers' Training
   Corps), 99
Rowan and Martin's Laugh-In (TV
   series), 170, 212, 213
Rubin, Jerry, 96, 97 (ill.), 159
Ruby, Jack, 24 (ill.), 25
Russell, Bill, 191, 192, 193 (ill.)
Ruth, Babe, 189

S

Saigon, fall of, 81
Santana (musical group), 220
*School Dist. of Abbington v.
   Schempp,* 33
Schulman, Bruce J., 31, 43
SCLC (Southern Christian Leader-
   ship Conference), 119–120,
   121
SDS (Students for a Democratic
   Society), 40–41, 51, 85–86,
   90, 91, 99–100, 152
Seale, Bobby, 96, 130
Searle Pharmaceutical Company,
   145
Segregation
   in American South, 5, 57–59,
      115, 123–124
   fight to end, 30

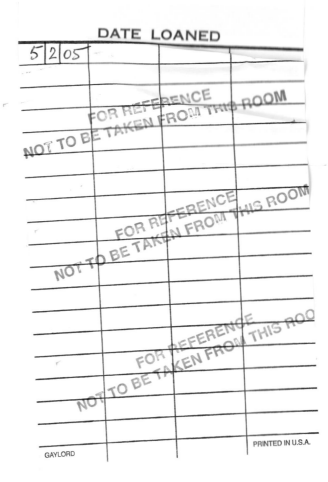

DATE LOANED

5 2 05			
GAYLORD			PRINTED IN U.S.A.